MARIE ANTOINETTE

CREATED AND PRODUCED
BY
EDITA LAUSANNE

PHILIPPE HUISMAN · MARGUERITE JALLUT

MARIE ANTOINETTE

PATRICK STEPHENS LIMITED
WITH
EDITA LAUSANNE

Not for sale, resale, or distribution in the United States of America,
its territories and possessions or in Canada

© 1970 Edita Lausanne

Published in 1971 by Patrick Stephens Limited
9 Ely Place, London EC1N 6SQ

ISBN O 85059 073 6

Printed and bound in Switzerland

CONTENTS

PREFACE

A little, fourteen-year-old princess, Marie Antoinette of Lorraine-Austria, gay, spontaneous, seductive, arrived in France in the month of May 1770 as the bride of the future king Louis XVI. She received a triumphal welcome for she incarnated an immense hope. The French had just made one of the great discoveries of modern times : they had invented happiness, not pleasure or passing satisfactions, but a life ideal which the whole of humanity could enjoy. A thousand years of wars, of economic instability, of epidemics and famines, had strengthened the religious conviction that man was on earth to suffer in order to merit eternal felicity after death. Then a half-century of general though unequal rise in the standard of living, thanks to the progress of science and technology, a new confidence in the power of the human spirit, had shown a growing number of French people the prospects and advantages of human welfare. Paradise on earth no longer seemed an impossible attainment.

In 1770, the throne of France was occupied by Louis XV, a king who had become unpopular and whose long reign seemed an obstacle to a universally desired evolution. The good-will of his successors, the grace and youth of the future queen were the very image of the happiness soon to come.

A quarter of a century later, on a cold morning of October 1793, before an indifferent or hostile crowd, Marie Antoinette, the last Queen of France, was led to the scaffold. Ten months earlier the Republicans had beheaded Louis XVI and ended the monarchy for ever. Marie Antoinette was executed because she was the personification of a happiness that had become detestable : her carefree and glittering life appeared as an insult to the austere and virtuous gladness of a revolutionary nation.

Whether hated or adored, triumphant or persecuted, Marie Antoinette symbolized an existence that still exercises a nostalgic fascination. In the conquest of happiness two attitudes have always been found in opposition, one sentimental and spontaneous, the other reflective and soon tyrannical. Revolutions begun in joy have often led to joyless societies and it is not only at the close of the eighteenth century that the tragedy of happiness has been experienced.

The tastes of Marie Antoinette would surprise no one of our times. She liked comfort : the supreme luxury is not to display one's riches but to bring together in elegant simplicity all the material pleasures of life. She had egalitarian thoughts : Marie Antoinette launched the fashion of cheap cotton dresses formerly worn only by the peasant women and the lower middle classes. In her Trianon hamlet she passed long hours in the midst of country people, for her own pleasure. Similarly she had a wish for social changes : along with her son and daughter the Queen brought up children from very simple backgrounds, including a small negro brought back by a traveller from Africa, and treated them all the same. The dreams of freedom for the colonials also raised the hopes of people in the reign of Marie Antoinette when France took part in the American War of Independence. Upsetting all the traditional rules and customs, boldly considering all possible transformations, such were by then the basic elements of the crusade for happiness, synonymous with movement and novelty.

The attempt to build a true picture of Marie Antoinette and to retrace the sources of the idea of happiness leads to a rediscovery of our own era and ourselves. Far from the bourgeois commercialism and the selfish nationalism of the nineteenth century, there was under the Ancien Régime a breadth of vision that is in close agreement with the hopes of our times. And it should not be forgotten that survivors of French eighteenth-century society always referred to that brilliant pre-Revolutionary period as *la douceur de vivre*.

In this world of frivolous aspect happiness is an art. The much-vaunted sociability of the French of that times was, in fact, a deliberate attitude. Upon his arrival in France the famous Italian adventurer Casanova received from a travelling companion a piece of advice which he was not to forget: "Never say no. This disobliging word is a disappointment. No is not French." There was a universal complicity to give an appearance of harmony to human relations, an incontestable goodwill to make them easier, in fact a predetermination to simulate joy even at times when it was not felt, which created an atmosphere of true well-being and affected gaiety.

Archives serve to trace events that form the framework of an era. Works of art express the intentions, the dreams, the atmosphere that are its underlying reality. Unpublished or neglected documents allow us to clarify certain points of the life of Marie Antoinette, but the works of contemporary artists constitute in themselves a captivating biography. It is ridiculous to try to prove the virtue or the shame of this woman. She was a sovereign comparable to the "idols" of our time. Deeply touched by the homage and then by the aversion to which she was subject, she was in turn the image of an adorably capricious queen chosen in universal admiration by the French, then of a mother made heroic by events. We must look at Fragonard's masterpiece *The Festival of St. Cloud* or read *Marianne* by Marivaux to understand the equivocal figure of Marie Antoinette. Fragonard's figures do not altogether stand out from the luxuriant vegetation of the Park of St. Cloud; his women seem to be flowers too. During the course of Marivaux's strange novel Marianne changes according to the circumstances she is in and the people she meets. The idea of happiness implied availability, an easy-going attitude, hope.

A breeze, light at first, blew over France and Europe in the eighteenth century to become by stages a tempest that raged over the whole world. The conception of religion, of nations, of society, of morality was progressively shaken then overturned. The world ceased to be acceptable as it was and suddenly appeared admirable as it ought to be.

What was more exhilarating than the caress of this radiant hope? Never was happiness so beautiful as in the early dreams of Marie Antoinette. Chimera or reality, the work of the painters or the writers give the truest image of it: the paintings of Greuze, Fragonard or David express an atmosphere, a state of mind which can be seen again, after a long lapse, in the attitude of governments. To discover in the acts of the life of Marie Antoinette, through the pictures, the furniture, the *objets d'art*, the books and the music she loved, the definition of the art of happiness is to reach to the source of the world in which we live and recognize the principles of our own successes and joys and of our failures and disappointments.

Philippe Huisman

"Le couronnement d'une rosière", drawn by Jean-Baptiste Huet as a model for a decorative toile de Jouy, is a naïve representation of various themes of the art of happiness as conceived by the contemporaries of Marie Antoinette. The dogs, flowers and lamb are an evocation of nature, but the fringed hanging gives a theatrical air to the scene. Virtue is accompanied by the passionate fires of love and peasant poverty goes side by side with luxurious elegance.

Spring

Portrait of Marie Antoinette aged thirteen and a half years, taken in Vienna by the French pastellist Joseph Ducreux.

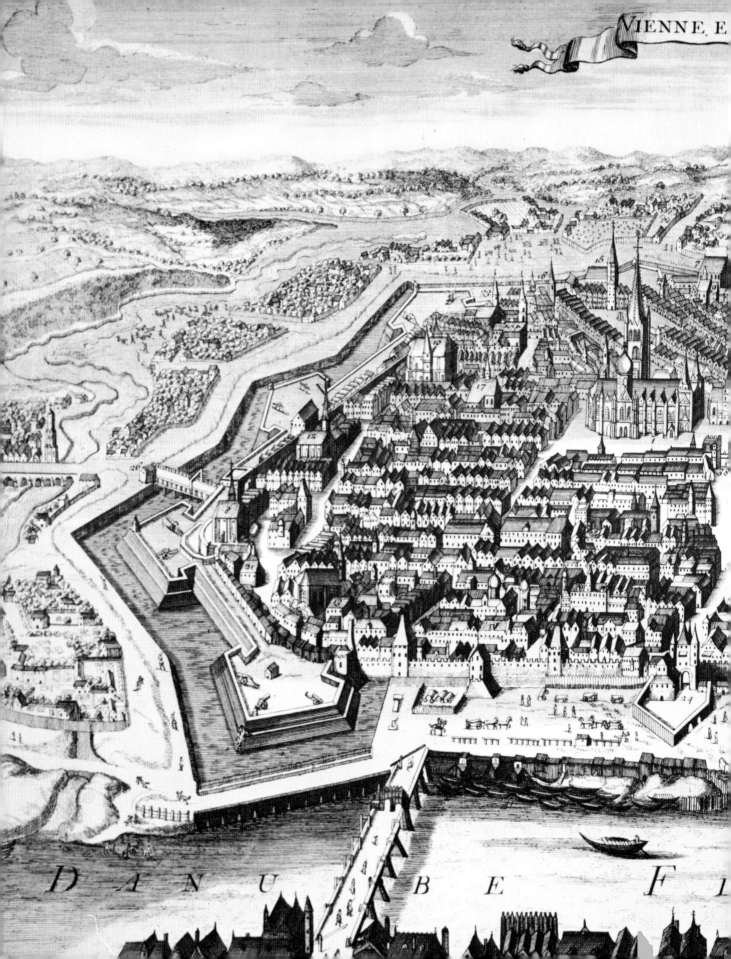

D A N U B E F

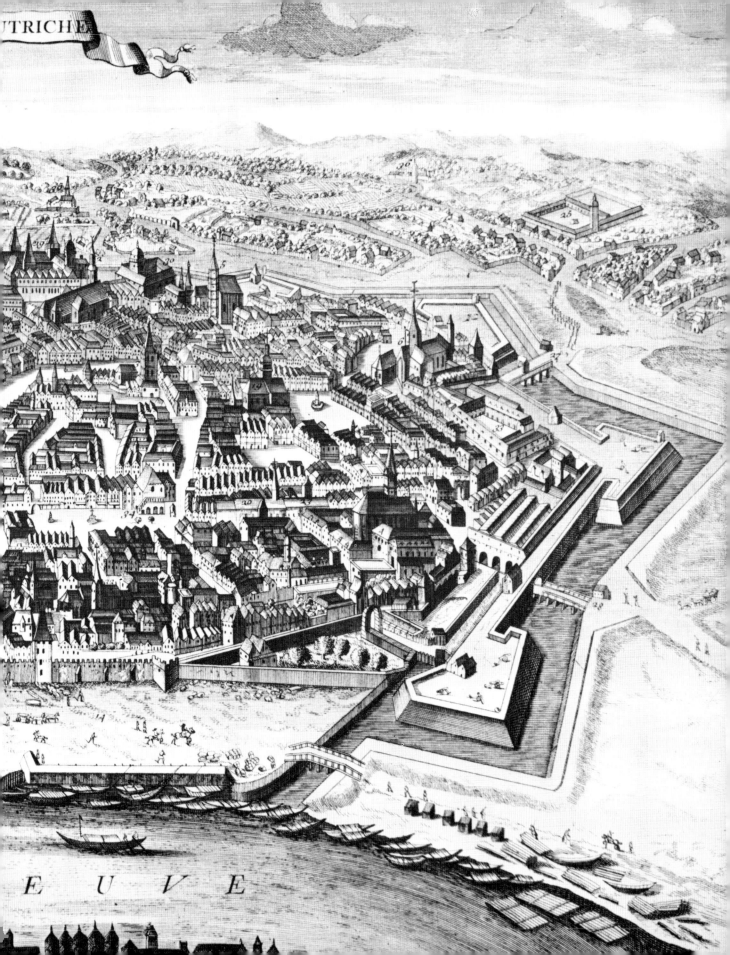

VIENNA, November 2nd, 1755. During the course of the afternoon, Maria Theresa of Habsburg, Empress of the Holy Roman Empire of the Germanic Nation, felt her first labour pains. Being an extremely strong and well-organized woman, she determined to put these pains to good use and asked her surgeon to extract a decayed tooth which had been troubling her for a few days. Then, in her chamber in the Hofburg Palace, seated in a low armchair following the old German custom rather than lying down on a bed as in France, she waited for her fifteenth child. In the meantime, she signed a few urgent papers and studied files. When she was finally forced to put down her pen, her husband, the Emperor Francis of Lorraine, was still attending the High Mass of All Souls' Day which was celebrated in the church very near to the Augustins. He was recalled in great haste. As soon as he arrived back at the palace, the Emperor issued instructions to keep his eldest son, the Archduke Joseph, who was then fourteen years old, away from the Empress's apartments "so that he may neither see nor hear things which are improper and unfitting for his age". Towards half-past seven, a little girl was born. There followed a blessing, Te Deum, and the presentation of the infant to the Court assembled in the Hall of Mirrors of the Hofburg. And on that very same evening, the Empress took up her files and the study of state affairs anew; in fact, she never had neglected them, taking childbirth in stride, for a numerous progeny is a dynastic precaution in a hereditary government.

The baptism took place the next day. The young princess received the names Maria Antonia Josephina Johanna, and as all the daughters of the imperial couple were named Maria, her relatives called her Antonia. After the ceremony, she joined her many brothers and sisters in a palace wing a long way from her parents' apartments. A grand mistress and a few ladies of the nobility were to take care of her and she was suckled by a nurse named Weber.

To celebrate Antonia's birth, popular festivities were held in Vienna on the fifth and the sixth of November. There were balls, food was distributed, and free theatrical and musical performances were given in honour of the small archduchess who was to disappear into a sort of anonymity for several years.

The middle of the seventeenth century marked a turning-point in the history of the world; the Middle Ages and the modern era lived side by side, collided and overlapped in all countries and in all hearts. Is man powerless, as traditional teachings say, when confronted with a universe governed by divine laws whose mystery he cannot penetrate; or is he, as the Frenchman Descartes, the German Leibnitz and the Englishman Newton recently affirmed, capable of finding a rational explanation of material phenomena and, consequently, of mastering them? Is conservatism the basic reality in the world, and resignation the aim of all morals; or should we believe in movement, change and progress? The mystical philosophy of the Middle Ages, the fondness for stability and mistrust of the future were always accompanied by indifference towards childhood. Until then—and this concept is particularly striking in paintings—there was no transitional period between an infant and a grown man, a cherub and a created being. Even the children of sovereigns were disguised as adults in their portraits.

Yet during this period in France, childhood was already considered as the most interesting and the happiest time of life. Rousseau was writing *Emile*, whose touching theories on the child-king strongly reflect common opinions among twentieth-century parents. But in Austria, if Antonia was forgotten, it was because childhood did not yet enjoy its proper status; the high rate of infant mortality certainly helped to discourage parents from becoming too deeply attached to beings whose future seemed so precarious. Physical weakness and the first stammerings of intelligence or sensitivity did not move them. In particular, they had no concept of a gradual development; the slow preparation and blossoming forth of a being who was to belong to the future and to another civilization were not realities of which parents were aware. They lived in the present, or rather, in eternity. Promises did not interest them.

Maria Theresa, a traditional head of state, was therefore obeying old precepts in giving little thought to her children of tender years. She thought about them at the time when the boys could occupy posts which were important for her policy, and when the girls could make useful matches. From this situation, Antonia at least gained the advantage of enjoying a perfectly carefree childhood and the freedom to play with other Viennese children of her age without close supervision.

Vienna, however, in more than one respect still lived in the Middle Ages. In 1755, England was a parliamentary democracy, and France already a united country. But the imperial monarchy still embodied a theocratic ideal born a thousand years earlier.

When the barbarian hordes invaded the Roman provinces during the first centuries of our era, the peoples of Europe found an essential spiritual refuge in Christianity, and the emperor, the head and defender of Christendom, became the representative of God on earth. Faced with mortal danger, in the midst of massacres, looting and frightening anarchy, both material and moral, the emperor assumed all power. Charlemagne, who re-established the Roman and Austrian Empire in A.D. 800, was the absolute master of Europe, and nine and a half centuries later the parents of Antonia were his successors.

Maria Theresa inherited very few of the powers exercised by her forefathers. Her pre-eminence over the sovereign kings and princes of Europe was purely honorary. But Antonia never quite forgot that she was the descendant of the Caesars.

Archaism, however, was sometimes combined with modernism. The hereditary possessions of the imperial couple certainly did not constitute a nation as we consider it today. It was an assorted mosaic of provinces, mostly separated from each other, with very different races, languages, laws and customs, and united only by chance inheritances.

Marie Antoinette would often contemplate a work-box given her by her mother and created in Vienna by an anonymous artist. When she opened it nine views of Vienna were revealed: left to right, Der Josephsplatz, Burgplatz, Michaelsplatz, Der Lobkowitzische Platz, Der Neumarkt, Der Graben, Der Hohemarkt, Universitätsplatz, Am Hof.

"Austria" said Hugo von Hofmannsthal, "is an organism which has grown like a plant, and which owes to God that it is what it is." Vienna lay in the heart of a German-speaking country, but not all of the present Austrian Republic's land belonged to Maria Theresa.

On the other hand, she was Queen of Hungary, a kingdom which encompassed a part of Yugoslavia and Rumania. Another of her provinces, Bohemia, extended farther than Czechoslovakia does today. In Italy, Maria Theresa owned a large part of the Po plain with Milan as its capital. Her spouse reigned over Florence and Tuscany. In Flanders, she was mistress of the Austrian Netherlands which occupied the same territory as Belgium does today.

This excessive partitioning presented a drawback and an asset. Maria Theresa had as many subjects and vaster states than the King of France, but she was the only really European sovereign. Every language was to be heard on her land: German in Austria, French and Dutch in the Netherlands, Italian in Milan and Florence, Czech in Bohemia, Magyar and Serbian in Hungary, etc... and as Vienna was a city full of fascination where rich lords built their mansions, Maria Theresa's court foreshadowed a Europe in which national rivalries would not exist. The Austrian authoress, Caroline Pichler, was to write fifty years later, "At that time, most of the Viennese society could say: I speak Italian like Dante, Latin like Cicero, English like Pope and Thomson, Greek like Demosthenes, French like Diderot, and German like... my nurse."

Thus, even as a child, Antonia spoke Italian, French and German and she never completely adopted nationalist prejudices.

Many of the future queen's characteristics were reflected in her father Francis I. His was the life of a rich and indolent man, full of goodwill towards everyone and with great artistic curiosity, especially for music; he had a fondness for dancing and festivities and a passion for horses, but very little perseverance.

His dynasty, descended from René of Anjou, good King René, the friend of painters in the fifteenth century, had reigned for three hundred years in the face of great obstacles over the little Duchy of Lorraine, a vassal land of the Habsburgs, but surrounded by territory belonging to the King of France.

This borderland had always been a battlefield, looted by both armies during the never-ending struggle between the Germans and the French.

In the seventeenth century Lorraine, repeatedly conquered, laid waste and re-occupied, was in a piteous state. Two artists have expressed this tragedy with overwhelming intensity. Long before Goya, Jacques Callot sketched and engraved the horrors of war; and Georges de la Tour, pathetic or ironical, took the martyrdom of saints or the words of the Bible to express the absolute despair of life when all is deceit, the birth of a child an agonizing trial, and death the only certitude of achieving peace. At that time, the people of Lorraine knew only famine, massacres and looting. Their dukes, devoid of armies, sometimes took refuge in France, but more often in Vienna. They thus became more and more Austrian. Antonia's great-grandfather, a brilliant leader of men, had played a large part in routing the Turks when they laid siege to Vienna. To seal a very precarious peace between the Emperor and France, he gave his son in marriage to a niece of Louis XIV. Francis's mother, the sister of the Duke of Orleans who was the French Regent while King Louis XV was a minor, had become fanatically Lorrainese. She willingly accepted having her sons brought up at the Viennese court and Francis, the hereditary duke, marrying the Emperor's heiress. But she passionately opposed the annexation of her country by France in exchange for Tuscany being granted to her son. She was powerless, yet she did not want to leave Lorraine, and so she closeted herself away, in exile in the country over which she no longer reigned, proudly waiting to die without ever having any contact with the representatives of the country of her birth. By her, Antonia descended from the kings of France Henry IV and St. Louis.

Francis I always retained a great longing for his Lorraine where his childhood had been spent and which had been snatched from him. In spite of his imperial title, he was not a German, nor, although the Duke of Tuscany, was he an Italian. He remained, all his life, a man without roots. He showed a sort of horror at the large-scale international politics conducted by his wife and the other European sovereigns. When he was very young he joined the Freemasonry movement, an association closely modelled on the old trade-guilds, the *compagnonnages* of the Middle Ages, which were forbidden and harried by employers and governments yet were essential for workmen who needed to help one another.

The Freemasons were rationalistic and anticlerical, but not unbelievers. They wanted to institute liberty, equality and the happiness of everyone through universal fraternity, and they sang its joyful coming :

> On a path covered with a thousand flowers
> The Freemason goes through life
> Searching for joy,
> Nature's cry, friend, is liberty!

Freemasonry in the eighteenth century played a large part in spreading philosophical ideas and in preparing the way for the French Revolution; the Emperor of the Holy Empire thus needed a certain amount of courage to remain faithful to his Masonic ideal. The Pope censured Freemasonry in vain; and in spite of all her authority, Maria Theresa never managed to make Francis resign, nor did she ever succeed in having him taken unawares in the Masonic Lodge in Vienna, where Mozart was later to be initiated and where he was to find inspiration for his opera *The Magic Flute.*

Francis often told his children how agreeable it had been to live under the government of Lorraine, whose duke, according to Francis, never asked his subjects to pay taxes, was content with passing the hat among the congregation after mass when he was in dire need of funds, and recoiled from applying compulsion or punishment. Antonia was always to be astonished that it was impossible to rule France like this dream Lorraine. Francis assuaged his nostalgia by hunting, gambling, love affairs, and by his children's company. In his letters, he made a confidant of his younger brother, Charles of Lorraine, governor of the Austrian Netherlands in Brussels. Should we smile at this emperor, who was so ignorant of spelling rules at the time when Frederick, the King of Prussia, wrote poems in French, or marvel at the innocence of heart of such a great monarch ? :

You talk about splene...do you no that it is the sam as talking of a rop in the hous of a hanged man for I do not hide from you that I suffer this yere more than any other but I fite nobly against it but can not overcom it and I only try to be suffered and I hide it as much as posible. One must not think and believe one is young....

A mediocre general and a bad politician, Francis I was nevertheless a very charming friend, lover, father and husband. No one evoked his personality better than the Prince of Ligne, a young companion of the ageing emperor and his smiling rival to the heart of the exquisite Princess Auersperg:

During the period when I shared the good graces of the prettiest woman in the world and the greatest lady in Vienna with the good, excellent, steadfast, kind, even handsome Emperor, Francis I himself, the Empress sometimes went to the theatre, and then the Emperor did not dare to leave his box. One evening, he saw that she was apparently well-occupied, and slipped into the box where I always went at that time. His mistress and I were slightly taken aback by his appearance, but we knew that he was fond of both of us. He asked me what the little play was called; it was *Crispin, His Master's Rival.* I did not know how to go about telling him. He insisted. I told him, half embarrassed and half dying of laughter, stammering out the words which described, in fact, the position for both of us, and I escaped as quickly as I could, leaving this pretty and charming woman to use her brilliant imagination to find a plausible explanation of our embarrassment and my precipitate exit....

Maria Theresa, on the contrary, was strong-minded, intelligent, convinced of the lawfulness of her rights as an absolute sovereign, very conscious of her position, and engrossed above all with her prestige and the success of her line.

Her career had been brilliant, but difficult. She came to the throne on her father's death at the age of twenty-three, and had to confront a coalition of the continental countries of Europe who were firmly decided to divide her states among themselves. Quite alone, for neither her husband nor her father's ministers proved capable of coping with these dangerous circumstances, she resisted with indomitable energy, raised armies, found new generals, negotiated essential alliances and set her enemies at odds with one another. In this way, she finally managed to achieve recognition of her rights.

All her life, Maria Theresa maintained this attitude of a commander-in-chief of an army. Her political philosophy was that of Louis XIV; she had no regard for the will of her subjects, her children, or her husband.

Paradoxically, at a time when national identities were gaining strength throughout Europe and ideas of liberty and well-being

acquiring such importance, Maria Theresa worked to transform her states into an absolute, centralized monarchy. She was gifted with a sharp intelligence and an acute sense of reality; she knew how to choose her ministers, and she succeeded triumphantly in going against the current of ideas of her time.

She was very pious, and with the Catholic religion helping to justify her authority, she led a real crusade in Vienna and her states against free-thinkers and philosophical theories. In this respect, she could congratulate herself on having slowed the blossoming of an Austrian literature, but she naturally could not prevent French writings from infiltrating into her very palaces nor prevent her husband, her ministers and her children from reading them with enthusiasm.

Maria Theresa wrote and spoke an elegant Italian, French and German. She painted in oils, indifferently, it is true; she sang well, was passionately fond of dancing, and rode with skill. She loved both pomp and simplicity. Her father, Charles VI, who in his youth had been a contender to the Spanish throne against Louis XIV's grandson, had brought back the tradition of a restrictive and majestic etiquette from Madrid. Maria Theresa organized splendid festivities, but the Hofburg's ceremonies were like theatrical performances: when the play ended, everyone reverted to his natural self again. Her son, the Emperor Joseph II, considered her an extraordinary actress. At the beginning of her reign, when she was obliged to call upon her Hungarian subjects for help, she appeared weeping before the magnates of this kingdom, with her eldest child, still an infant, in her arms, and Joseph claimed that he remembered his mother pinching him hard to make him cry, in order to move the rough Magyars to pity....

Maria Theresa was certainly impassioned, but she possessed frightening lucidity and was of an arrogant egoism. In her letters to her children, although they are countless, we rarely find simple words of tenderness, and even more rarely real effusiveness. But in the Empress's strength and superiority there was an attraction to which everyone yielded.

She was an arbitrary sovereign: one day in a foreign country—Switzerland—she had a Viennese couple abducted. Both were married and had abandoned their spouses to live there —oh, for shame!—in adultery. On other occasions, however, her spontaneity was charming; one winter evening in 1768, a messenger arrived from Florence, over which her second son Leopold, the Grand Duke of Tuscany, reigned, and announced the birth of her first grandson Francis, the future emperor, adversary and father-in-law of Napoleon I. Without even changing her clothes, Maria Theresa rushed to the nearby Burgtheater, entered the imperial box and, in the middle of the performance, cried out to the audience *"Mein Leopold hat einen Buben!"* — "My Leopold has a son!" Maria Theresa was an empress to the core; the irresistible arbitrariness of her vocation enabled her to make use of even the most natural joys of her existence as a mother to serve her popularity, her authority and her prestige.

With respect to the great western nations, Maria Theresa was in a peculiar position. The Emperor of the Holy Roman Empire was the sovereign of a jutting-out borderland of Europe; he acted as a sentry in the East, which was the source of great invasions during thousands of years, and he was the champion of the borderland's cause, for he had to protect a large common frontier against the Turks, for centuries the Moslem adversaries of Christendom, who constituted such a real threat that Vienna underwent a long siege during Antonia's great-grandfather's reign, and both her grandfather and father waged a long war in the East.

This dangerous position explained the capital's characteristic appearance. Paris, London, Rome and Madrid had already been open cities for a long time. In 1755, Vienna still remained a stronghold engirdled with sturdy ramparts. The Hofburg, the residence of the imperial court, was an ancient, medieval fortress very near the town's fortifications. The first impression given by the narrow streets and old churches was that of a city rooted in its past. Vienna's medieval character was reflected in many aspects of its social and artistic life. Thieves were still displayed to public view on a platform with their thumbs crushed by an iron ring, and murderers

In order to dominate the south of Italy, Maria Theresa married Carolina, the favourite sister and confidante of Marie Antoinette, to the King of Naples, a mediocre descendant of Louis XIV through the Spanish Bourbons.

Sovereignty over Florence, the capital of Tuscany, was held by the Grand Dukes of Austria: first Maria Theresa's husband reigned and after him her son Leopold. Leopold, the future emperor, was a successful ruler in Florence because he adapted himself to the Italian way of life.

Budapest, the capital and heart of Hungary, recognized Maria Theresa as queen but had difficulty in accepting the directives of the Austrian government and the weight of its administration.

20

were tied to crosses by twos, one on each side of a large baroque figure of Christ. Antonia could not help seeing these terrible sights, nor meeting men and women who had been arrested for immorality and left tied at the town gates for months, relying on the charity of passers-by for their subsistence.

It is astonishing, however, to find a new town with elegant, sumptuous and original architecture in the heart of this medieval city. After the defeat of the Turks, Vienna underwent a truly feverish building period. The imperial family set the example, but many great Austrian, Hungarian, Italian and Czech lords also built splendid mansions. The architects came from various European countries, particularly from Italy, France and Germany. The result was a style which was both varied and original. During this period, no other capital could boast of such a luxuriant architectural blooming.

The most spectacular work was carried out in the Hofburg's grounds. Following the plans of that greatest of Austrian architects, Johann Bernard Fischer von Erlach, his son, Joseph Emmanuel, built the Hofbibliothek, a large edifice with great central eaves and two perfectly symmetrical wings. The abundance of sculptures is the only feature characteristic of Viennese baroque, for the building is of classical elegance. To complete this structure, which was finished at Maria Theresa's accession, the architect Pacassi constructed equally severe buildings at the two ends and at the right angle; these were almost completed when Antonia left Vienna for Paris. An admirable complex was thus formed. Farther away, but still adjoining the Hofburg, Joseph Emmanuel von Erlach added an enormous, high room, with a span like a church nave; it was the winter riding-school. From the gallery, copied from the Versailles chapel gallery where she was later to hear mass, Antonia admired the prowess of the horses trained in the famous Spanish school.

Throughout the city, Antonia could see sumptuous mansions. The Starhemberg Palace was built by the Italian, Domenico Martinelli, as was that of the sovereign princes of Liechtenstein. Fischer von Erlach the elder built, among others, Batthyany Palace and Lobkowitz Palace, and Lukas von Hildebrandt built Fondi-Schwarzenberg Palace and Harrach Palace. Lembruch Palace was erected by Anton Ospel and Esterhazy Palace by

Giovanni Petro Tencala. Together with the Wilzech, Caprara, Kinsky and many other palaces, these made Vienna, a town without manufacturers and almost without suburbs, a very aristocratic city. The most perfect evidence of Austrian baroque was the Belvedere Palace at the town gates where, in 1770, Emperor Joseph II was to organize the festivities in honour of Antonia's marriage. The German Hildebrandt here created this most sumptuous and elegant edifice for Eugène of Savoy, a prince brought up in France who afterwards became the best general and the most-consulted minister of the German emperors. This architect gave free rein to his imagination with a medley of stone ornaments, but their over-elaborate forms never appear ridiculous. The interior was decorated by such French sculptors and painters as Louis Dorigny, who extolled in vast compositions the Austrian victories over his countrymen. This residence contained the finest collection of engravings and sketches in Europe, a legacy to the imperial family from the Prince.

During Antonia's childhood, Austrian architecture was increasingly influenced by France. At the time of her birth, Nicolas Jadot, a Lorrainese architect called to Vienna by the Emperor Francis I, completed the new building of Vienna university, which was of such elegance and simplicity that it might almost have been constructed in Paris. At the Hofburg, Jadot had just copied the monumental Ambassadors' Staircase, built by Louis XIV at Versailles and destroyed by Louis XV. Two hundred years later, most of these buildings still exist. Vienna has faithfully kept its baroque appearance and Antonia's memory lives on in these stones which she knew when they were still white.

Maria Theresa liked to spend the summer with her children at her Schönbrunn Castle, a few miles from Vienna. There was a great, uncompleted structure there, built in 1770, which had been waiting forty years for the final touches when Maria Theresa acceded to the throne. From 1743 onwards, the Italian architect, Nicolas Pacassi, following the Empress's instructions, transformed the buildings and progressively arranged all the rooms. During two hundred years, almost nothing has been changed; today we can see the palace, the furniture and decoration exactly as they were chosen, painted and arranged at the time when Antonia was a Viennese.

21

This intimate scene in the domestic life of the imperial family was painted by one of Marie Antoinette's sisters, Maria Christina. It is the occasion of the feast of St. Nicholas, 1762, and the children have received gifts. The Emperor Francis I has taken up a rather bourgeois position by the fire and behind him stands his wife, Maria Theresa.

Schönbrunn, much less vast, is not a Versailles. Here there are neither marble nor precious stones, and the outside of this large palace, painted light ochre, has a modest appearance. If Versailles is the masterpiece of the art of grandeur, Schönbrunn is a typical example of the art of comfort and *Gemütlichkeit*. It is a large house, very pleasant to live in, with good German stoves in every room. The interior is characteristic of Maria Theresa's eclectic tastes, and of the curiosity about the whole world which was typical of the Austrians. In one room there is Chinese lacquer-ware, in another Persian designs; others are decorated by Italian or French painters, and over all there is a superabundance of stucco decoration painted in various colours. This slightly superficial sumptuousness is very characteristic of Austrian rococo. One study is decorated solely with works painted by the children of the

Emperor Francis and the Empress Maria Theresa. In Vienna, art was a common embellishment and a distinction was not always made between the work of professionals and that of amateurs. One gallery is decorated with mediocre paintings showing the Archduke Joseph's marriage in 1760; they were souvenirs and not real works of art. Maria Theresa rarely called upon the greatest painters of the period; she probably found their prices too high. She did not commission Tiepolo to paint her frescoes, but Guglielmi, one of his second-rate disciples. It was Bellotto, and not Guardi or Canaletto, who depicted Schönbrunn in 1760. In the same way, the Empress did not order pastels by Latour or Perronneau, but by Liotard, a good Swiss artist who visited her from time to time. When Maria Theresa wanted to show her artistic aspirations, however, she found much of her inspiration in the Versailles ideal of

22

a century earlier. Thus she had her gardens designed according to Le Nôtre's style at the time when "Chinese gardens" were fashionable in France. She had a miniature Hall of Mirrors built, with the ceilings, which Antonia saw painted, showing the exploits of Maria Theresa portrayed as a goddess, in the style invented by Lebrun for Louis XIV a century earlier and which was already considered fairly ridiculous in France. Schönbrunn was the magnificent house of a woman who liked her comfort as much as great art.

In literature, too, Austria played no more than a modest role. All the great German writers and philosophers of the eighteenth century lived in the provinces and cities of the North. Vienna, however, possessed more theatres than any other city in the world. Even the Benedictines, Jesuits and Piarists organized performances in their schools, but these were acted in Latin. At court and among the great lords, by contrast, Italian opera was particularly fashionable. But in little theatres popular German plays full of frankness were acted. Lady Mary Wortley Montague, who attended a performance of *Amphytrion* in Vienna, reported about it:

I thought the house very low and dark; but I confess the comedy amply recompensed that defect. I never laughed so much in my life. It began with Jupiter's falling in love out of a peep-hole in the clouds, and ended with the birth of Hercules.... But I could not easily pardon the liberty the poet has taken of larding his play with, not only indecent expressions, but such gross words as I don't think our mob would suffer from a mountebank. Besides, the two Sosias very fairly let down their breeches in the direct view of the boxes, which were full of the people of the first rank, that seemed very well pleased with the entertainment, and assured me this was a celebrated piece.

The most characteristic sculptor of this period was certainly Balthasar Ferdinand Moll. He was often called upon by the court, and his masterpiece was the sarcophagus of Francis I and Maria Theresa, which the Empress commissioned him to do just before Antonia was born. The spouses are shown face to face, awakening from the sleep of death. They hold the sceptre together with their right hands, and a naked cherub holds a crown of stars above them. It is brilliantly painted and skilfully composed, but the peculiar combination of minute realism,

Many of Marie Antoinette's features can be seen in her father, Francis I. He is here portrayed in red chalk, supposedly by the little girl herself when she was ten years old.

opera and balls. Her grandfather, the Emperor Charles VI, was an outstanding harpsichord player and, as was then the custom, regularly led his court orchestra on this instrument. Most of the Habsburg family, and particularly the Empress Maria Theresa, were excellent musicians. The archdukes and duchesses, the children of Francis I and Maria Theresa, often formed an orchestra, but Antonia was too young to take part.

At that time, Vienna was the musical capital of the world. The generation of great classical musicians, Bach, Scarlatti and Händel, lived in the four corners of Europe, in Germany, Italy, France and even in England during the first half of the century. Thanks to its international character, its vast public enthusiasm, and the passion for music of its sovereigns and great lords, Austria towards 1750 became the source of an artistic revolution which was to give birth to a new music. Georg Christoph Wagenseil, the Empress Maria Theresa's music-master, invented the

The street vendor gives a particular animation to a town and he adapts his wares to its tastes and its needs: thus the birdseller is a symbol of eighteenth-century Vienna, a city impassioned by music and joie de vivre.

political and religious propaganda and theatrical mythology makes us want to smile.

At the same time, the unyielding and rather pathetic faith of Austria was expressed in the numerous sculptures of baroque crucifixes which Antonia admired along the paths she walked during her childhood, and which still arouse the same fervour today. The cross is always richly decorated, and the personages at its foot are full of strength and health and draped in sumptuous robes. But Christ twists in agony and on the pedestal a skull recalls the brevity of human existence. Popular Austrian artists passionately extolled the joys of a world whose vanity and perversity they denounced. The country was at the same time pious, untamed and very sentimental.

Antonia was steeped in a musical atmosphere. She probably never became a very good singer; according to the kindest reports, her voice was not very true and she did not play any instrument regularly enough to achieve real skill. But she adored concerts,

The Habsburg emperors had established a magnificent collection of carpets and tapestries from Flanders. Their taste was shared by their Viennese subjects and the rugseller was a popular figure in the eighteenth century.

24

The Vienna street cries added greatly to the charm of the city. "Poine! Poine!" yelled the seller of curd-cheese, much eaten by the Viennese; "Kauft Dinten!" chanted the inkseller who supplied the public writers.

concerto for piano and the modern symphony; and it was in Milan, also on Austrian soil, that San Martini, one of the chief reformers of Italian music and the admired master of Gluck and Mozart, worked until 1775.

In the sixties, when Antonia listened to her first concerts, two composers held sway over Viennese life. Joseph Haydn, with an ease, verve and rapidity which recalled the way in which Voltaire composed short stories for the Duchess of Maine at Sceaux, improvised his first string quartets for a group of friends at Melk, near Vienna, shortly after Antonia's birth. He wrote his finest symphonies between 1760 and 1770 either in Vienna or in Hungary. Haydn delights and touches the heart. With great restraint and seeming lightness, he knew how to be simple and human. His compositions link music with painting, for his works, as do those of Mozart, recall the finest achievements of Fragonard. The knight Gluck, who was born in 1714 in the north of Germany and who was much older than Haydn, was really worshipped by the Viennese during Antonia's youth. The imperial family were his passionate supporters, and he wrote and conducted his principal operas in Vienna: *Alcestis* in 1761 and *Orfeo* in 1762. His dramas captured the imagination and his heroes loved or suffered intensely in real situations. When Antonia, who had in the meantime become dauphine and then queen, heard Gluck in Paris, the enthusiastic fervour of her childhood swept her up again; to achieve the success of the Viennese composer's operas she was to plot, intrigue and fight more efficiently than she ever would to obtain a political decision.

The arrival at Schönbrunn Palace of the conquering hero of the battle of Kunersdorf (1759) by Bernardo Bellotto. He has been summoned to recount the story of his victory to the Empress and her ministers. ▷

The "Millions" Room, one of the most beautiful reception halls in the Schönbrunn Palace, is so named because of the million florins (over £800,000 or about two million dollars) spent on its decoration. Maria Theresa commissioned the ambassador of the Holy Empire at the court of the Sultan to gather together the extraordinary collection of ancient Persian and Hindu miniatures that adorn this room and that make it look like something out of the Thousand and One Nights. The gilt picture-frames are elaborately ornamented in a French-influenced rococo style. This is Vienna in her essential role of a city situated in the confines of Christian Europe; a borderland under the constant threat of the Moslem Turks, the centuries-long opponents of Christianity; a city with one eye turned towards the East.

Curiously enough, Mozart did not have the same effect on her. Yet they met several times. The author of *Don Juan* was three months younger than the future queen and died a few months before her. The first accounts of their acquaintanceship come from Mozart's father and sister. Leopold Mozart took his six-year-old prodigy son on his conquest of Europe. After leaving his native town, Salzburg, the first stage of the journey was Vienna, where they were received in a very flattering way. On October 16th, 1762 Leopold Mozart wrote to his friend Hagenauer, who had remained behind in Salzburg:

I have only time to tell you this about our session at court; we were received with so many marks of favour by their Majesties that if I told you about it in detail, my account would be taken for a fairy-tale. We remained with the Empress from three to six o'clock, and the Emperor took me into an adjoining room to hear how the Infante played the piano.

Mozart's sister was to recount that the performance which they gave to their imperial majesties lasted more than three hours, and the archdukes and archduchesses were also present. Among other things, Emperor Francis said to Wolfgang that it was not difficult to play with ten fingers, but a more arduous exploit would be to play on a harpsichord which was covered over. Thereupon the child began playing with a single finger with the greatest agility, and then had the keys covered over with a sheet and played on this, just as if he had often practised the feat.

Later, much later, other real or imaginary details, which in any case are very touching, came to light about this reception, which certainly made a great impression on the small musician. Was it from the lips of Mozart himself that his wife heard the account of his fall on the over-polished floors of the Hofburg? Antonia rushed to help him up and consoled him. Mozart, touched by the Princess's consideration, said, "You are kind; I would like to marry you." The children recounted the incident to the Empress who diverted herself by asking the little musician why he wanted to marry her daughter. "Out of gratitude," said Wolfgang. And Antonia is supposed to have kissed him. In any case, the solemn etiquette at the court did not exclude such familiarities.

Five years later, Mozart made another and last appearance in the Archduchess' life. He was known throughout Europe for his virtuosity and his first works were esteemed. But the atmosphere at the court of Vienna had greatly changed. Since her husband's death, the Empress, as Leopold Mozart remarked, had no more "music" and no longer went to the opera or the Comédie. She warmly recommended the Mozarts to her son, the Emperor Joseph II, but he had a horror of spending. Moreover, this was the period during which Gluck, who was supported by the whole imperial family, enjoyed his greatest success. On January 23rd, 1768, Leopold Mozart wrote:

On the 19th, we stayed at the court from three o'clock to half past five. The Emperor came to meet us and took us in himself. Prince Albert and all the archduchesses were there, but no strangers. The Empress was very kind...and the Emperor talked to me and Wolfgang about music....

Mozart's youthful works then seemed to the Viennese, who only admired his virtuosity as a prodigy, as if they were copied from Joseph Haydn and therefore lacking originality. Antonia left Vienna too early to be able to judge differently, and she probably did not have the possibility of hearing Mozart's finest works in Paris. Yet their destinies ran parallel, and because of a meeting which is perhaps unique in history, the gay, light-hearted, brilliant and tragic Marie Antoinette is the quintessence of the fascinating, equivocal beauty of Mozart's masterpieces.

The events of the little archduchess's childhood are very little known. She had twelve brothers and sisters, for three of her parents' sixteen children were already dead when she was born. Most of them, however, were considerably older, and not playfriends.

Her contemporaries were Ferdinand, born in 1754 and the future governor of the Milanese, and Maximilian, born in 1756, who, thanks to the Queen of France, was later to become the Archbishop of Cologne. But among her own family, her most faithful friend was her sister, named Maria Carolina, who was born just before her. Until her death, Maria Carolina was to cling fiercely to the guillotined queen, and was even to cause anti-French coalitions to be formed under the Empire, and protect and help Nelson before the decisive battle of Trafalgar.

The Empress Maria Theresa had the Blue Drawing-room at Schönbrunn papered with a Chinese wall decoration. All the paintings on the walls of this vast room are original works executed in the Celestial Empire. Things oriental had long been in vogue in Europe but the eighteenth century saw an accentuation of this curiosity. In France, Chinese and Japanese lacquers were greatly appreciated and cabinet-makers would go to great expense to send furniture to the Far East to be lacquered on the spot. But in spite of assimilated borrowings decoration remained homogenous and completely in French taste. In Austria, however, the Empress accepted the usages and art of an unknown country, and created a truly exotic room that could give scope to the romantic imaginings of its inhabitants.

29

The Emperor's children were not brought up alone. German and Austrian princesses lived with them, sharing their games and receiving the same education. Antonia always remained very attached to the two princesses of Hesse of whom one, Charlotte, was to become Princess of Mecklenburg, and the other, Louise, hereditary princess and afterwards *Landgräfin* of Hesse Darmstadt. These childhood links always remained very strong, for, on the eve of her trial and her transfer to the Conciergerie prison, when an inventory was drawn up of the objects which the Queen carried on her, two miniatures of the princesses were among her few treasures.

When she was two years old, Antonia suffered a severe attack of measles. On January 31st, 1758, the Count of Kevenhüller, the great chamberlain at the Viennese court, noted in his diary: "During the first days of this year, she was very ill to such a point that we were very anxious about this amiable and pretty princess." Nevertheless, her recovery was rapid. The following year, on October 5th, 1759, she took part in a children's performance, given by the Empress to celebrate her husband's birthday. Antonia, who was not even four years old, wore a sumptuous court dress and already sang verses in French. On that evening, each of her brothers and sisters showed their talents: Ferdinand beat a drum, Maximilian recited a poem in Italian, Charles played the violin, Joseph the 'cello, and Maria Anna and Maria Christina a duet on the piano....

In 1760, great festivities were held in Vienna to celebrate the marriage of Archduke Joseph, heir to the imperial throne, to the Infanta Isabella of Parma, the child of the daughter of the French king Louis XV and the son of the King of Spain. In spite of the Seven Years War, in which Austria, France and Spain suffered many defeats, there were splendid celebrations. The small archduchess, then five years old, attended the immense parade of the nuptial procession, admired the balls, the theatrical performances, and also the roundabouts, banquets and fireworks.

On December 10th, 1763, Maria Theresa wrote to her faithful follower, Count Sylva Tarovca: "Antoinette has convulsions; she has been unconscious for the last hour." Once again, she recovered rapidly. On June 13th, 1764, a celebration was held at Schönbrunn to mark the event of her first communion. On January 24th, 1765, she danced a ballet with her brothers Leopold and Ferdinand during the merry-making organized on the second marriage of her brother Joseph, whose first wife had died. In August at Innsbruck, in the Tyrol, where the whole court had gone to celebrate Leopold's wedding, a misfortune occurred which certainly affected her deeply. Her father, Francis I of Lorraine, who seemed to be in excellent health, was walking down a staircase with his eldest son when he fell as if struck by lightning. He had suffered an attack of apoplexy and died in the Archduke Joseph's arms. Maria Theresa was so distressed at her husband's passing that the atmosphere at court changed completely; she no longer had any desire to organize festivities or attend performances. She even considered giving up the government, but decided instead to include the Archduke Joseph in the direction of state affairs and had him elected emperor. In April, 1766, Antonia again attended a banquet in honour of her sister Maria Christina's marriage to Prince Albert of Sachsen-Teschen. A month later, according to Kevenhüller, she was ill again.

Towards the month of April in 1767 —Antonia was eleven years old—an event took place of which she was to speak often at Versailles. From this time onwards, she felt respect mixed with fear for her mother the Empress, who was probably rather terrifying in her mourning. As a consequence of smallpox, a contagious illness which at that time was mostly fatal, Joseph II had just lost his second wife, Josephine of Bavaria, who was not greatly lamented in Vienna, for she was neither brilliant nor beautiful nor amiable, and her husband had not loved her. The Empress, however, instructed her daughter, Maria Josephina, then the fiancée of the King of Naples, not to leave Vienna on any condition before meditating in the family tomb where her sister-in-law had just been interred. The future queen of Naples was convinced that the contagious disease would inevitably infect her if she obeyed, yet she did not feel

In this painting, preserved at Schönbrunn, van der Meytens reproduces a scene in the Redoutensaal in Vienna in 1760, on the occasion of a concert attended by Marie Antoinette and given in honour of the marriage of her eldest brother, the future emperor Joseph II.

strong enough to resist an order which she considered as a death sentence. Before going down into the crypt, she took her little sister Antonia on to her lap, confided her fears to her and bade her farewell for ever. Maria Josephina actually was infected in her turn by this terrible sickness and died two weeks later. The Queen of France was never able to rid herself of the tragic impression that the Empress' severity had caused the death of one of her daughters. In obeying the precepts of religion or family morality, has one the right to risk the life of one's child?

A few weeks later, Maria Theresa decided to arrange a marriage between the King of Naples and Archduchess Maria Carolina, in Maria Josephina's stead, and her first precaution was to separate her two youngest daughters, for she considered their closeness dangerous. On August 19th, 1767, she wrote to Carolina:

I warn you that you will be totally separated from your sister Antonia. I forbid any secrets, contact or speech with her: if the little one were to begin again, you need only to pay no attention to her or to tell Lerchenfeld [Carolina's grand mistress] or your ladies. All these intrigues will thus come to an end immediately; in any case, these secrets only consist of remarks against your neighbours or your family or ladies. I warn you that you will be closely watched and that I rely on you as the elder and therefore the most sensible to make your sister behave.

The following spring, Maria Carolina became the Queen of Naples, but did not forget her little sister. Ten days after her marriage on April 17th, she wrote to the Countess of Lerchenfeld, who was now responsible for Antonia's education:

Write and tell me the little events concerning my sister Antonia; what she says, what she does, and almost what she thinks. I beg and entreat you to love her very much, for I am very interested in her.

Then on August 13th:

I was pleased to learn that my dear brother, the Emperor, took Antonia into his box at the theatre; I know how these little honours give pleasure and nothing would make me happier than to know that people recognize how amiable my sister is and that they sing her praises.... I beg you to tell my sister that I love her extremely.

The prospect of a French marriage existed for the Empress' youngest daughter from the time of her birth. 1775 was, indeed, the year which marked the reversal of alliances. Louis XV, betrayed by Prussia during the Austrian War of Succession, and frightened by England's progress throughout the world, was thinking of re-adopting a policy thought up by Louis XIV during the last years of his life, the Franco-Austrian reconciliation. And according to political philosophy such agreements were sealed by marriages.

In the eyes of all Frenchmen, Austria, however, seemed to be their hereditary enemy. Since Charles Quint, nearly three centuries earlier, France had resisted being encircled by the house of Habsburg, which had reigned over the Netherlands in the north, over the Empire in the east and over Spain in the south. The Austrian threat had, in fact, disappeared a long time ago. But hate is not easy to eradicate.

Negotiations followed by an Anglo-Prussian agreement in 1756 threw France into the arms of Austria, but this alliance born of necessity had a difficult beginning. It was the work of two brilliant politicians, the Prince of Kaunitz, Austrian ambassador to Versailles in 1753 and afterwards Chancellor of the Empire, and the Duke of Choiseul, the French ambassador to Vienna and later Louis XV's chief minister.

Since the son of Louis XV had a wife and children, the only possible connection between the two crowns would have been the marriage of the eldest of the Dauphin's sons to an archduchess of the same age. The Dauphin, however, who was very enamoured of his wife, a Saxony princess hostile to the Empress, and who was himself the avowed enemy of Choiseul, decided to refuse his consent. His death on December 20th, 1765 hastened the diplomats' action. Choiseul obtained an agreement in principle from Louis XV. The Prince of Starhemberg, Austrian ambassador to Versailles, considered the decision as being definite. But Louis XV still hesitated.

In Vienna, the Marquis of Durfort, the French ambassador, was shown all kinds of attention. Once Maria Theresa herself asked him for the portraits of the entire French royal family, and also gave him the name of a painter capable of painting those of her children. Another day, Starhemberg was chatting to Durfort in the presence of Antonia, then thirteen years old:

"What do you think of her?" asked the Austrian with typical Teutonic frankness.

"Very charming," said Durfort politely.

Francis I and Maria Theresa had sixteen children of which six attained adulthood. In those days a large family gave the opportunity to make many alliances and Maria Theresa was always careful to marry her children in the most useful way possible. This portrait was simply copied and adapted as each new addition was made to the family.

Starhemberg looked at him laughingly and said: "His Highness the Dauphin will have a delightful wife there." All at once, the old lord, who found Antonia exquisite, was ready to forget diplomatic prudence: "She is a dainty morsel" he replied, laughing too, "and will be in good hands...if it is to be."

From 1769 onwards, French masters were assigned to Antonia in Vienna. They were two French actors, a profession very much scorned in Paris. Durfort became worried. Could the education of a future queen of France be neglected? Choiseul, without officially taking a hand in choosing a tutor, nevertheless advised the Austrian ambassador, Mercy-Argenteau. The Abbé Vermond was

thereupon engaged in Paris in 1768 by the imperial ambassador; he remained to the end of his days in Austria's service, even after returning to France.

Definite negotiations commenced at the beginning of 1769 with a portrait being ordered. Choiseul, for economy's sake, sent a little-known pastellist, Ducreux, to Austria. To avoid giving the painter's journey the appearance of a decisive diplomatic step, he was instructed to paint the portraits of three archduchesses and even of a son-in-law of the Empress. Two months' work, and the son of the French ambassador was able to take Antonia's portrait by Joseph Ducreux back to Versailles.

33

This pastel seemed to influence Louis XV more than Choiseul's subtle intervention. On June 7th, 1769, the King of France suggested celebrating the marriage during the month of April 1770. Indeed, no fewer than ten months were necessary for the laborious negotiations on the marriage contract and the preparation of all the festivities.

During the fifteen years of diplomatic discussions, there was never any question about the inclinations or ideas of Antonia or Louis Auguste. Never at any time was the chance offered to one or the other to accept or refuse their fate.

The unknown prince for whom destiny and politics intended Antonia was, however, neither handsome nor brilliant nor gay. He was a lonely child, weighed down by the burden of his future responsibilities even before he had to carry them.

Louis Auguste, born a year earlier than Antonia and named the Duke of Berry by his grandfather, Louis XV, was the second son of his pious, conscientious and mournful parents, Louis, the Dauphin of France, and his wife, Maria Josephine of Saxony. He was neither very strong nor very gifted intellectually, and during the first years of his life he served the purpose of showing up the intelligence of his elder brother, the Duke of Burgundy, who was heir to the throne according to the laws of the kingdom. Burgundy, proud and witty from his earliest childhood, seemed a born king. His childish remarks delighted his family and the court. During the Seven Years' War, when France often suffered disastrous defeats, he declared one day when the situation was particularly depressing: "Why do you look sad? I am very well." And again, "I shall subjugate England and take the King of Prussia prisoner. I shall do everything I wish. Why was I not born God?"

Berry listened admiringly to his brother who embodied the hopes of a gloomy court.

In 1760, however, Burgundy fell seriously ill. It seemed completely natural that Berry should live day and night at his brother's bedside to take his mind off the pain. Louis Auguste, then six years old, witnessed his adored brother's slow decline; he listened to his complaints and confessions and was probably marked for life by this inhuman trial.

On the day that Burgundy, heroic and fully conscious, was finally freed from his sufferings by death, Louis Auguste became seriously ill in his turn. His convalescence was long, but he managed to survive the sickness, most probably tuberculosis, which had carried off his brother.

Now heir to the throne, and surrounded by tutors, gentlemen-in-waiting and valets, Louis Auguste was still not happy. His younger brothers, the Count of Provence and the Count of Artois, who were more gifted for learning and more skilful courtiers, played the same ill-omened part with regard to him as the Duke of Burgundy had done.

As he grew older, Louis Auguste was more and more alone. He was little loved and always retired within himself. One day, the Duke de la Vauguyon organized a lottery for Berry, his brothers and a few courtiers. According to the rules, each winner had to give his prize to the person present whom he loved the most. The game was gay and lively. All the winners gave their prizes to Provence and Artois. Berry won in his turn, and without saying a word, he put the prize in his pocket. La Vauguyon asked him to comply with the rules. "Who do you expect me to love the most here," he asked, "where I see I am loved by no one?"

Louis Auguste, taciturn and with fits of violent joy and anger, put people out of countenance. His misanthropy was considered as a sign of insufficient intellectual development in an age in which human relationships were so important. He hunted often, and read very widely, but only books on history or science. He was interested neither in art nor music, and did not dance. He only aroused the sympathy of his grandfather and other attentive observers who esteemed his knowledge and his real common sense. Others considered him a savage and an imbecile; the ambassadors, in spite of the restraint of their diplomatic style, said this plainly in their dispatches. "He seems to have been brought up in a wood," wrote the King of Naples' emissary and Maria Theresa's representative.

The watercolourist Carmontelle portrayed the six-year-old Mozart with his father and sister on the occasion of the young musician's first voyage to Paris. Not long before, Mozart had met Marie Antoinette in Vienna. Strangely enough the future queen was never to become familiar with the works of this Austrian composer.

"If appearances are to be believed, nature seems to have refused His Highness the Dauphin every gift. His countenance and remarks herald only a very limited intelligence, little comeliness and no sensitivity."

Antonia's education was completely neglected in her childhood. In the eighteenth century, it was not the custom to devote as much care to girls' education as to that of boys, and if Maria Theresa was exceptionally well brought up, it was because her father knew that she would be called upon to succeed him. The clearest proof of Antonia's ignorance was to be seen on her arrival in France; at that time she wrote so badly that she was unable to sign her marriage contract without making a spelling mistake and a great blob of ink. On the eve of her departure, Maria Theresa severely pointed out to her "her little inclination for any serious application, her superficiality, and her indolence". Later, the Queen herself was freely to admit that she had learnt almost nothing in Vienna. She told her chambermaid, Madame Campan, that

... the Empress received news of her children from her doctor, and sometimes only saw them every eight or ten days. The grand mistresses responsible for supervising the archduchesses' education tried to make themselves popular with their pupils by following the very common path of indulgence, which is so fatal to progress.

Antonia, as Madame Campan also reported, had her grand mistress dismissed by admitting to the Empress that she had her pages of writing prepared in pencil by others.

We have proof of this in a letter written in French to this accommodating teacher, the Countess of Brandeis; the text is elegant, but not very natural; it was probably written to offer her wishes for New Year's Day in 1768:

My very dear Brandis, I wish you the compliments of the season. Believe me, my dear Brandis, that the wishes I express for your happiness spring from a most grateful heart. I hope that in the future my obedience will compensate for the care which you expend on my education. Continue, my dear friend, and rest assured of the affection of your faithful pupil.

The pencil marks can still be seen today under the ink covering them; the letters had been traced beforehand for Antonia who, at this time, still did not know how to write, although she was already twelve years old.

The Countess of Lerchenfeld, the former grand mistress of Archduchess Maria Caroline, was Countess Brandeis' successor in April, 1768. She does not seem to have achieved any more spectacular results. One day someone at Versailles mentioned to the Queen a drawing which she had done and which the Empress Maria Theresa had given to a Frenchman, M. Gérard, the first clerk of the Foreign Ministry, on the occasion of his visit to Vienna in 1769 to negotiate the marriage contract. "I would blush," said the Queen in the presence of Madame Campan, "if I were shown this evidence of the cheating in my education; I do not think that I put a pencil once to this drawing."

When she arrived in France at the age of fourteen, she had to take a few music lessons in secret so that her complete ignorance would not be revealed to her first official teachers.

When the Abbé Vermond arrived towards the end of 1768, Antonia's tuition was probably better organized, but the education, lasting fifteen months, does not seem to have borne much fruit. Abbé Vermond's letters to the Count of Mercy-Argenteau in Paris, which were intended to keep the latter informed of Antonia's slow progress, provide an extremely suggestive picture of the future dauphine during the months preceding her marriage. Already in January 1769, he wrote:

After using my first lessons to learn Her Royal Highness' turn of mind and the extent of her learning, I drew up a list of the subjects and the method which I thought most useful. I included religion, French history, a general smattering of French literature, and gave special attention to the language and spelling. To lessen the boredom of these lessons, I bring them down as much as I can to a conversational level. I cannot praise Her Royal Highness' gentleness and willingness enough, but her liveliness and frequent distractions thwart her wish to learn in spite of herself. It would be desirable for the conclusion of her education to be less near.... I am completely convinced that the court and the nation will be charmed with our future dauphine; she combines

Both art and sport had a part in the feasts given by Maria Theresa at Vienna. The mother of Marie Antoinette was an excellent horsewoman and herself directed sumptuous "caroussels" in the riding-school at the Hofburg Palace. After two hundred years the magnificent hall of the Hofreitschule remains just as Martin van der Meytens shows it in this painting.

all the graces of bearing with a delightful appearance, and if, as it is to be hoped, she grows a little, she will possess all the charms to be desired in a great princess.

Then during the month of June, from Schönbrunn :

I was very contented in Vienna, and I am even more so at Schönbrunn. I cannot describe to Your Excellency how much goodness, attention and fear of troubling me this young princess shows me every day. She does not, however, doubt the pleasure I take in being with her. I was extremely flattered by the truthful and naive answer she gave recently. H.M., making her give an account of how she spent her time, had the goodness to add : "You are subjugating the abbé too much." "No, Mama, I well see that he likes it." I would like this kind of life to last until I leave ; I regain by her conversation what H.R.H.'s liveliness makes me lose when teaching.

It hardly requires these letters as proof to understand that Abbé Vermond first of all wished to forewarn Mercy-Argenteau against a disappointment. The Archduchess was certainly pretty, amiable and gay ; she learnt very easily, but she wrote with difficulty, spoke French with German sentence constructions and syntax mistakes, and knew little history and catechism. Yet all this was perhaps not necessary in order to please.

From 1768 onwards, in order to learn French dances, Antonia was entrusted to one of the most famous ballet masters at the Paris Opéra, Noverre, who had been invited to Vienna to organize the performances in honour of Maria Carolina's marriage to the King of Naples. We know that Antonia often danced in Vienna and was passionately fond of this diversion. But at the Hofburg balls easier German dances were preferred to the subtle and complicated French figures. Here too, Antonia learned nothing, or almost nothing, for in spite of her wonderfully dexterous master's efforts, which were perhaps too brief, she felt incapable of dancing the minuet at her own marriage festivities at Versailles and preferred to look on. In two respects, however, the care of her retinue provided satisfying results. A French dentist, summoned by Durfort on Abbé Vermond's advice, succeeded in healing the child's decayed teeth within a few months, and by the beginning of 1769 her teeth were pretty and well-spaced. A complete success was also achieved with her hair. It was fine and

supple, of a beautiful ash-blond colour, but it grew slightly too low down on her forehead and her family were anxious about this shortcoming. Larseneur, a Frenchman sent by Choiseul, invented a new hairstyle which enchanted the Viennese and which the Dauphine wore in her portrait by Ducreux. The Count of Neny, Maria Theresa's private secretary, declared : "It is simple and decent, but at the same time very flattering to the face," and he added, "I am convinced that our young ladies, who for some time have been wearing mountains of curls, will abandon them forthwith and dress their hair like the Dauphine." Antonia was probably satisfied, for she continued for a long time to have her hair dressed by Larseneur, in spite of the criticism he was to undergo in France.

From the beginning of 1769, when her marriage with Louis Auguste appeared probable, until her departure for Paris, Antonia's life was supervised by the ambassadors.

In January, she had a sore throat, and to her great regret was unable to take part in the New Year receptions. But her mother, to console her, gave her a jewel as a present, and even arranged a new ball in honour of the Count of Logres, the French ambassador's son. This time, Antonia danced the minuet, which she had just learned from Noverre, with the young man, but she only danced one and then preferred eight easier quadrilles.

During the month of April, Antonia often posed for Ducreux, and found it boring, for the same pastel had to be begun again several times. Then on June 13th, Louis XV's marriage proposal arrived. Her mother, who was rather superstitious on great occasions, took her on a pilgrimage to a small village in Styria, Mariazellen, where a twelfth-century Virgin in wood was supposed to bring luck to young married couples. After spending the summer at Schönbrunn, festivities were begun again in the autumn on returning to Vienna.

When the French ambassador came to offer his wishes at the Hofburg on January 1st, 1770, Antonia was in too much of a hurry to receive him in her apartments. "If you will come with me," she said, "I will show you something that you have perhaps never seen !" and she whisked him along to the Archduchess Theresa, who was eight years old and the only daughter of Joseph II. The child had just received a magnificent toy with movable scenes, showing the main events of the Old

At the age of ten Marie Antoinette applauded a ballet danced by her brothers and sisters in the Schönbrunn Gardens. The picture is by Greipel.

Testament. Antonia was enthusiastic about the mechanical theatre, and the ambassador politely pretended to share her delight.

Two deaths, one after the other, put a sad note on this year's beginning. First of all, little Theresa was carried off on January 23rd, after a lightning illness. As she was Louis XV's great-grandchild, the whole French court wore mourning for her, but in spite of the Emperor's grief the court of Vienna did not follow this example; the death of a child younger than twelve was not considered a bereavement in Austria. On February 23rd, the Countess of Lerchenfeld, who had been Antonia's grand mistress for two years and her friend for even longer, was brutally carried off by death. She was replaced by the Countess of Trautmannsdorff.

In spite of these distressing events, the Empress, who wished to initiate her daughter as much as possible into society life, ordered gambling twice a week. They played at Cavagnol, and Maria Theresa reproached Antonia with not being interested enough in the game. At the *Krammerfest*, a ball given by the Emperor in February, Maria Theresa informed Durfort that Antonia had become a young woman and asked him to tell the French court the happy news. On February 28th a ball was given by the Prince of Kaunitz. Antonia did not attend it nor was she to be seen at the other Carnival festivities. Officially, she had a sore throat and her mother wished to save her strength in these last few weeks before the marriage ceremonies, but it is possible that she sincerely suffered from the death of her beloved Lerchenfeld.

On April 3rd, Durfort brought Antonia and her mother two portraits of the Dauphin. His fiancée sweetly asked for permission to hang up hers in her own apartments and this greatly pleased the ambassador. During the first week of the month, the delegations of official bodies followed upon each other's heels to offer their congratulations to the future dauphine. Antonia answered the represent-

These six portraits form part of a series of miniatures of Maria Theresa's family. From left to right : Maria Christina, who was to marry Prince Albert of Sachsen-Teschen ; Maria Carolina, future queen of Naples ; Maria Amalia, future duchess of Parma ; Leopold, Grand Duke of Tuscany and the future emperor ; Maximilian, who

atives of Vienna University, who made a speech to her in Latin, by a few sentences in the same language, which had probably been written by Vermond and which she had hastily learnt by heart.

Then the festivities suddenly came to a halt for Antonia. In the instructions left to his children, the Emperor Francis had asked them to make a few days' retreat each year to prepare themselves for death. Alone with Abbé Vermond and far from the preparations for the celebration, Antonia devoted three days to edifying reading and reflection on death. Against all expectations, this experience interested her; she became enthusiastic and declared to Vermond: "I would need more time to explain all my ideas to you."

Her mother also decided—rather late, it is true—to take a personal interest in her. For a few days, the Empress had her daughter sleep in her bedroom, spoke to her tenderly, and initiated her into the mysteries of married life. But the ageing sovereign also tried to ensure the faithfulness of the future queen of the most powerful kingdom in Europe for herself and her dynasty.

On Easter Sunday, the Marquis of Durfort, who as ambassador to the court of Vienna had taken leave of the Empress a few days earlier, made his public entrance as the envoy extraordinary of Louis XV, instructed to represent the king at the marriage of his grandchildren. The enormous procession of forty-eight coaches each drawn by six horses, including two of the king's carriages built specially for the event in Paris, slowly rolled through the streets, accompanied by one hundred and seventeen valets or equerries wearing Durfort's livery. From a window, Antonia admired the extraordinary pomp displayed in her honour.

Emperor Joseph II and the Empress-Queen received Durfort officially the next day. After the ambassador had presented a new request for Antonia's hand in marriage, she was brought in. On a sign of agreement from her mother, she accepted a miniature of the Dauphin and it was fixed to her bodice.

On that evening, new festivities took place, with a reception and a grand gala. At the Hofburg theatre, *La Mère Confidente* by Marivaux and *Les Bergers de Tempé*, a ballet whose choreography had been composed by Noverre, were acted. On April 17th, a much more impressive ceremony took place: in the Hofburg's conference room, in the

was to become Grand Master of the Teutonic Order and the Archbishop of Cologne; and Marie Antoinette, portrayed here at the age of thirteen. Few of Maria Theresa's children were playmates for Marie Antoinette and her most loyal friend among her brothers and sisters was Maria Carolina, three years older than herself.

presence of her mother's ministers and counsellors, and before the Emperor and Empress, Antonia signed the acts of renunciation of all her rights as a descendant of the Habsburgs, and renewed her oath on the Bible.

The marriage was celebrated on Thursday, April 19th, at six o'clock in the evening. The Empress-Queen and the Emperor, followed at a respectful distance by Antonia, who according to eye-witnesses was gay and smiling, walked through a guard of honour of grenadiers to the Augustins church adjoining the Hofburg. The future dauphine wore a dress of silver drape whose long train was carried by the Countess of Trautmannsdorff. Archduke Ferdinand, Dauphin Louis Auguste's representative by proxy, kneeled next to Antonia in the church and slipped on to her finger a wedding ring which she was to wear until the eve of her death.

A banquet followed the nuptial mass. Henceforth Antonia, already Dauphine, took precedence over her brothers and sisters; the Emperor Joseph seated her next to him.

Several letters were prepared on Sunday, April 20th. They were all addressed to King Louis XV, the head of the family, and not one was sent to the young dauphin. Maria

Theresa, in addition to a very official letter, wrote a more spontaneous note of introduction entrusting her daughter to the former enemy who had now become her ally. In spite of the pompous style customary among sovereigns, nothing was hidden; the Empress was anxious about her daughter's superficiality, but had confidence in her desire to do well. In reality, Antonia was a pledge of alliance and mutual profit between the two states. In her turn, the dauphine recopied as well as she could the text prepared for her:

Sir, my brother and very dear grandfather, I have wished for such a long time that I might be able to show Your Majesty at least some of all my feelings for you, and it is with great satisfaction that I seize the first occasion permitting me to do so. Allow me, Your Majesty, to inform you herewith that my marriage to His Highness the Dauphin was celebrated here yesterday.... It will be with as much sincerity as respect and affection that I shall have the honour of personally repeating to him all the feelings which I shall, all my life, bear towards Your Majesty, Sir, my brother and very dear grandfather; I am your very affectionate sister, servant and granddaughter.

Antonia

41

In 1756 François Hubert Drouais portrayed the second and third grandsons of Louis XV in their sumptuous court clothes ; on the right is the two-year-old Duke of Berry who was destined to become King Louis XVI of France and the husband of Marie Antoinette : on the left the Count of Provence who was to reign from 1814 as Louis XVIII.

For the last time, she signed with her childhood name. In France, this Christian name did not exist; she was to be called Marie Antoinette. She was not to take any of her friends or companions to Versailles. Only her tutor, and her little dog, stayed with her.

The long journey far from Austria, which she had never left before, to the richest kingdom in the world and the Palace of Versailles whose majestic beauty still dazzles all Europe, began for Antonia on Monday, April 21st, at half-past nine in the morning. In front of the Hofburg where she was born, she entered the coach before the whole court, with her brother Ferdinand escorting her to its door.

A long caravan of carriages went with her, in which were the Prince of Starhemberg, a minister greatly esteemed by Maria Theresa and her special ambassador to Louis XV to deliver Antonia; her grand mistress; the ladies of her retinue; her tutor, and the French ambassador Durfort. Everything leads us to believe that this was a joyful procession, for such journeys were the occasion for festivities organized along the way by princes, cities, and even ecclesiastical communities.

Early in the afternoon, after a few hours' journey, Antonia arrived at Melk. This monastery, built by Charles VI and decorated by Maria Theresa, was like a palace. No other eighteenth-century edifice better recalls the epic nature, the taste for sumptuousness and the typical grandeur of Theresian art. The two architects, Prandauer and his successor Munggenast, aimed at striking the imagination. The enormous buildings, erected on a rocky peak, can be seen from a great distance. Contrary to the medieval custom, the church, instead of being hidden by conventional structures, stands apart from the other buildings, and its beautiful façade with two towers attracts all eyes. Some motifs were taken from Palladio, but the influence of Michelangelo is the most striking. The shape of the buildings skilfully follows the relief of the rocky hill on which they are constructed and emphasizes even more the impressive height of the whole. The abbey of Melk is Italian, French, and even Byzantine with its bulbous bell-towers, and it is typically Austrian by the very fact that it adopted artistic styles from all over Europe.

Antonia's brother, the Emperor Joseph II, had gone to Melk before her; in the evening, she attended a German opera with him. The singers were monastery pupils and the Benedictine monks had formed an orchestra. This was another performance by amateurs like so many she had seen as a child. Durfort found her sad that evening; in his opinion, her bad mood was not due to the sorrow of parting, but to the mediocre performance.

The next morning, Antonia bade her brother farewell and the retinue left for the castle of Enns where Prince Auersperg was waiting. The weather was cold and rainy. The stages were calculated to last seven or eight hours at the most, to avoid tiring a child whose health had until then been rather delicate. On the 23rd, Antonia was at Lambach, on the 24th at Altheim, on the 25th at Alt Ettingen in Bavaria, after crossing the Inn. On the 26th and the 27th, the latter a Sunday, she attended festivities at Nymphenburg Castle, very close to Munich, which were given in her honour by the Elector of Bavaria. One of Europe's richest sovereigns, passionately fond of the arts, the Elector Maximilian Joseph certainly made her admire the poetic decoration of his Amalienburg shooting-lodge in his castle gardens. These had been conjured up by his architect François Cuvilliés, a Germanized Frenchman, who had created a style which combined French elegance, a German atmosphere and Italian gaiety.

Starhemberg sent news of the journey to Vienna and Versailles, and was very pleased with the Dauphine: "Everyone seems charmed with the Princess I am bringing you, and I can only hope that she will enjoy as great a success in France as she has at all the places we have visited until now."

Their way crossed little states which formed the Holy Roman German Empire and which were theoretically under her brother's and mother's suzerainty. On April 28th, still in the rain, Antonia arrived at Augsburg, one of the most powerful free cities in Germany, made wealthy by banks and trade, although it was governed by a prince-bishop. Her aunt, Charlotte of Lorraine, her father's sister, received her the next day at Günsburg where she was the abbess, for her family reigned everywhere in a small way. Antonia had a cold and several ladies of her suite were indisposed. This stage in the journey was lengthened to care for the sick persons, but in spite of this, the ceremonies and festivities still continued. On May 7th, everyone was in sufficiently good health for the journey to be undertaken again. On that evening, they arrived at Riedlingen, next to the Danube, in the Duchy of Württemberg, whose sovereign, Charles Eugène, had squandered his fortune so rapidly that the great European powers had to intervene that same year to protect his subjects. On the 3rd, Antonia was at Stockach in Baden, and on the 4th, the Prince of Fürstenberg received the future queen and her suite in his beautiful castle at Donaueschingen, which had been built in the baroque style during the first years of the eighteenth century at the source of the Danube, whose waters lap against the walls of Vienna.

On the 5th, their halt was at Freiburg in Breisgau. After a journey of several hundred miles, Antonia was once again on Habsburg soil. Breisgau, with its capital Freiburg, was one of the great intellectual and commercial crossroads of Germany. It had in fact belonged to Austria for four hundred years, but as it was a remote territory of the imperial

The Marquis of Durfort, Louis XV's ambassador for the marriage of Marie Antoinette, organized a coach parade through Vienna which surpassed in splendour the parade for the future Joseph II's wedding, an event shown in this painting by Martin van der Meytens. ▷

The Duke of Choiseul, chief minister under Louis XV, in his bedroom in a hotel in the Rue de Richelieu, Paris.

The Duke had commissioned van Blarenberghe to portray on a gold box these episodes of his daily life.

Choiseul dictates to his secretaries in the study, where all the King's other ministers come to work with him.

As Minister of War Choiseul visits the Louvre to inspect the plans kept there of the country's fortified towns.

Choiseul in his Octogonal Room. Three rows of pictures line the walls, two by the landscapist Claude Lorrain.

Choiseul has removed his dressing gown and slipped on a jacket. His valet holds ready the Order of the Holy Ghost.

dynasty, hardly any modern buildings were to be seen. Finally, on June 6th, the retinue arrived at Schüttern Abbey near Kehl, where the little princess was to spend her last night on Austrian soil. The Count of Mercy-Argenteau, Austrian ambassador to France, had already been there for twenty-four hours to supervise last-minute preparations for the next day's ceremonies. A few members of the French delegation arrived from Strasburg to be presented that very evening to their future sovereign. The ambassador chosen by Louis XV was the Count of Noailles, a duke and lord of France, lieutenant-general of the armies and governor of Versailles. His wife, the Countess of Noailles, who accompanied him, had been appointed as the Dauphine's own lady-in-waiting. She had already held sway over the "household"—that is, all the noble or commoner servants of the former queen of France, Maria Lesczinska, who had died a few years earlier. The Countess of Noailles was very conscientious, very pious, very much aware of her prerogatives and clung very much to court traditions. Her tastes and character had been well adapted to those of her former sovereign, but they were much less suited to the fancies of a young princess. Nevertheless, Antonia received the Count and Countess so amiably that they both declared they were charmed with her.

The place where the ceremony was to be held had been chosen several months earlier. It was the Isle des Epis, situated at Strasburg's gates between two arms of the Rhine. Although within the French border, this little island on this occasion was to be considered as neutral territory. For want of a sufficiently large building, a temporary wooden lodge had had to be built which looked like a French-style palace. It was naturally divided into two parts, one Austrian and the other French. The furnishings, which moreover were extremely assorted, came from France, which was nearer. All the rich Strasburg subjects had provided furniture, but their contributions proved insufficient so that it was necessary to call upon the crown's property and many objects were sent from Paris. The result was both sumptuous and very ill-suited to the event.

Everything would have been perfect on May 7th had it not rained so much on that day. At half-past eleven, the retinue, after leaving Schütten a few minutes earlier, arrived at Kehl to cross the Rhine bridge. Carpenters wearing their trade's traditional clothes, with their axes on their shoulders and soaked to the skin, surrounded the coach during the bridge crossing, while six boats loaded with sailors in full uniform stood guard over the river.

At midday, in the centre of two rows of soldiers and a large crowd, the Dauphine arrived at the make-shift lodge on the Austrian side, and was greeted by an artillery salute. A brief meal followed. Antonia changed her travelling clothes for a ceremonial dress and talked for a little while with her retinue in the drawing-rooms reserved for imperial personages. Then, accompanied by Starhemberg and other Austrian dignitaries, she entered the Tapestry Drawing-room and sat down alone on a raised armchair under a canopy.

The French loved her immediately. An Alsatian, the Baroness of Oberkirch, with other girls of noble birth, saw her for the first time that day; years later she was to write:

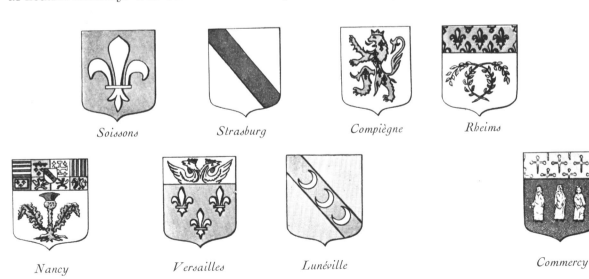

Soissons Strasburg Compiègne Rheims

Nancy Versailles Lunéville Commercy

EUROPE

divided into its Empires,
Kingdoms and Republics

By S. ROBERT DE VAUGONDY Geog?
ord? to the King, the late King of Poland,
the Duke of Lorraine and Bar, and the
Royal Academy of Science
and Literature at Nancy

1778

To get from Vienna to Paris Marie Antoinette crossed a Europe which, as can be seen from this contemporary map, was not yet a collection of states with clearly defined borders, nor a simple agglomeration of principalities in the possession of hereditary and independent sovereigns as would seem to accord with the laws and traditions of the times. In theory only Spain, France and England were nations in the modern sense of the word. But cartographers were reflecting the general feelings of their contemporaries when they delimited Germany and Italy, although these were countries divided into a great many states, and when they isolated Bohemia and Hungary, lands that were hereditary possessions of the family of Marie Antoinette. The Ancien Régime, whose institutions were founded on a respect for rules established by long usage and not by an objective analysis of reality, was not in the slightest degree discomfited by such contradictions. In this domain as in many others the Revolutionary state of mind would consist in taking the opposite point of view to that of the old order.

Vienna

Munich

Augsburg

Lambach

Ems

The union of the Archduchess of Austria and the Dauphin of France was more than a princely marriage. For two centuries war had thrown against each other the two most powerful royal houses in Europe. At the beginning of the sixteenth century a king of Spain, heir to the Italian, Austrian and German possessions of the Habsburgs, had become the Germanic emperor. For years after France was beseiged and the Austrian menace became an obsession in the public mind. But in the eighteenth century France and Austria were on the defensive before the expansionist policies of England and Prussia. A young girl of fourteen was the pledge of a definite end to their seemingly interminable conflict. Below is a hitherto unpublished plan of a pavilion constructed for the delivery of the girl, Marie Antoinette, to Louis XV's representatives.

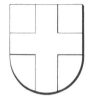

Freiburg-im-Breisgau

Altheim

On the left-hand and right-hand pages are the arms of the different towns passed through by the young dauphine.

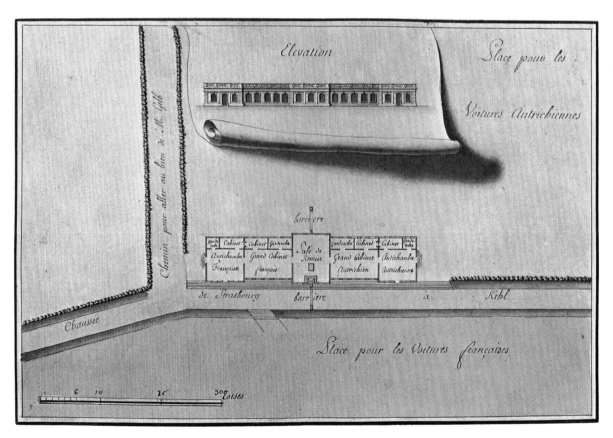

51

At that time, Her Highness the Dauphine was tall and well-made, although a little slim. She has changed but little since then; her face is still the same, long, with regular features and aquiline nose, although it has a Roman bridge; a high forehead, and lively blue eyes. Her tiny mouth already seemed slightly disdainful...she had the Austrian lip.... Nothing can describe her dazzling complexion, literally milk and roses. Everything about her betokened the greatness of her line, and her gentleness and nobility of heart. She appealed to all.

There followed the reading of legal acts, long speeches, showers of water on to the toilets of some of the ladies present, for the lodge's roof could not withstand this deluge of rain; farewells by the Austrian lords and ladies to their archduchess, official presentation of some members of the Dauphine's household to her by the Countess of Noailles and of the main French personages by the Count.

Marie Antoinette suddenly found herself alone in the midst of foreigners whom she did not know. None of her friends or servants were allowed to remain with her; she was to be accompanied exclusively by the French. She left the lodge on the French side by the door opposite the one by which she had entered it. A coach sent by Louis XV was waiting for her. The procession got under way to the episcopal palace of Strasburg, with numerous stops owing to the vast crowds.

The magistrate, who was also the mayor of the city, had a famous lawyer hold forth to her. It is said that he did not speak in Latin or in French, but in German, the language spoken at that time by all the inhabitants of Strasburg. "Do not speak a word of German," the Dauphine is supposed to have said. "From today, I only wish to hear French."

In any case, the young princess knew instinctively the art of captivating people and during these first festivities in her honour she showed a natural talent for repartee.

For a day and a half in Strasburg, the festivities for Marie Antoinette were practically continuous, except for a short night spent in the episcopal palace, the most beautiful building in the city. There was something of everything: a theatrical performance, a ball, a high mass at the cathedral, a carnival-like procession through the streets with drinking songs, buffoonery, acrobatics and dancing. Political and religious demonstrations were combined with all kinds of folklore, and musical and artistic merry-making. The gaiety was expressed with the greatest amount of noise possible.

During the afternoon of May 8th, to the sound of cheering and bells rung at full peal, the Dauphine left Strasburg for the castle of Saverne on the way to Paris, the second residence of the Cardinal of Rohan, the Bishop of Strasburg. More festivities, more presentations.

The Gazette de France, one of the principal newspapers of the time, wrote:

The Cardinal introduced a woman of about one hundred and five years old, who has never been ill, to the Dauphine. This woman said to her in German: "Princess, I pray to Heaven that you may live as long as myself and as free of disabilities." "I wish it may be so," replied the Dauphine in the same language, "if it is for France's well-being."

Was this little dauphine of fifteen French or German? The question was already almost unimportant. Carried away by the whirlwind of ceremonies and merry-making, she learned with pleasure, grace and skill how to make believe that she was happy, and she had neither the desire nor the possibility of tearing herself away. As the heroine of festivities given in her honour, she embodied to her future subjects' complete satisfaction the happiness which they longed to feel and which she wished for them, for like them, she had no other ideal.

Résumé of the Wienerisches Diarum.

The Wienerisches Diarum of May 26th, 1770 gives a precise if rather colourless description of the crossing of the Rhine by the Archduchess. For the young girl this was a solemn moment: she was leaving the imperial lands to pass into France. On an island on the Rhine, at the gates of Strasburg, the Austrian and the French escorts met to transfer the Dauphine's guards. In a pavilion built for the occasion the ceremony took places in three stages: first Marie Antoinette took leave of her imperial escort; then the two commissaries transferred the charge of guarding the Dauphine; finally the latter made the acquaintance of her new escort, commanded by the Count of Noailles, lieutenant-general of the royal armies and Grandee of Spain. Having crossed the Rhine, Marie Antoinette made her way to Strasburg, the first town to welcome her to France.

Nro. 42. Sonnabend den 26. Maymon. 1770.

Wienerisches Diarium,

oder

Nachrichten von Staats, vermischten,

und gelehrten Neuigkeiten.

Verlegt bey den von Ghelischen Erben.

Von dem neulich in unseren Blättern abgeschilderten Empfang Ihrer königl. Hoheit der Durchl. Erzherzoginn Maria Antonia, nunmehrigen Dauphine von Frankreich, zu Straßburg, haben wir nun eine andere umständlichere Nachricht, samt der Beschreibung der daselbst errichteten Ehrenbogen erhalten, die wir hiemit unseren Lesern mitzutheilen, keinen Anstand nehmen wollen.

Straßburg den 8. May.

Gestern Vormittags um 11. Uhr langte der Dauphine königl. Hoheit mit Dero Gefolge in der zwischen beyden Rheinbrücken gelegnen kleinen Insul an, stiegen bey dem auf derselben errichteten schönen Gebäude ab, der Graf von Noailles, zu Dero Empfang und Begleitung ernannter königl. Commissarius, Generallentenant der königl. Armeen, und Grand d'Espagne, erwartete Ihre königl. Hoheit allda, in Begleit des Herrn Marschalls von Contades, des Hrn. Marquis von Voghue, des Hrn. Baron von Wurmser, und des der Dauphine zur weitern Begleitung bestimten Gefolges; beym Aussteigen wurden Höchstdieselbe durch den

---

The Vienna newspaper devoted its issue if May 26th, 1770 to an account of the young dauphine's voyage to France. The titles of the great lords who participated in the various festivities and ceremonies, the inscriptions on the triumphal arches, the richness of the apparel prepared for Louis XV at the Palace of Versailles, all are carefully described for the delight and entertainment of the Viennese readers.

SUMMER

Marie Antoinette at the age of twenty-eight, painted here by L. A. Brun, is the living picture of youth and beauty.

The Palace of Versailles presented to the wondering eyes of Marie Antoinette on the morning of May 15th, 1770 was almo

same as we see it today. To make it more pleasant Louis XV ordered Jacques-Ange Gabriel to build the Opéra.

On May 14th, 1770, a large crowd gathered at dawn on the outskirts of the forest of Compiègne, whose trees were decked out with gay, spring colours. The most brilliant companies of the French army, the bodyguards, light infantry, musketeers and life-guardsmen in their braided uniforms, formed a rank of honour. The new dauphine had crossed the whole of the east of France, passing through Nancy and Lunéville, the capital cities of Lorraine where her ancestors on her father's side had reigned, and through Commercy, Châlons, Rheims and Soissons. Some towns had erected triumphal arches in her honour; religious celebrations, military parades, popular festivities, firework displays or theatrical productions were given to welcome her. Her gratitude and her wonderment in the face of so many new and joyful scenes contributed to increasing the enthusiasm along her way from town to town. Much later, she was to say that it was then that she had understood the happiness which being a queen entailed. Louis XV was informed of the success of his unknown granddaughter's journey. He came to meet her well beyond his Compiègne residence, which he left on the morning of May 14th; the King of France's coaches stopped at the side of the road near the Bern bridge, just before the Dauphine's procession, coming from Soissons, arrived.

Louis XV then stepped down from his coach. At 59, the King was still the most handsome and certainly the most attractive man in his kingdom. He was tall, and his curious mixture of majesty and simplicity was touching. He was also an impressive sight in his magnificent court dress. Marie Antoinette, wearing a sumptuous gown, came forward between the Count of Saulx-Tavannes, her knight of honour, and the Count of Tessé, her first equerry, followed by five ladies of her house. She carried off her first curtsy very well. Louis XV embraced his new granddaughter, and seemed delighted with her joyful expression and her already well-rounded figure. He presented her to the scowling dauphin, who was frightened at greeting this unknown wife before so many people.

In the coach taking them back to Compiègne, Louis XV placed Marie Antoinette next to him. Louis Auguste and the Countess of Noailles were seated opposite them. A certain familiarity was established between the intelligent, sensitive and curious sovereign of the most powerful kingdom in the world—on whom, however, most of the pleasures of life had already palled—and this little princess filled with the desire to savour the unheard-of homages, riches and scenes which surrounded her. The Court was struck by his playful mood when he presented the Dauphine first to the princes of the blood and then to the great dignitaries at the palace of Compiègne.

Slowly, very slowly, the royal procession rolled towards Paris the next day. So dense was the crowd all along the way that they only arrived at the Muette castle in the evening. A cosy supper had been prepared there for the royal family. This gave Marie Antoinette the opportunity of meeting her brothers-in-law for the first time. The Count of Provence was just her age; a great reader, he was completely convinced of his superior intelligence, but his hypocrisy and his love of intrigue alienated all who knew him. The Count of Artois, a year younger, was handsome, witty, very talented at dancing and games, and already only concerned with his own desires and pleasure. Right from the beginning, his sister-in-law was much more drawn to him than to his brother.

A gay and charming young woman, who had never been introduced to the royal family, attended this rather informal meal. She was said to be the Countess du Barry. Marie Antoinette was completely unaware of her position. In fact, Louis XV, giving in to a whim, had invited his new mistress to his grandchildren's table; he was certainly very much in love with her, but in spite of her youth she had had a great deal of experience before knowing the King. On the eve of the two adolescents' wedding such a gesture was not only immoral but indecent. Later, when Marie Antoinette became aware of the situation, she was to feel embittered by this insult and was always to harbour a stubborn grudge against the Countess du Barry.

But on that evening, she thought of something completely different. The King had had a fabulous casket of jewels placed in the little dauphine's chamber. The jewels of the

Louis XV was thirty-eight when de la Tour painted this portrait. In 1770 when the monarch welcomed Marie Antoinette to Versailles he was fifty-nine and still the most fascinating man in the kingdom.

queens of France were given to this child, and as a more personal present, Louis XV had even added a sumptuous set of diamonds. Marie Antoinette had always loved precious stones. She went to sleep intoxicated with weariness, gratitude and happiness.

The palace which met Marie Antoinette's wondering eyes from a great distance away on the road to Paris on May 15th, 1770, was almost the same as it is today with its rectilineal perspectives and the immense esplanade framed by the royal stables and the ornate iron-work gateway. Yet there was a fundamental difference. Versailles was not a museum as now, but a picture of bustling life. An entire population lived in, moved about among and invaded these enormous buildings which were always poorly maintained, always being repaired or transformed, and always encumbered with parasite buildings. Indeed, the smallest corners of Versailles were not only occupied by the court dignitaries and the king's attendants who were granted the privilege of living there, but also by a great number of guards and servants, who slept in makeshift quarters. Moreover, the palace was invaded every day by swarms of curious people who had access to most of the rooms of the royal residence and either came to negotiate business matters with the government or out of simple curiosity to see how the sovereign lived. Peddlars and merchants also besieged Versailles, setting out their wares in the open-air passages and taking advantage of temporary tolerance to prop up against sumptuous buildings their sordid sheds made of planks which the royal edicts never completely succeeded in abolishing.

For all its splendour, Versailles was an ambiguous place. Louis XIV, Louis XV's great-grandfather, had had the palace built with the aim of edifying the sanctuary of a king who considered himself a superior being. It was the temple of a deified monarch. The enormous edifices surrounded and encircled an archaic style building to whose removal Louis XIV had never agreed; it had been his father Louis XIII's hunting pavilion. The King's room was here, the Holy of Holies of Versailles. Its windows, behind a balcony, could be seen right from the back of the courtyard by the visitors from Paris. People moved very freely through the maze of the palace drawing-rooms. The King's room was one of the few which were really inaccessible: only the high priests of the royal cult were allowed to enter it. The King's retirement and his rising were ceremonies attended by the highest court dignitaries or the lords designated by the sovereign. The most solemn audiences also took place there.

Louis XV loved Versailles; he felt an almost superstitious respect for the customs and institutions created or modified by his great-grandfather, but although he was the splendid incarnation of royal majesty, he felt very ill at ease playing the part of a demi-god for which he had no calling at all. During the fifty years of his reign, he took part with conscientious weariness in ceremonies that he accepted as being necessary without really believing in the reality of which they were the outward sign. Every morning and evening, he came to this room to go to bed and to get up, repeating the ritual gestures of the part imposed on him. But he did not sleep in his great-grandfather's room; he had a personal suite set up a little farther away, where he could receive whom he wished. In 1770 Versailles seemed like a church where the rites lived on through force of habit, thanks to the power and intelligence of the ministers, but where faith had given way to the overriding dictates of efficiency. For the people of the towns and the country, the King, whether loved or detested, was still a superior being, but in his daily life Louis XV did not worry at all about acting this part.

The work undertaken at Versailles for the last marriage of a dauphin of France which was ever to take place did not, however, aim at making the palace more sumptuous, but more pleasant. In spite of enormous financial difficulties, Louis XV undertook to build the large theatre which had already been planned by Louis XIV, but whose construction had always been postponed. It was given the name of Gabriel's Opéra, after the architect who had drawn up the plans, but this room should rather have been called the Marie Antoinette Theatre, as it was erected in honour of the last queen of France and it was here that, until 1789, the decisive moments of her life were to be played out.

Jacques-Ange Gabriel had the task of surpassing all existing theatres in splendour and artistic perfection. A few years ago, thanks to skilful and patient repairs, the former beauty of the place he built was restored, and today it is unequalled throughout the world. The whole was created to be used as a stage equipped with the most extraordinary refinements in machinery to provide infinite variations in scenery and the decor. Arnoult, a brilliant technician, had invented all kinds of new processes: for example, the floor of the orchestra pit could be raised to the level of the stage to form an immense ball-room. The material chosen was mainly wood, and the shape a half-oval; these two factors contributed to the quality of the acoustics. The decoration was carried out with extraordinary care. Only the rough work was entrusted to carpenters. Louis Delanois, a cabinet-maker and one of the most brilliant furniture makers of the period, was commissioned by Gabriel to execute the moulding of the boxes, which meant all the visible wooden surfaces which did not require actual fine sculpture. Guibert and Rousseau, panelling specialists and wood sculptors, who were also very well-known, carved the countless wooden ornaments themselves. Finally, the figures, inset-work and bas-relief in gilded wood were not given over to decorators; they were entrusted to the imagination and chisel of Pajou: he was perhaps the best-known sculptor in France. The ceiling was painted by Durameau, an artist who has unjustly been forgotten and who would appear to deserve equal fame with Pajou. The azure which was the dominant colour of this large scene matched that of the woodwork and the drapings. The stage curtains showed fleurs-de-lis, the symbol of the kings, worked in golden thread on a blue background of France. How can we fail to be astonished at all the arts, even the finest, such as architecture, painting and sculpture, which were used to produce such a theatre? Such things were possible because life at that time had a quality for many of Louis XV's contemporaries which it has lost for us. Festivities, gambling and theatre were its essential and, if one dares to

Two months before the date fixed for her daughter's marriage, Maria Theresa noticed that she still did not have any picture of Louis Auguste. Louis XV had this print sent of "The Dauphin Toiling", a pastoral scene in rather doubtful taste. At the beginning of April two portraits of the Dauphin in ceremonial robes were sent to the young bride.

From Strasburg to Compiègne, where she was to meet the Court, the new dauphine received an enthousiastic welcome.
Some towns, such as Rheims shown here, raised triumphal arches and organized shows and popular festivals : there
were military parades, religious ceremonies, firework displays and theatrical performances on topical subjects.

say so, its truest elements. A child of fourteen dazzled by all these splendours would in no time have confused dreams with reality.

Marie Antoinette arrived at Versailles at ten o'clock in the morning. She had very little time to change and dress her hair. Louis XV again came to present to her the Dauphin's younger sisters—Clotilde, who was eleven years old, and Elisabeth, who was six—and other important personages at court. Hundreds of curious watchers were crowded together in the rooms through which the nuptial procession was to pass. No one was able to approach without showing a special invitation signed by the Duke of Aumont, the presiding groom of the bedchamber. Enormous sums had been spent by the wives of the kingdom's great dignitaries

to outdo each other in elegance. At one o'clock, the grand master of ceremonies appeared to lead the way. Marie Antoinette, elegant and smiling, wearing a white brocade dress with large hoops, gave her hand to Louis Auguste, who was embarrassed and awkward, ill-at-ease in the golden doublet decorated with diamonds of his uniform of a knight of the Order of the Holy Ghost. Behind them walked the royal children of France, then the princes of the blood surrounded by their gentlemen-in-waiting, and finally Louis XV, dressed in the finest suit he had worn since his own wedding, as was duly noted by the Duke of Croy, always the precise and faithful analyst of this reign.

The procession slowly reached the chapel built by Mansart for Louis XIV. As in all

61

During the first months in France the Dauphine was often depressed; at these times she would amuse herself with her dog Mops, a sort of miniature boxer.

watch the royal family as it left the chapel. Marie Antoinette returned to the apartments which were to be hers for twenty years, and received the allegiance of the officers of the house, then the homage of the ambassadors and ministers of foreign courts.

When all these tedious ceremonies were over, she doubtless took great pleasure in opening an admirable casket, of a simple shape but richly decorated. The greatest Parisian craftsmen had worked together to produce the wedding present which Louis XV now offered to his granddaughter. Within it Marie Antoinette found an elaborate set of blue enamel with a chain of diamonds, a pocket box, a watch, and a fan encrusted with diamonds; only Parisian craftsmanship could have produced such objects.

In the late afternoon, in accordance with tradition, a few privileged persons played cards in public. Thousands of people, whether they possessed an invitation or not, came to watch the King playing *lansquenet* with the Dauphine seated at his right. During the evening, the members of the royal family attended a dinner alone in the new theatre, which on this occasion had already been changed into a banquet hall. An orchestra right at the back of the stage, which had become a music room, played continually. Thousands of spectators encircled the guests who were protected by balustrades. Finally, at midnight, the Dauphin and the Dauphine went to the nuptial chamber, accompanied by the royal family, the great men of the kingdom and the bands of the French and Swiss guards, dressed as Turks. The great almoner of France blessed the bed; according to tradition, the King gave the Dauphin his nightshirt and the Duchess of Chartres held out Marie Antoinette's night-dress to her. The bed curtains were still held open for endless curtsies and bows by the courtiers, who enjoyed this privilege by right. The two children, sixteen and fourteen years of age, exhausted by so many ceremonies and still complete strangers to each other, simply went to sleep.

On the next day, a Thursday, the festivities continued with more introductions, which seemed endless. That evening, a theatrical performance, the first to take place in the new opera house, was planned. The choice was surprising: it was *Perseus*, a play written a century before. But it enabled the marvellous machinery which had just been installed

the other royal and princely weddings for more than a century, the Dauphin and the Dauphine knelt at the foot of the altar. Mgr. de la Roche Aymon, the Archbishop of Rheims and grand chaplain of France, conducted the service. A silent crowd watched the Dauphin put on to Marie Antoinette's finger the ring which had already sealed their union during the marriage by proxy in Vienna. After the mass, as was the custom, the parish-priest of Notre Dame of Versailles brought his church register in which the baptisms, marriages and deaths of all his parishioners were noted, including even the members of the royal family. Louis XV signed the marriage act at the top in his clear, decisive hand. Louis Auguste carefully wrote his name. And the Dauphine did not manage to write her four Christian names in a straight line nor avoid an enormous ink-blot.

In the drawing-rooms and the great gallery, there were more than five thousand persons to

to be used. Papillon de la Ferté, the steward of the Light Amusements, who was responsible for organizing the details of the festivities, said that he was partially satisfied; in his diary, he noted:

This production was much better than could have been expected after such hasty preparations and with machines whose intricacies were still so little known to the workmen. It did not seem to be to the taste of Madame the Dauphine. It is true that it is a very serious opera for someone who is not familiar with it....

On Saturday, the festivities were to reach their peak. Once again, the Opéra was transformed. The stage had been set up as a very large ballroom; it was decked out with garlands and even with paintings ordered for the occasion from an excellent painter in Paris. The seats had been removed from the boxes and the auditorium, and the royal ball took place. Louis Auguste and Marie Antoinette danced the first minuet alone; the Dauphin moved stiffly and Marie Antoinette with her usual grace. She then hazarded a few country dances with her brother-in-law Provence, but she did not dare to take part in the quadrilles in which her future friends, the Princess of Lamballe and the Countess of Polignac, shone. To close the ball, the Duke of Chartres, who was later her relentless enemy under the name of Philippe Egalité, gallantly suggested dancing an allemande in which she showed all her spirit and charm.

On the same evening, a great popular celebration had been planned in the Versailles park. At least two hundred thousand persons attended it; the main attraction was to be a firework display. Behind a latticed window of the great gallery, the King, with the Dauphin, gave the signal to begin. The variety and length of the display were prodigious. "The great bouquet at the end," noted Papillon de la Ferté, "consisted of 20,000 rockets; it was the largest which had ever been seen." An hour later, the Versailles park was illuminated; at the end of the Great Canal a sun-temple of startling height had been erected. Torch-lit boats in which the musicians were seated acted out a water-ballet. All the groves were centres of light, and the high spray of the fountains completed the picture. Orchestras scattered among the crowd enlivened the dances of the people. There were also open-air spectacles, with boatmen, actors, acrobats, and tightrope dancers. Marie Antoinette could not resist all this and made the rounds of the illuminations, which were said to be the most beautiful since Louis XIV's reign, in a coach. Everywhere, she was greeted with cries of joy from the public.

On Monday, a masked ball; on Wednesday, the theatre with a famous actress, Mademoiselle Clairon, taking the title part in *Athalie* by Racine—altogether, the wedding festivities lasted two weeks. After the wild enthusiasm of these hectic days, Marie Antoinette felt strangely alone in this immense, unknown palace where she had been given the cold and sumptuous suite reserved for the queens of France. It was an impressive series of rooms facing south, and some of them had a view of the park; very little had been changed since Queen Marie-Thérèse, the wife of Louis XIV, had lived in the palace a century earlier. Today we see the setting almost as Marie Antoinette left it; an impressive marble staircase leads to it. A large room for the bodyguards, which was very vast and cluttered, called the "warehouse", was opposite the staircase; in the eighteenth century, merchants, lackeys and curious watchers crowded together here. A second room, 33 feet long, was reserved for the Queen's guards; they lived there day and night. We can imagine the piles of screens, beds, weapons and the noise of conversation, the games of men condemned to perpetual idleness. The Queen's ante-chamber, which was no more intimate, was the domain of her numerous attendants. The ceiling was still decorated with heroic paintings ordered by the Sun King a century earlier. In this room, where Maria Lesczinska one day received the young Mozart, Marie Antoinette was to attend the "Great Table", the official meal of the King and Queen in public, which all decently dressed visitors were allowed to watch. The large office or the office of the nobility also had a ceiling painted by Michel Corneille for Louis XIV; it was used for public audiences.

The Queen's room was just as vast and austere; it had been redecorated for Maria Lesczinska around 1730, but in a mythological and sumptuous style. Although not everyone had access to this room where Marie Antoinette was to sleep for almost twenty years, tradition did grant the kingdom's dignitaries, who had their small and important entrées, the unimpeachable right to enter it.

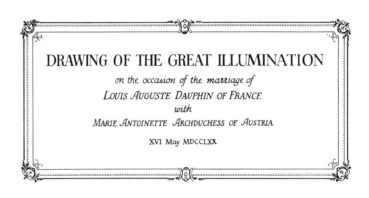

DRAWING OF THE GREAT ILLUMINATION
on the occasion of the marriage of
LOUIS AUGUSTE DAUPHIN OF FRANCE
with
MARIE ANTOINETTE ARCHDUCHESS OF AUSTRIA

XVI May MDCCLXX

The marriage of Marie Antoinette, Archduchess of Austria, to Louis Auguste, heir to the kingdom of France, was the occasion of numerous brilliant festivities. The night feast of May 19th was particularly successful : the fireworks, the most magnificent ever seen at Versailles, consisted of more than twenty thousand rockets. The entire park was illuminated. On the Grand Canal torch-lit boats performed a water ballet. Music everywhere. The show was beheld by over two hundred thousand delighted spectators.

Finally, the last room of this endless suite, which is still as impressive today as it must have been two hundred years ago to a fourteen-year-old child, was the Queen's Games Drawing-room, also called the Peace Drawing-room. It was at the end of the fabulous Gallery of Mirrors facing the park, and whose pompous decorations were spread over nearly a hundred yards : a simple frame and movable drapes separated the Peace Drawing-room from the Gallery of Mirrors. The Queen held her public games here, gave concerts, held court, and the public was generally admitted.

These descriptions would give a false impression of the official Versailles of 1770 were one not to try to recall the aspect, both tumultuous and sordid, of these sumptuous premises of which today only the ostentation has been preserved in the museum. Countless varletry, visiting provincials, merchants, intriguers, parasites, the forced idleness of the whole court when there was no official ceremony, gave the luxury an air of negligence which is unconsciously revealed in the memoirs written during this period. The Queen's suite was both sumptuous and dirty ; only a sense of decency prevented the artists from evoking a sordid aspect of the place which the honest memorialists did not fail to note. Viollet-le-Duc, the great architect who restored so many ancient monuments in the nineteenth century, provided some interesting evidence on the odour which reigned in the palace :

Versailles was provided with so few privies that all the personalities of the court had to keep commodes in their dressing-rooms. We remember the odour which spread throughout the corridors of Saint-Cloud at the time of Louis XVIII [the Count of Provence in 1770], for the tradition of Versailles was scrupulously preserved there. This fact concerning Versailles is not at all exaggerated ; one day, when we were very young, we visited this palace with a respectable lady of Louis XV's court. Walking through a reeking corridor, she could not help exclaiming with regret, "This odour reminds me of a very wonderful time."

To flee ! This was certainly Marie Antoinette's first impulse, faced as she was by a universe which was so strange to her after the simple, more homely and more comfortable setting of the Austrian court. Fortunately, a door hidden behind the bed of the state chamber led to a few private rooms where, before Marie Antoinette, Maria Lesczinska

had succeeded in finding refuge. Marie Antoinette, as Dauphine and Queen, continually changed and improved these chambers. But during the first period of her stay in France, she was only able to hide her loneliness there. The Abbé Vermond was the only man in France whom she had known for more than a few days. When he came to visit her, he noticed her sadness. In a secret letter to the Prince of Kaunitz, he wrote : "Her Highness the Dauphine amuses herself with the little dog ; I feared this would be a drawback ; M. de Starhemberg thought it might be useful ; it is but a momentary distraction, then she goes into a brown study again. It cuts me to the heart."

Many intrigues were woven about this lonely child. She felt their danger, but could not succeed in unravelling the threads. Louis Auguste, who was awkward with women, was incited by his former tutor, the Duke of Vauguyon, to mistrust this Austrian who was Choiseul's protégée, and he remained friendly and aloof. Everyone at court knew that the marriage between the Dauphine and the Dauphin was still unconsummated. Louis Auguste hunted a great deal. He did not fail to visit his wife, and sometimes even accepted to share her bed, but he was still as little effusive in words as in deeds. "While I was with Madame the Dauphine this morning," noted Vermond, "His Highness the Dauphin came in. I moved a little farther away without leaving. His Highness the Dauphin said, 'Did you sleep well ?... Yes !' and he went out."

Marie Antoinette's aunts, Louis XV's daughters, Adélaïde, Victoire and Sophie, and Choiseul and his friends, all violently hostile to the Countess du Barry, thought to use the keen interest shown by Louis XV in his granddaughter as a weapon in their efforts to remove his favourite. Marie Antoinette, easily persuaded, gallantly plunged into the fray. She ingenuously wrote to her mother :

The King has shown me a thousand kindnesses and I love him tenderly ; but it is pitiful to see his weakness for Madame du Barry who is the stupidest and most impertinent creature imaginable. She has played with us every evening ; she was next to me twice, but did not speak to me and I made no effort to strike up conversation with her. As for my dear husband, he has shown me great friendliness and has even begun to show confidence in me. He certainly does not

Madame Elisabeth, the younger of the sisters-in-law, was six years old when the Dauphine arrived at the French Court. She was later to share suffering and imprisonment with Marie Antoinette under the Revolutionary régime.

Louis, Count of Provence, was the same age as Marie Antoinette but there was never any sympathy between the two. An ambitious and intriguing man, he was later to work his way to the throne as Louis XVIII.

Charles, Count of Artois, later Charles X, was a gay and charming boy who, like the young Dauphine, was only concerned with his own amusements. From the start his sister-in-law preferred him to Provence.

LOUIS STANISLAS XAVIER DE FRANCE
MONSIEUR Fr. DU ROY
Né à Versailles le 17 Novembre 1755.

CHARLES PHILIPPE COMTE D'ARTOIS
Fils de France et Petit Fils du Roy
Louis Quinze le bien Aimé
Né à Versailles le 9 Octobre 1757.

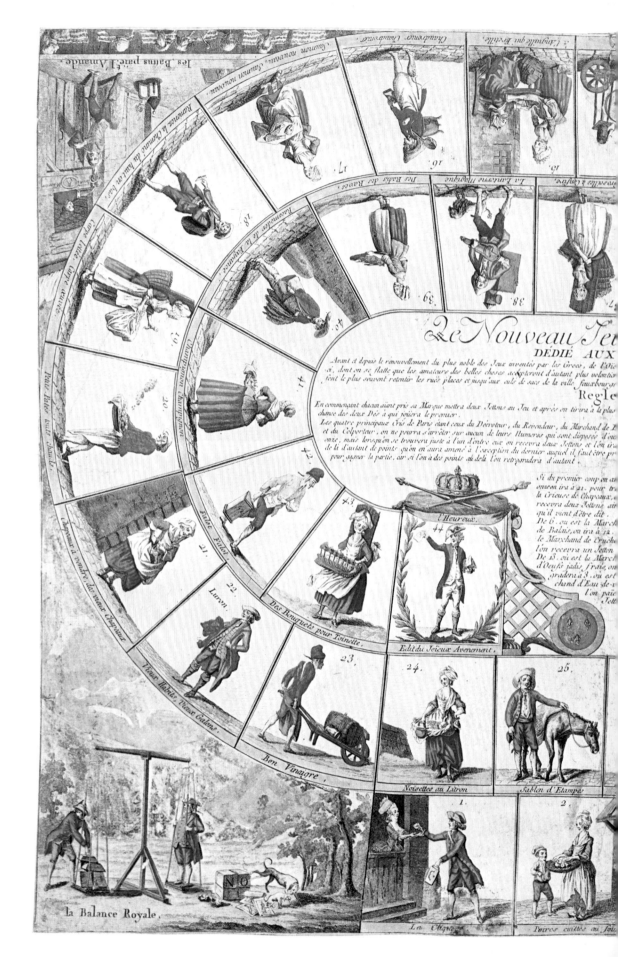

Le Nouveau Jeu

DÉDIÉ AUX

Règle

Edit du Joïeux Avenement.

la Balance Royale.

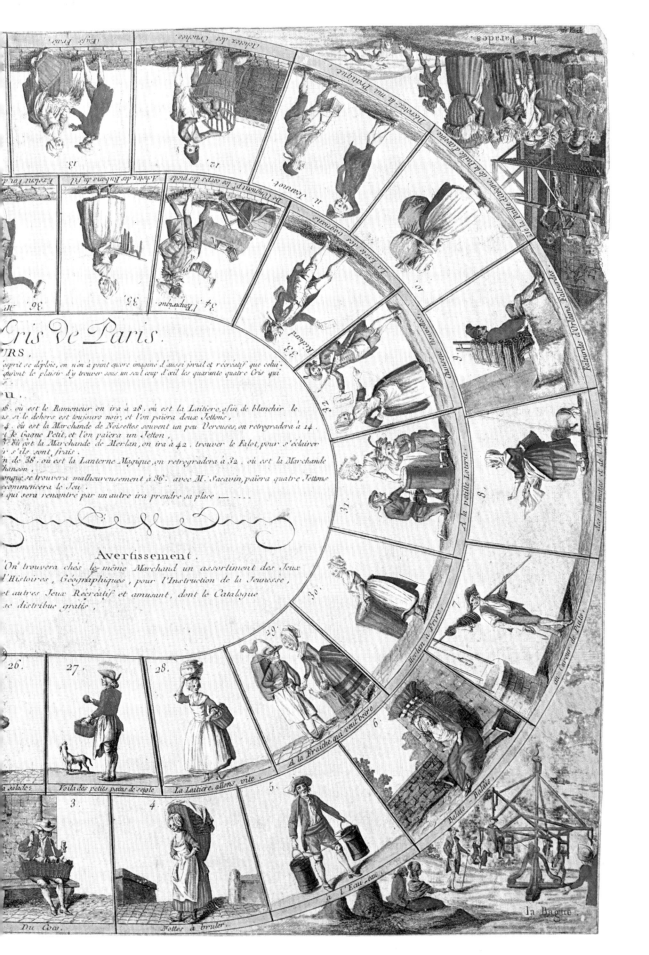

like M. de la Vauguyon, but he is afraid of him. A curious event took place the other day. I was alone with my husband when M. de la Vauguyon hurriedly came to the door to listen. A manservant who is either a fool or a very honest man opened the door, and the duke stood rooted to the spot like a stake without being able to retreat. I then pointed out to my husband the disadvantage of letting people listen at doors....

She was conscious to such a degree of the spying on her that she wrote to her mother in secret and tore up her answers for fear of not even being able to keep anything locked away. She did not imagine for a second that her mother had woven a network of supervision about her which was just as tight. Mercy-Argenteau was more than an ambassador, he was an intelligence agent. He himself wrote to Maria Theresa:

Her women and two menservants give me an exact account of what happens in private. Every day, I am regularly informed of the Archduchess' conversations with the Abbé Vermond, from whom she hides nothing...and I have more people and more means of knowing what happens when Madame the Dauphine is with the King...so that I am able to give an account of what Madame the Archduchess may have said, done or heard at any time of the day....

The situation became even more complicated when one considers that Mercy-Argenteau did not content himself with sending "public letters" to the Empress, i.e. letters also intended for the Emperor or her ministers, and with suggesting to the mother and daughter what they should write to each other, but that he also kept up a secret exchange of letters with Kaunitz, the chancellor of the Empire, unknown to the Empress; and another secret exchange with the Empress, supposedly unknown to Kaunitz. But La Vauguyon was certainly not the only spy of Louis XV or on du Barry's behalf; the ambassadors of the great powers were past masters in the art of securing a great deal of intelligence, particularly about the secrets of the bedchamber. The Dauphine, who was the object of constant supervision and subjected to influ-

ences worked out by minute calculations, abandoned any serious occupation. She had become a toy in the hands of much older politicians or intriguers, without ever encountering serious and sincere friendship. Marie Antoinette quite naturally adopted the attitudes of a doll and, not without complacency, accepted the rôle of a puppet tossed about on the eddies of fate.

Instinctive coquetry encouraged her to appear, with regard to the King, even more of a child than she really was. One day, she arrived at Louis XV's suite in a boudoir wrap, without even being announced, then ingenuously asked permission to appear dressed in this fashion. The King gallantly replied: "I like being asked to grant a privilege which one has already arrogated to one's self."

Another time, Madame de Grammont, one of Marie Antoinette's ladies-in-waiting, was expelled from court for having lacked respect towards Madame du Barry. The Dauphine coaxed the King to have her recalled; this time, the King was adamant. "But Papa," begged Marie Antoinette, "apart from reasons of humanity and justice, think how afflicted I would be if a woman in my service happened to die in your disgrace." And the sovereign, his heart softened, gave in to these coquettish, childish tricks.

If we judge by her writing or her occupations, Marie Antoinette, at fifteen, sixteen or seventeen years of age, was very far from behaving as an adult. It is true that when she wrote to her mother, she described a serious use of her time:

I rise at ten or at nine o'clock and after dressing, I say my morning prayers, then I have breakfast and afterwards I visit my aunts where I generally find the King. At eleven o'clock, I go and dress my hair. At midday, the chamber is called together and everyone may come in. I put on my rouge and wash my hands before everyone, then the men leave and the ladies remain and I dress in front of them. Mass is at midday. After mass, we dine with His Highness the Dauphin, but by half-past one we have finished, for we both eat very quickly. I then go to His Highness the Dauphin's suite and if he

is busy, I return to my own apartment. I read, write or work, for I am making a jacket for the King.... At three o'clock, I visit my aunts again, and the King also comes at this time; at four o'clock, the abbé comes to visit me, and at five o'clock every day, the harpsichord or the singing teachers. At half-past six, I generally go to my aunts', if I do not take a walk.... At seven o'clock, we play cards until nine. We then have supper, and if the King is not there, my aunts come to us for supper, but when the King is there, we have supper in their suite; we wait for the King who generally comes at a quarter to eleven, but while waiting, I am allowed to lie down on a large sofa and sleep until the King arrives; when he is not there, we go to bed at eleven o'clock. This is all our day.... I must finish now because it is time for the King's Mass.

And she added, even more childishly,

With regard to what you asked me about my devotions and *la générale* [a familiar expression used for the menstrual periods] I may tell you that I have only been to communion once: as for *la générale*, this is the fourth month that it has not come without a good reason....

The witnesses were in agreement about the studious nature of the Dauphine's days. Vermond vainly tried to induce her to undertake serious reading. Mercy fiercely struggled, often through the intermediary of the Empress, to turn her aside from amusements which were unfitting for her high position. He wrote to Maria Theresa:

Madame the Dauphine has taken up the habit of playing with children again, and unfortunately her first lady-in-waiting has two of them, a boy of six or seven, and a girl of twelve; both are very noisy, ill-kept and full of drawbacks. But the Archduchess spends a large part of the day with these children who spoil and tear her clothes, break the furniture, and cause the greatest disorder in the apartments.

To the great disapproval of Mercy-Argenteau and the Empress, the Dauphine nourished a real passion for following the royal hunts, sometimes on a donkey, later on horseback, and often in a carriage. She took with her an extremely varied selection of provisions which she distributed with very little regard for etiquette to the young participants who were ravenous after their lengthy escapades.

With her indifference not only to rules but also, to a certain extent, to social classes, Marie Antoinette ingenuously bore witness to new ideas in a court which still stoutly upheld tradition. She was spontaneous and sensitive in the manner of a heroine of Jean-Jacques Rousseau, whose works were already then enjoying success.

One day in November, 1770, returning from a hunt near Versailles, a postilion of the Dauphine's carriage fell on to the road and was trampled by the horses. Mercy recounts:

He was pulled out covered with blood and unconscious. Madame the Dauphine sent messengers right and left to find surgeons. They wanted to carry the wounded boy in a chair.... Madame the Dauphine was against this, and very wisely pointed out the disadvantage of jolting an unfortunate person who was black and blue with bruises.

The wounded boy was finally transported to Versailles in the carriage, accompanied by two surgeons, and Marie Antoinette rejoiced when her servant regained consciousness. She gave a voluble account of the incident. "I told everyone that they were my friends, the pages, the grooms, and the postilions. I said: 'My friend, go and fetch surgeons; my friend, run and find a stretcher, see if he speaks, if he is conscious.'"

Another hunting accident was publicized because of its seriousness. Almost before the Dauphine's eyes, a vine-grower was wounded by a stag pursued by the King and his pack. The hunters were naturally not stopped by this mishap. Marie Antoinette, by contrast, watched over the wounded man and was concerned about his family's fate until the father was healed. Another day, she met orphans with their rather wretched grandmother. The Dauphine suggested that one of the young boys should be brought up in her own suite at Versailles. Little Armand was to live amidst the Dauphine's attendants when she became queen and to receive the same education as her own sons, but during the Revolution he was to forget his benefactress completely.

Childishness as well as a genuine sense of decency kept Marie Antoinette, despite the strong insistence of her mother and her ambassador, from ever associating with the Countess du Barry. Pushed by his mistress to win her recognition, Louis XV used every means at his disposal to overcome his granddaughter's resistance. He even summoned Mercy-Argenteau and urged him to make her listen to reason: "Until now you have been the Empress's ambassador, but now I ask you to be my ambassador for a while."

Marie Antoinette, carefully indoctrinated by Mercy and Vermond, promised everything they wished. The day, the time and the manner in which the Dauphine was to address her grandfather's mistress were carefully contrived. The whole court waited for the enthralling scene. Mercy-Argenteau, accompanied by Madame du Barry, started towards the Dauphine, but Marie Antoinette, swept off by her aunt, Madame Adélaïde, escaped once again. The scandal reached its climax. "Well, M. de Mercy," thundered the King, "your advice bears hardly any fruit. I shall have to come to your assistance."

But the struggle was, in fact, a long one. The King had to wait until January 1st, 1772, to obtain satisfaction at last. On that day, once again, the entire court was assembled and everyone came to pay homage to the Dauphine. Without even looking at the woman she loathed, Marie Antoinette said in the most indifferent way imaginable: "There are many people at Versailles today." Then, in a voice full of rancour, she declared to her mother's ambassador: "I have spoken to her once, but I am determined to leave it at that, and this woman will not hear the sound of my voice again." For the Empress and the Austrian court, who were fully conscious of the diplomatic difficulties with France at that time, as well as for the opposing factions of the French court, this comparative capitulation of a Dauphine who was very little aware of her responsibilities implied political consequences of vital importance.

The first years of Marie Antoinette's stay in France were indeed decisive for France's destiny. Was it the fault of a child if, during the year in which she abandoned the country of her birth for her adopted country, so much was changing in so many different spheres and France's destiny seemed so uncertain?

Marie Antoinette was a sensitive and spontaneous girl. One day in 1773 the Court was chasing a stag without heeding a wine-grower they had accidently wounded. The Dauphine stopped to help him and looked after the welfare of his family until his recovery. She never hesitated to break with etiquette when it went against her feelings or desires.

The Countess du Barry is here portrayed by Drouais as a page. She never managed to please the Dauphine, who from her first letter to Maria Theresa spoke of her as "the stupidest and most impertinent creature imaginable". Nothing would make her forget her prejudice or change her decision to ignore her grand-father's mistress.

77

In 1770, by pure coincidence, two great painters died, the Frenchman François Boucher and the Italian Giambattista Tiepolo. Both had been pre-eminent in their century. With realism, the taste for naturalism which was typical of the French nature, and the splendour and spirit of an idealistic imagination which characterized Italian art, they both remained faithful to the traditional mythological inspiration of the previous century, but adorned it with gaiety, humanity and irony. Louis XV no longer represented the Sun King, like his great-grandfather, but he was as handsome as a god for his painters, and his mistresses were very human Venuses. Yet everything was to change again when the last great painters of Olympia were to stop painting. It was also in 1770 that Beethoven was born; his music was to illustrate and galvanize a new heroic generation in which the last echoes of the time when life was sweet were to be lost and forgotten.

Into the life of every Frenchman, that year brought even greater changes. Since the beginning of Louis XV's reign, France had acquired a great deal of wealth; to use a modern expression, the gross national product had greatly increased. But it was distributed very unfairly. Although the standard of living of the poorest people had improved (famines were far more rare, and painters, by contrast to the artists of the previous century, no longer portrayed the peasants as barefoot but showed them at least wearing clumsy shoes), the proprietors, in particular the middle classes, took great advantage of the increase in prices, the depreciation of currency and the loans of the government.

At the same time, the analyses, studies, criticisms or even the panegyrics of the philosophers, of whom Voltaire was certainly the most influential, had stripped the royal government of its sacred and religious nature. The sole justification for its existence was its efficacity: it seemed to be the best government possible for a large country. Louis XV had, however, suffered a whole series of setbacks in his foreign policy. By imprudently plunging into the continental war, he had helped to strengthen his former ally, Frederick II, the King of Prussia, who was now, through his repeated aggressions, a menace to the whole of Europe. In spite of overthrowing the alliances and the union with Austria, of which Marie Antoinette's marriage was the pledge,

France had recently found itself still committed to a costly continental war which did not leave sufficient resources to defend the colonies in India, Africa and America, which were conquered one by one by England.

Choiseul championed a policy of revenge which also flattered the self-esteem of the French. He built up a war fleet again, set himself to finding new allies on the continent, and even increased the size of France by buying Corsica in 1760. But the fulfilment of these ambitions was naturally costly. The royal finances were in a deplorable state. The middle classes, through the instrumentality of the Parliaments, which the King only considered as courts of justice and registration, challenged the government's decisions on taxes. Nor did the nobility hesitate to go against the King's wishes. Choiseul, who had married a wealthy middle-class woman and was very involved with the intellectual élite, was not lacking in sympathy for the development of a movement which was gradually to lead France to a constitutional monarchy.

But at court there was a strong contrary current which was frightened by this development. Grouped about Catholics who were strongly bound by tradition, it considered the only safeguard of the established order to be the re-establishment of royal authority. Since Choiseul had desired the Dauphine's marriage, the adverse party relied on the Countess du Barry. The whole year of 1770 was taken up with procedural struggles between the royal government and the Parliaments supported by the nobility and also, to a certain extent, by Choiseul. In December, Louis XV decided to dismiss his minister and exile him to his lands in Touraine.

Now surrounded by an active team—the Duke of Aiguillon in Foreign Affairs, the Chancellor Maupéou, and the finance assessor Terray—the King began rapidly to try to restore order in the country. In 1771, he suppressed the Parliaments, replacing them with ordinary courts of justice which no longer had the right to express political opinions. Terray used all the means at his

Thanks to this portrait by Desfossés we have an idea of the features of little Armand, the orphan boy that Marie Antoinette adopted and brought up with her own children. Under the Revolution he was to forget his benefactress.

command to reduce the state's debts and did not hesitate to use any expedient to tax the nobility and the wealthy middle-classes—who had practically escaped before—as heavily as possible. He even reduced or abolished the pensions or annuities which the King had granted to privileged persons. The Duke of Aiguillon followed a disengagement policy. Prussia, Russia and Austria each agreed to annex a province of Poland, France's traditional ally; D'Aiguillon did not intervene either before or afterwards to defend the Poles. Louis XV contented himself with thundering forth against this breach of faith of his ally, Maria Theresa. The Dauphine's position at court was made more difficult, for it was evident that France no longer gained any political benefit from her marriage.

The year 1770 was also important for the development of French art, and the year during which Louis XV took possession of the Petit Trianon. Although this house in the fields is linked with Marie Antoinette's memory, it was neither built for her nor by her. The King had ordered its construction while Madame de Pompadour was alive, and he resided there with the Countess du Barry. "On September 3rd, 1770" wrote the Trianon's architect, Jacques-Ange Gabriel, "His Majesty will go to supper at Louveciennes (the Countess du Barry's property) and on the 9th, I think he will sleep at the Trianon for the first time." It is difficult to explain the perfection of a work of art, but it would seem that the Little Trianon was a success to a degree rarely achieved throughout human history. The building was perfectly adapted to the piece of ground on which it stood, with a variation in the level enabling the servants' entrances to be hidden completely, and the construction of four façades which were both harmonious and different. But, in particular, Gabriel succeeded in finding the perfect balance between the often over-abundant ornamentation of the seventeenth and the first half of the eighteenth century, and the barrenness of an excessively denuded construction. The Trianon struck a happy medium; it was a masterpiece of harmony in its shape and a perfect adaptation to its use. For Louis XV, like Marie Antoinette later, tried to find a place where he could be alone with very few companions: a ground floor, which at the same time was a cellar-kitchen, a first floor

where they lived and spent their time, and a second floor with a low ceiling if they wished to have privacy. A mechanism only just perfected even made it possible to take meals without servants; the dining-room table was automatically lowered to the floor below and the floor closed over it; then the table was sent up again with another course. Thus was artistic discretion complemented by discretion in practical life. At the Trianon, happiness meant supreme comfort.

It was the custom for the heirs to the throne to enter Paris officially one day, and to be presented to the local authorities and the people of the capital. This city, which with almost three hundred thousand inhabitants was vast compared to other European cities, was at the same time the heart and the centre of the active forces in the kingdom, its most beautiful ornament and an enormous menace. Louis XV was aware of this: during his childhood, he had experienced the insurrection known as the Fronde, a civil war which had obliged the Regent, his mother, to take him away from Paris when the city rose up against the legal authority. During the eighteenth century, Louis XV's tolerance, his dislike of authoritative measures and quick decisions, and his lack of enthusiasm for being seen in public had reduced the royal government's prestige and strengthened the city's actual independence. The pace of economic developments had also thrown the growth of Paris into confusion. A large increase in population and the beginning of industrialization was attracting to the capital an immense, often wretched horde who could not find work in rural areas. At the same time, the nobility and the middle classes, who had become wealthy not only through the general progress but also through inflation, had a large number of splendid residences built. The contrast was striking between the pomp of princely mansions, whose numbers it is difficult to imagine today, and a populace which was often on the brink of famine.

During his visit to Paris in 1764, Mozart's father gave an unfavourable description of the capital:

You would have difficulty in finding a spot thronged with so many wretched and crippled people as Paris. One can hardly enter a church or take a few steps in the street without a blind man, a paralytic or a tatterdemalion approaching one and stretching out his palms....

Leopold Mozart probably saw mostly semi-rural villages, while Paris was already a metropolis; but he also met a fair number of wealthy music-lovers who wished to hear his children give a concert. From Germany, Italy, even England, Sweden, and much farther away, came painters, writers, sculptors, cabinet-makers, architects and musicians, thinking to develop their talent by coming into contact with better artists and especially to find clients in Paris. The genuine tolerance towards strangers enabled a real Paris school to develop. In supporting her own countrymen, Marie Antoinette was only to emphasize a trend which was already well-rooted in Parisian customs. From this period onwards, it was Paris and not Versailles which was the intellectual, theatrical and, to a great extent, the artistic capital of France. The success of the immense work undertaken by Diderot and d'Alembert, the Encyclopaedia, was ensured. The Opéra and the Comédie Française, subsidized and controlled by the royal government, acted in Paris and only went to Versailles for an occasional few plays. And many private theatres were kept alive by the abundance of the Parisian public. Great painters such as Watteau and Chardin, and many other artists of lesser fame, never relied on court commissions.

Paris was beautiful, attractive, and not only captivating because of its numerous

On her arrival in France the Dauphine knew only unsophisticated Austrian steps and on the occasion of her marriage celebrations at Versailles she felt incapable of dancing a quadrille. She opened the ball by dancing a

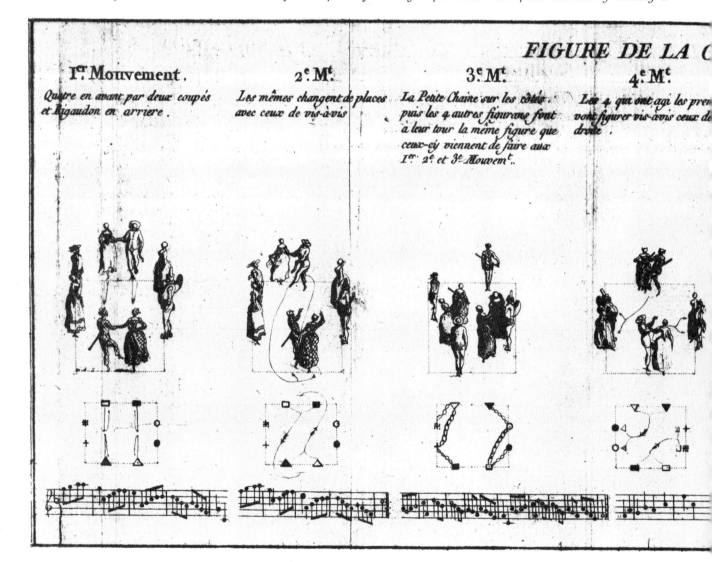

monuments built by successive generations, but because of its violent contrasts and its incomparable picturesqueness. The city was a noisy hubbub, a kaleidoscope of bright colours. How can we, who are so receptive to the charm of the oriental bazaars and relatively untouched towns and villages of Africa or Asia, fail to understand the spellbinding attraction for Marie Antoinette of a more colourful city than any metropole in the world of today? It was impossible to walk in a street without being assailed by the various grating or melodious cries of the countless pedlars in their wide variety of colourful clothing. The princes and, very often, the middle class persons chose livery for their servants. The uniforms varied from one regiment to another. Rich men wore shot-silk suits, and the provincials kept their traditional dress in the capital. Herds of sheep or cattle were driven through the town in which factories were being built. Frequent processions took place during religious festivities, and everyone had access to the promenades, such as the King's Park at the Tuileries or the Dukes of Orleans' garden at the Palais Royal. Due to the progress in the standards of living and of taste, ancient traditions came into full bloom at the end of the eighteenth century. The Parisians, aware of the usefulness of being attractive and interesting, lent themselves to the extraordi-

minuet with the Dauphin but was afterwards content to join her brother-in-law, the Duke of Provence, in some country dances. She was eventually to acquire a taste for the French measures and learned to perform them with grace and skill.

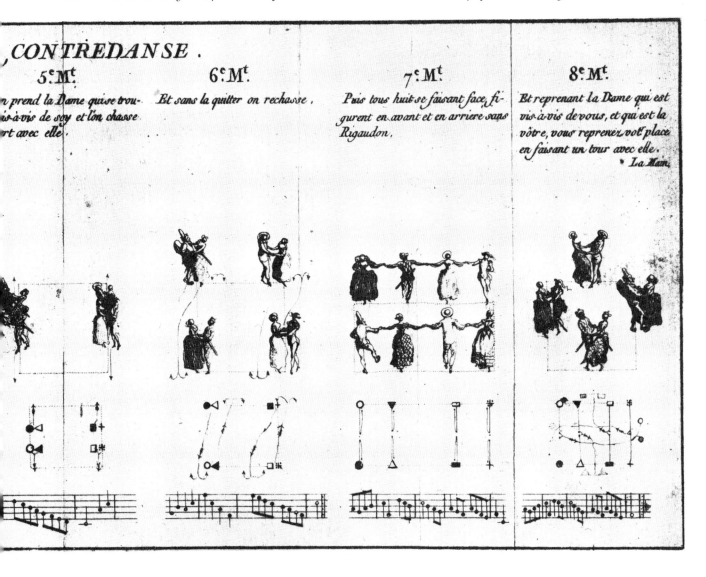

nary scene in their dress, their mannerisms and way of talking. Marie Antoinette was subjected to all of this indisputable fascination, like many contemporary artists who increased the curious comments on their town. A new liberty characterized social relationships. Leopold Mozart said in surprise : "One has great difficulty in recognizing the mistress of the house; everyone does as he wishes."

Marie Antoinette and Louis Auguste sometimes visited the capital incognito and the young dauphine was enraptured from the outset by the difficult game of being attractive both as a woman and as a future queen. Louis XV feared the dangers for his grandchildren of an official confrontation with the city. He was also fond of Paris, however, and continually tried to make it more beautiful. On the advice of Gabriel, his favourite architect, he developed the town towards the west; he had the Ecole Militaire built, and drained the enormous plot of the Champ de Mars, which until then, owing to the Seine's high waters, had been a swamp.

On the right bank, he had planned the admirable vista which spreads from the Tuileries to beyond the Champs-Elysées. Hundreds of out-of-work labourers had been set to levelling a hill at the spot where the Arc de Triomphe of the Etoile was later to be erected. The square Louis XV, which today is the Place de la Concorde, was already partly constructed, and from the time of their entry into Paris until their deaths, the decisive moments of Marie Antoinette's and Louis Auguste's brief existence were to take place here. This square, which had already been designed in 1750 during the reign of Louis XV, underwent repeated improvements to make it more beautiful. In its centre, an extremely beautiful statue of Louis XV on horseback was erected; this was why it had been constructed in the first place, for all the large squares in Paris had been built in honour of a sovereign. But by contrast with the other royal squares, there are no attendant monuments. This was more a case of wedding architecture and nature. At the northern end, two large palaces with simple and majestic lines were built. Beyond them, the Rue Royale unfolded, with its symmetrical façades, and this vista was to end with the Madeleine Church, which was to be built much later. To the south, a bridge to cross the Seine was planned and was to be built by Louis XVI, with the Bourbon Palace beyond it, constructed in an antique style by the Prince de Condé, the King's cousin. The real originality of this square, which was one of the finest in the world, lay in the transition from one garden to another. The green terraces of the Tuileries overhung its vast area, and beyond this, the immense walk of the Champs-Elysées which was still almost completely pastoral. Here, architecture aimed at ambitious town-planning, and building consisted in emphasizing the beauty of the scene offered by nature. Marie Antoinette was never completely to abandon this concept.

By dint of skilful and tender entreaties, the King finally resigned himself to allowing his grandchildren to make their solemn entrance into Paris. The date, which had been postponed for a long time, was June 8th, 1773.

Radiant sunshine lit up Paris on that day. The spectators were numerous even on the road to Paris from Versailles, and still more so at the entrance to the capital. The merchants' prefect made a long and very boring speech when the procession arrived, but the Duke of Brissac, the governor of Paris, instead of haranguing the Dauphine at length, simply said as he showed her the crowd come to cheer her : "Madame, there before your eyes are two thousand people who love you."

The market women, allowed by a custom dating from time immemorial to speak to the sovereigns, whom they received with the greatest liberty, did not fail to give the young couple extremely ribald instructions on their marital teething troubles, of which the news had spread throughout Paris a long time ago. Everyone laughed, but was it really sincere ?

The halts in Paris were many and tedious. They had to stop at the Conti quay to receive the homage of the prefect of the Mint, at the Pont Neuf where the lieutenant of the Criminal Department was waiting with a company of soldiers; at Notre-Dame where mass was celebrated with great pomp and the archbishop and his chapter welcomed the heirs to the throne in the cathedral square. The princely couple, at the gate of the Louis

This portrait of Voltaire is the work of Maurice Quentin de la Tour. From his residence at Ferney the writer held sway over all the enlightened minds of his time and his influence was felt throughout the whole of Europe.

Le Grand high school, had to listen to a long speech by the rector of the university. A young pupil, lost in the crowd, saw for the first time the Dauphine whom he was later to hate so intensely; his name was Maximilian de Robespierre. Dinner was served at the Tuileries Palace. It was a public ceremony; the crowd passed along, constantly renewed, before the guests. At the end of this hectic day, the Dauphin and the Dauphine appeared on the balcony above the gardens which were swarming with people. Marie Antoinette insisted on mixing with the throngs; the Dauphin followed her and on the Tuileries terrace adjacent to the Place Louis XV, they were cheered, pushed, jostled, and left happy. Marie Antoinette enthusiastically described this triumphal visit to her mother:

As for honours, we received all those imaginable, but although this was all very well, it was not this which moved me the most, but the tenderness and eagerness of these poor people, who in spite of the taxes heaped on them, were beside themselves with joy. When we went for a walk at the Tuileries, there was such a large crowd that we remained three quarters of an hour without being able to move either forwards or backwards. His Highness the Dauphin and I instructed the guards several times not to strike anyone. There was such good order during this day that in spite of the enormous number of people who followed us everywhere, no one was hurt. After returning from the walk, we went to our open terrace and remained there for half an hour. I cannot describe the joy and affection which we were shown from that moment onwards. Before withdrawing, we waved to the people, which gave them great pleasure. How happy one is in our position when one gains the friendship of a whole people so cheaply! Yet there is nothing as precious as this; I felt it deeply and I will never forget it.

Happiness consisted in pleasing others and in being loved. As Mercy-Argenteau also explained to Maria Theresa, Marie Antoinette was well aware that her husband did not play the main part that day, but that her gracefulness and her charming femininity had won thousands of hearts. An idyll was drafted between Marie Antoinette and the French people which was to experience terrible vicissitudes and come to a tragic end. Reciprocal hatred was to be born of a great thwarted love and the future queen had already reached a height of popularity that she was never again to attain.

The art which surrounded Louis XV all his life and which he bequeathed in a changed form to his grandchildren after half a century, was a repudiation of the shapes and styles which his great-grandfather had wished. Eighteenth-century houses and their interior decoration formed a striking contrast with the Great Century residences as great as that between the characters of Louis the Beloved and Louis the Great. In many respects, it shows the reaction to an era in which the King's glory was ample justification for the whole country's efforts, war was man's natural occupation, religion above all a means of escaping from misery on earth, and discipline the normal attitude of peasants, middle classes, nobles, thinkers and artists. A system had existed into which the most original and gifted personages had willingly or unwillingly been integrated, artists such as Mansart the architect, Le Nôtre the gardener, and Lebrun the painter and decorator; but also dramatists like Molière and Racine. All, like Louis XIV, searched for an absolute ideal, and all desired to contribute to the glory of the greatest king in the world.

The eighteenth century, on the contrary, marked the explosion of all liberties and challenged all concepts. Although the great thinkers, novelists and memorialists like Montesquieu, Voltaire, Marivaux or Rousseau give us an idea of this far-reaching revolution which was born several decades before it was called by its name, the furniture, ornaments and even the objects which men and women of this period liked to have about them provide us with more concrete information on this philosophy of happiness which gave rise to an art of living so agreeable, so gentle and also so wise that nothing comparable to it has ever been known. The sumptuous furniture with its frequently heavy and splendid ornamentation, but with austere, geometrical shapes, was succeeded by a riot of imagination in the design of seats and cupboards as well as in decoration or skilfulness in fulfilling the need for comfort and pleasure. The century of the "chest of drawers", the "escritoire", the "desk", the "confidant" and the "silent attendant" was also the one permitting the greatest freedom of conduct, on the sole condition that no one was caused any pain. The men of the eighteenth century loved variety and novelty in their life and their furnishings.

No fashionable residence could be without a music-room complete with musicians and music-lovers. Here the works of Couperin and Rameau are being played and discussed. Rousseau's "Devin du Village" also had a great success.

The development increased rapidly. In behaviour and decoration, during the reigns of Louis XV and Louis XVI, the revolt was first of all directed against the architectural sobriety of the Louis XIV style. Then, under the influence of the classical antiquity only lately rediscovered in excavations in southern Italy, as well as because of a natural progression in taste, a more simple, if not more sober harmony slowly appeared. In any case, a happy balance was struck before the advent of the excessive starkness of the Directory or Empire styles towards the end of Louis XV's reign and during that of his successor. At the time of Marie Antoinette, decorative art still profited by the fabulous powers of imagination and execution which had developed since the beginning of the century, but it had shed its baroque appearance. Moreover, it was increasingly adapted to the needs and convenience of men. To

use an adjective which then did not exist, it was functional art, in which the care for comfort did not at all detract from the concern for aesthetic beauty. It was characteristic of the philosophy of the times, in which the feeling of eternity or even of a distant future was mitigated and in which immediate desires increasingly governed everyone's attitude, to emphasize decoration at the expense of architecture. Louis XIV, Louis XV, and the latter's favourites the Marquise de Pompadour and the Countess du Barry had, it is true, built fewer and fewer vast palaces and houses. Marie Antoinette, who was accused of having spent so much on buildings, did not have a single large mansion erected for herself during the fifteen years of her reign. The plans carried out under Louis XVI were those which had been decided upon during the preceding reign. On the other hand, the Queen had a passion for furniture,

*Life for the French aristocracy was a pleasant and lighthearted game : the salons were graceful and the guests elegant ;
at the gambling, dancing and other amusements courtesy and language rose to heights of exquisite delicacy and charm.*

arranging and decoration. In this respect, too, she behaved like her noble or middle-class contemporaries. Mercier, a chronicler, noted with some exaggeration :

When a house is built, nothing has yet been done ; not even a quarter of the total expense has been reached. Then come the carpenter, upholsterer, painter, gilder, sculptor and cabinet-maker, etc.... Afterwards, mirrors are needed, and doorbells everywhere ; the interior takes three times longer than to build the mansion ; the antechambers, secret entrances and private staircases are all endless.

The high quality of furniture during Marie Antoinette's time was first of all the fruit of a long tradition in perfecting the taste of enthusiasts, and of the skill of craftsmen throughout several generations. It is not an exaggeration to say that, from the aesthetic point of view, we must thank a system of social privileges which had existed in France

since the Middle Ages, and whose injustice was brought out most strongly at a time when it produced in a certain area its most beautiful results. The middle classes and the aristocracy of upstarts which sprang from the Revolution and the Empire were never to form the exacting, knowledgeable and subtle clientele (even to the point of esteeming and sometimes supporting their worst enemies) constituted by the Ancien Régime families whose taste had evolved through several centuries. This situation was reflected among the craftsmen. They were a closed society, a social class which had been confined to its own members for several hundreds of years ; people were only admitted if they were born into it or gave evidence of really exceptional talent. Each manual trade, cabinet-makers, goldsmiths, joiners and so on, formed a guild which was an association of a small number of "masters", privileged craftsmen with the exclusive right to make

On April 20th, 1776 Marie Antoinette presided at the first horse races to take place in France. In spite of a lack of enthusiasm on the part of the King, racing was soon to become very fashionable throughout Europe.

certain types of objects. They were obliged to guarantee the quality not only of the articles which left their own workshops, but also those of their colleagues; and they themselves elected the replacements for deceased masters. They very naturally favorized the son, or the relative whom the deceased master had selected as his successor after a long apprenticeship. Just as there were noble and royal dynasties, so there were famous families of cabinet-makers like the van Riesenburghs and the Migeons, and joiners like the Senés, of whom one or more members worked for Marie Antoinette. Thus people were born into a craft and were led to practise it from their earliest youth until their death. No training school has ever been able to replace such an initiation.

But the masters were naturally helped by apprentices or craftsmen who were not born into the guild and of whom some had exercised their trade in other countries. At the time of Marie Antoinette, several craftsmen of German origin therefore worked in Paris, and whether consciously or not, the Queen sometimes particularly favoured them. The noteworthy cabinet-maker Jean-Henri Riesener was first employed by Oeben; then quite naturally, as was his talent's due, he took over

his master's workshop on the latter's death and also married his widow.

Each trade and each guild was strictly specialized and the masters guarded against any encroachment with jealous care. A cabinet-maker could thus make a wardrobe, but not a chair, which was reserved for joiners; and he had to call upon a bronzer if he desired to decorate a piece of furniture. Such narrow rules may seem to us, probably wrongly, to be exaggerated. But long practice and untiring patience enabled their talent to gain in refinement throughout a career which did not allow any possibility of diversification. The most beautiful furniture was the fruit of the work of several artists who, like the musicians in an orchestra, played the part in which they excelled.

This, for instance, was the case with Marie Antoinette's jewel chest, which was ordered by Louis XV and delivered at Versailles on May 4th, 1770, on the eve of the Dauphine's arrival. It was designed by an extremely gifted young architect, Jean-François Bellanger, whose masterpiece was to be La Bagatelle. The main work was carried out by the cabinet-maker Evalde, who had been elected a master five years earlier. On the inside, the crimson velvet embroidered with gold had been woven and inserted by the tapestry-maker Delanoue. The sculpting in gilded wood was carried out by the joiner Auguste Bocciardi, and the ornaments in gilded bronze were carved by the best bronzer of the period, Pierre Gouthière. But for the medallions of the Dauphin and the Dauphine which decorate the centre of the main panels, he had only to copy the models provided by Jean-Antoine Houdon, the sculptor. At that time, the complete modesty of the most famous artists, and the advantages of extreme specialization and well-organized co-operation enabled works of art to be achieved of such taste that a single man, gifted as he might have been, would never have been able to imagine them nor execute them. Very fortunately, no discrimination was made, as was to become the habit during the following century, between the workers and the creators.

Such co-operation was not only to be found in the execution of orders for royalty; the role of merchants was to be decisive in the eighteenth century. They were in contact with the clients and thus spared the craftsmen most commercial dealings. They also ordered articles which they sometimes kept in stock for a long time, so regularizing the craftsmen's activity and sometimes guiding public taste.

For during this period, in which scientific discoveries and research were so highly prized, patrons had an unrestrained appetite for new things, and a variety of techniques were tried and discovered which no other age, particularly our own, has known. The craftsmen did not have many workmen at their disposal. There was no question of mass production; a great deal of the work was adapted to the patron's taste. The most beautiful pieces of furniture, the splendid suites were often unique pieces. This concept of furniture obliged the craftsmen to call upon all kinds of imaginative and technical resources. The inlaid woodwork of different colours, the endless choice of the motifs generally ordered from painters who were already well-known, all opened limitless horizons. Under the reign of Marie Antoinette, very different woods, preferably of bright colours which have unfortunately faded with time, were popular; the variety of veneers was enormous and they were obtained from all parts of the world. Mahogany, kingwood, amboyna, cayenne wood, lemonwood, thuya, Brazilian rosewood, coral, ebony, rosewood and violet-coloured wood—the list goes on and on. Curiously enough (but was it not this generation's characteristic to fluctuate between the most abstract day-dreams and the most easily attainable pleasures?) the decorations were sometimes solely geometrical, the interlacing lines simple or complex, and sometimes very down-to-earth, with flowers, fruits, and agricultural or handicraft tools. Not only raw materials from other continents were used, but the talents of craftsmen from all over the world were called upon; ships bore chests-of-drawers, desks and all kinds of furniture to the Far East, where they were decorated with many different kinds of lacquer in Japan, or Southern China (particularly in Canton which was very receptive to trade with the west), or in Northern China. There was also a much less expensive French imitation of these specialities of far-off countries, from which the furniture sometimes only returned after several years. Thus Martin varnish was a paint used on wood which replaced lacquer without really imitating it. Nor was it exceptional to see decorations in grisaille of certain painted

pieces of furniture being entrusted to artists of secondary importance. At the end of Louis XV's reign and under Louis XVI, the ornamentation of furniture varied greatly. Work inlaid with mother-of-pearl, copper and silver came back into fashion, but a novelty which enjoyed great success was furniture covered with plaques of Sèvres china, made for royalty and very popular, with excellent painters producing very gay and realistic designs. The suppliers were sometimes foreign manufacturers, from Meissen in Saxony, for instance, or the Englishman Josiah Wedgewood, whose white figures copied from antique statues contrast with a blue background; for the discovery of the buried Roman cities of Pompeii and Herculaneum had not only given wings to the imagination of the times, but had also greatly enriched the scope of ornamentation. Bronze statues in furnishings were thus often inspired by Roman, Greek or Egyptian antiquity.

To emphasize the purely aesthetic quality of furnishings in the art of Marie Antoinette's time would mean risking a serious misconception. For when it was a matter of making life more beautiful, this could only be achieved

Marie Antoinette had a ruinous passion for cards and extravagant bets and on one occasion played for thirty-six hours at a stretch. At the end of 1776 her accounts showed debts amounting to about a hundred million francs.

For the royal apartments Jean Honoré Fragonard painted "Hide-and-Seek", one of a series of panels illustrating "the progress of love in the heart of young girls".

dressmakers, one can imagine what was represented by the chairs, couches and tables which were adapted or invented according to the client's fancy. From the armchair *à la Reine* with a flat back to the *cabriolet* armchair with the back curving slightly inwards, moulded to the shape of the body, and the "shepherdess" provided with a cushion or the "convenience armchair" with an adjustable back to change the angle, there were numerous and curious types. An office chair sometimes had an additional leg in front and an indented seat to allow the legs to reach well under the desk, and it could generally swivel around; the "toilet chair" had a curved back to make the hairdresser's work easier, and it was sometimes completely bare if it was to be used when powdering hair. The passion for card games gave rise to chairs called *voyeuses* on which a person could sit astride and place his arms on a low, upholstered back, or even kneel if the seat was nearer the ground. Nor can we fail to mention, too, the countless kinds of tables—of which several are still in existence—which were made for Marie Antoinette. Desks, sometimes very small, could be changed into writing or reading tables at will. Each game provided the pretext for a new invention : a triangular table for backgammon, round ones for *pan royal*, and square ones for quadrille ; work tables with candlesticks with two spikes, a painting table with a tray equipped to hold the bottles and the paints, and tables with pin-trays. The pieces of furniture which seem most superfluous are made with prodigious care to conceal their faculty of being used in unexpected ways by means of the system of trays, drawers and hiding-places. As for toilet articles which were the least fit to be seen, they were still generally very refined during this period; thus there were chamber-pots in sculpted silver, tin, or finely decorated china.

All kinds of furniture and ornaments encumbered these rooms meant to be "very elegant"; scarcely an idea can be conceived of them from our museums, where every object is so carefully placed. Chairs for sitting "in state" were placed all around the room, but they were rarely used; everyone sat on more easily movable chairs placed near the middle of the room, with pedestal tables and other small pieces of furniture. No surface was left entirely free. On the mantelpiece and the tables there were vases or other

by making it above all easier and more comfortable. The variety of shapes and decorative colours corresponded to the practically endless number of objects and furniture adapted to all circumstances and the habits and condition of each person. When one thinks of the custom of making clothes to measure and the unique models of a few great

objects serving the same function. For here, too, reality and fiction were constantly combined. Marie Antoinette adored flowers. They were replaced every day and were gathered in the Versailles or Trianon rose-gardens. But she also loved artificial flowers in china, silk, gauze or enamel. Like her contemporaries, she was very sensitive to perfumes and possessed a large number of perfume-braziers and also "oil-pots" in which flower essences were steeped, prepared according to skilful recipes and very often enriched by new scents. Objects of superb beauty were in reality often false vases, perfume-braziers or "oil-pots". They were sometimes made of rare china, or wondrous shells, skilfully set in gilded bronze. The Queen had loved lacquered articles since her childhood. Her mother, the Empress, was to leave her a great number of them. They decorated her private suites with no other purpose than that of pleasing the eye.

The need to furnish a room to excess, to make its atmosphere as warm as possible, was also noticeable in the care devoted to covering the ground and draping the beds and windows with thick curtains. The French textile manufacturers outdid themselves for Marie Antoinette. Lyons silks had occupied a privileged position in Europe from the eighteenth century. During the last quarter of the century, by the new berclé process which consisted in slipping a woof combining both tones between the two weaves, they achieved the extraordinary hangings of the Queen's room. These she owed to Philippe de la Salle, who created a vibrant general harmony with a setting of drums, shepherds' crooks, birds, baskets and trellises in a surprising range of different colours.

But Marie Antoinette was also fond of much more economical materials, such as printed linens. In particular the Jouy-en-Josas factory near Paris, founded by Ober-kampf, descendant of a family of Bavarian dyers, produced the most popular and typically French work. Oberkampf called upon painters, particularly Jean-Baptiste Huet, who supplied charming designs with cameos of country life or even work in factories: it was the same gentle poetry which was to characterize the building and decoration of the hamlet at the Trianon.

On the other hand, in the offices of her small suites, the Queen wished to have

The delightful Frago continued his flirtatious theme with "The Escalade", a prelude to the tender moments in "The Declaration" and "The Lover Crowned".

extremely richly decorated walls. The Gilded Drawing-room, the Rest-room at Versailles, and the Fontainebleau boudoir which have miraculously been preserved from the ravages of time, enable us to appreciate Marie Antoinette's tastes. The wood or stucco, the gold and colours, large mirrors, geometrical or realistic designs with flowers, cupids, sphinxes or goddesses worked and invented under Mique, the Queen's architect, or the Rousseau brothers, give an impression of splendour heightened even more by the curtain loops and all the other trimmings which it has been possible to restore.

Nothing used by a Queen could be ordinary or mediocre. Her books were sumptuously bound, and her library was a room with fine woods skilfully combined. Her dinner service and her instruments for weaving and sewing were of truly royal refinement. This was the opposite of the austerity of many modern homes, and also of the sumptuous solemnity of mansions during the time of Louis XIV. At the time of Marie Antoinette, when decoration was perhaps at its most costly, the expense was unavoidably caused by the extreme care given to each detail of a curtain, a piece of furniture or an object. Thus a time comes when refinement reaches its limits. It is certainly always easy to create vaster and more sumptuous buildings. But it is possible to reach the stage where the adaptation of things to their use, to the pleasure of the eye and all the other senses, can no longer be exceeded; when an everyday thimble, handbag, vase, wall-bracket and fire-dog attain such heights of perfection that working unceasingly to improve such delights becomes blasphemy. The superiority of decorative art at the time of Marie Antoinette owed its strength to its vitality and its continual renewal. It could not remain static, yet how could it be endlessly perfected? Its success seemed to ask for the cataclysm in which everything would be destroyed, for only isolated vestiges were to survive in the lifeless setting of museums. The nineteenth and twentieth centuries were to savour the nostalgia of a pleasant and gentle life which seemed the necessary condition for a certain happiness never to be known again—for it was the fruit of a period in social development which allowed a few personalities to blossom whose genius perhaps lay in their very frivolity.

For a few years, those at court and the ambassadors of foreign powers had noticed that Louis XV's strength was declining. But the king was still not old and it seemed that this reign which had lasted nearly sixty years was never to end. Returning after a hunt on April 27th, 1774, Louis XV felt unwell and went to sleep at the Little Trianon. On the next day, finding him feverish, the doctors moved him to Versailles where a king could be officially ill. On the 28th, the first symptoms of smallpox appeared, at that time a terrible disease from which people rarely recovered and which was very contagious. The Dauphin and the Dauphine were given instructions to remain in their suites, as were the Count of Provence and the Count of Artois. But Louis XV's daughters, Adélaide, Victoire and Sophie, and their enemy the Countess du Barry closeted themselves with the King at the risk of catching the disease. A few days later, in spite of their care, Louis XV himself felt death coming and asked for religious solace. This was the chance for the priests and the cardinal bishop of Paris to take their revenge, and a way to prove the Church's power even over sovereigns. The mightiest monarch of Europe was not only obliged to expel his mistress before being given communion, but he also had to proclaim his faults publicly. After giving the dying Louis XV absolution, the bishop went to the door of the royal chamber, and in a loud voice, proclaimed to the hundreds of courtiers assembled there:

Gentlemen, the King has charged me to tell you that he asks God's pardon for offending Him and for the evil example he has given his people; if God gives him back his health, he undertakes to show his penitence, support religion and succour his people.

Following this cruel humiliation, everything was to contribute to abase the esteem of the royal majesty, now personified by a dying man who had been increasingly unpopular in his later years, in the eyes of the general public. As on his great-grandfather's death sixty years earlier, a candle was lit behind the bedroom window at the end of the marble courtyard. Louis XV's resistance was surprising. The people were to wait impatiently for a long time before the candle went out. The body, covered with pustules, gave forth a nauseating smell, and his daughters needed real courage to watch over this being who was barely alive. When at half past three on Tuesday afternoon, May 10th, the candle could at last be blown out, the corpse was carried to its sepulchre at Saint-Denis almost in secret to avoid contagion, and also the insults of a populace ready to be unleashed. Marie Antoinette wrote to her mother:

Mercy has certainly instructed you of the circumstances of our misfortune; this cruel illness fortunately left the King conscious until the last moment and his end was edifying. The new King seems to have captured the hearts of his people; two days before grandfather's death, he had two hundred thousand francs distributed to the poor, which made a great impression. He does not stop working and answering in his own hand the ministers whom he cannot yet see (for they were in contact with Louis XV during his illness) and many other letters. It is certain that he possesses the quality of having a taste for economy and the most fervent desire to make his people happy. In everything, his wish to learn corresponds to the need to do so, I hope that God will bless his goodwill.

The public expected many changes; the King has restricted himself to putting the "creature" [Madame du Barry] in a convent and expelling all those accused of being scandalous from the court. The King himself owed this example to the people of Versailles.... The King has left me the liberty of choosing the persons to fill the new positions in my house as a Queen. Although God let me be born to the rank which I fill today, I cannot fail to admire fate's arrangement in choosing me, the last of your daughters, for the most beautiful kingdom in Europe.

And Louis XVI added in his own hand:

I am very pleased to have the occasion, my dear mother, to give you evidence of my tenderness and affection.... I should be extremely delighted to please you and thus show you all my affection and my gratitude for granting me your daughter with whom I could not be happier.

This showed a strange lack of awareness by this royal couple, now twenty years old, who had suddenly been invested with supreme responsibilities and who gave the impression of being so far from understanding the reality of political problems. Marie Antoinette had played at being the Dauphine for four years; evidently she only thought of the pleasures offered by a new rôle with vague and vast perspectives. And Louis XVI's goodwill hardly gave him any idea of how to achieve his people's happiness. Acclaimed by the crowd and fawned upon by courtiers for whom they represented the future, the young couple very quickly forgot this pathetic illness and their mourning and indulged in the joy of being loved and of being a source and a hope of happiness for others.

Who were these two young people who had now suddenly come to power? The judgement of their contemporaries certainly does not entirely agree, but it was not contradictory either. Louis XVI, tall, strong and a great eater, was neither handsome, nor of noble bearing, nor had he any gift for pleasing in society. "Beneath a slightly rough exterior," wrote Mercy, "he gives promise of frankness, strength of character, regular habits and the desire to do all the good which is in his power." But a very good observer, the Abbé de Véri, also noted that "he is a child king in his twenties who has never shown any sign of aptitude for governing". He had always been timid and awkward, and his grandfather had never given him the chance of taking on any responsibility. The non-consummation of his marriage had doubtless given him an inferiority complex which was often to paralyse him even in the private conversations with his ministers or assistants of lesser rank. His relationship to his wife is difficult to define. They had had the feeling of finding a refuge in each other when they were very young, and the husband certainly felt a keen gratitude for the affection and tenderness which his young wife showed him, in spite of his inability to answer her ardour. Yet their tastes were as different as they could be. Louis was fond of solitude; his greatest pleasure was to undertake long gallops on horseback in the country, to read, in particular historical works, or to carry out such difficult and complicated mechanical work as locksmithing. And his wife loved society, balls, music, and the theatre....

The opinions expressed about Marie Antoinette have naturally varied. If she was not, strictly speaking, beautiful, she was certainly very attractive. Horace Walpole was enthusiastic about her and described how she moved through a room "like an aerial being, all brightness and grace, and without seeming to touch earth". One of her protégés, Besenval, whose attitude was often critical, offered a more precise judgement: "Without being classically beautiful or pretty, her extraordinary complexion, the very graceful way in which she carries her head, and the great elegance of her whole person place her in a position to challenge many other women who

Fragonard's "Fête à Saint-Cloud" is a perfect picture of happiness as Marie Antoinette conceived it : to be beautiful, to be gay, to live in a fantasy world beneath a blue sky and in the midst of a smiling and benevolent nature. Did she live her happiness or only dream it? ▷

are more favoured by nature." And the Count of Lamarck, who was generally a very objective witness, asserted:

Marie Antoinette did not have a very large scope of intelligence, but she rapidly grasped and understood the things about which one talked. Her gay nature gave her a certain inclination for jesting...and as, at that time in France, a light-hearted tone accompanied by much graciousness and subtlety reigned among the high society, they assiduously amused and pleased the Queen by flattering her taste for mockery. Marie Antoinette's heart yearned for friendship.

The popularity of this oddly-assorted couple was undeniable and deep during the first months and years of their reign. It was noticed as soon as the sovereign appeared in public and even when the Queen was alone. Véri, who did not like her, noted in his diary on January 15th, 1775:

The day before yesterday, the Queen came to the Iphigenia Opera by Gluck; at the end of the second act, the piece has a chorus in which Achilles and the people say:

Let us sing, let us celebrate our Queen,
The Hymen which under
                    its laws captivates her
Makes us eternally happy.

At the same moment as the chorus began, I saw the spectators turn by a common impulse to the Queen's box and show her their satisfaction by repeated cheers. These same cheers were repeated at every pause in the music, and when the chorus had finished, the cry of "bis" rang out as with a single voice on all sides. During the chorus' entire repetition, the cheers were renewed several times. They were so lively and natural that I saw my neighbours moved to tears and we among the public learned that the Queen had been so moved that she had wept with happiness.

Popular enthusiasm was probably at its height at Louis XVI's solemn coronation at Rheims, during the very period when bad harvests and insufficient food might well have caused the peasants to rise up against the central power. Marie Antoinette described to her mother the atmosphere which reigned:

The anointing was perfect in every way; it seems that everyone was very pleased with the King; he must be with all his subjects, great and small, who all showed him the greatest interest, the church ceremonies were interrupted at the time of the crowning by most moving cheers. I could not contain myself, my tears flowed in spite of my efforts and people were most grateful to me. During the whole journey, I did my best

to answer the people's eagerness. It was both a surprising and very happy occurrence to be so well received in spite of the expensiveness of bread, which unfortunately continues. It is certain that on seeing people who treat us so well in spite of their misery, we are even more obliged to work for their happiness. My dear mother would have shared our joy.

But the tragedy of Louis XVI, Marie Antoinette and the French of all classes was the very fact that they desired a common ideal to which they were far from giving in practice the same meaning.

Few works by the greatest artists have ever recalled so keenly the qualities and shortcomings of a period, and its real characteristics, as did painting at the time of Marie Antoinette. As Dauphine or Queen, was she enthused by this art? Nothing proves this. Marie Antoinette visited the Salon and inspected the great exhibitions such as that at the Colisée in 1776, but she did not single out the best painters, nor did she think of enriching the royal collections with masterpieces. She was fond of good artists who were talented portraitists or decorators, such as Madame Vigée-Lebrun, Châtelet, und Hubert Robert. Yet she herself personified the most beautiful painting of her time.

From 1770 onwards, pompous and sensual mythology became increasingly rare, even at the Salon. On leaving Olympia, painting became more human and hewed more closely to the simple scene of nature and daily life. At the 1773 Salon, probably to commemorate the five hundredth anniversary of St. Louis' death, many well-known persons portrayed him—Hallé, Vien, Lagrenée, Amédée van Loo, Doyen, Lépicié, Taraval and Durameau—choosing a subject nearer to life than Hercules or Achilles. But there were also still-life paintings, simple landscapes and even a painting of events of the moment: *Their Highnesses the Dauphin and the Dauphine at the Tuileries going towards the Swing-Bridge on June 23rd, 1773.* Leprince did not hesitate to illustrate one of those accounts which delighted feeling hearts more often gratified by men of letters. He exhibited a painting with the evocative title: *A young girl who believed herself ill consulted an old doctor who, on taking her pulse, informed her that her sickness was in her heart.* The best sculptors, Pajou and Houdon, portrayed the Countess du Barry and Catherine of Russia respectively.

On December 19th, 1778, after ten hours of labour pains and in public according to the custom, Marie Antoinette gave birth to a girl, Marie Thérèse Charlotte, who was to be called Madame Royale.

At the Salons of 1775, 1777 and 1779, the same tendencies were seen, with an additional preference for ancient or contemporary history. It was noteworthy that van Loo was interested in portraying *Electricity* from 1777 onwards, while under Aubry's brush, tearful subjects became increasingly complicated, as witness the title of one of his canvasses : *A young man and girl are about to receive the nuptial blessing. At the instant when the priest is writing the act, a woman arrives, preceded by an usher, who presents a caveat and a promise of marriage. This woman throws herself at the young man's feet and tries to soften his heart by showing him two children, the fruit of their secret love. The future husband, seeing his intended swoon in her mother's arms, hastens to her assistance and asks her pardon for his unfaithfulness. Moved by the sight of the unfortunate offspring, the young man's father makes his son look at his children. Feeling his heart torn asunder, the son capitulates and paternal love triumphs.*

But the most brilliant painter of this generation and the most truthful witness of this period in history was omitted from the Salon, probably because he was weighed down with orders and hardly solicited academic honours : this was Jean Honoré Fragonard. Born in 1732, he was thirty-two on Marie Antoinette's arrival in France, and painted most of his masterpieces in ten years : the decoration of the Louveciennes pavilion for Madame du Barry, which today is in the Frick Museum in New York; the *Fête à Saint-Cloud* which decorates the Bank of France and was perhaps ordered by the Duke of Penthièvre, like the two large paintings in the Washington National Gallery; the *Cache-cache* and the *Escarpolette*, probably part of a single decoration.

There was a real unity of inspiration among these paintings. They were the definition of happiness such as it could have been imagined by Marie Antoinette or Fragonard. The anecdotal subjects resemble each other and have neither a very great meaning nor much importance : the *Escalade*, *L'amant couronné*, *Le colin Maillard*, the *Saltimbanques* were more pretexts than subjects, for they were always concerned with games and joyous occupations of little importance. Life in Fragonard's paintings was a play; spectators and actors in the picture of *La Fête à Saint-Cloud* all took part in a theatrical production like the protagonists in the gallant scenes of the Frick collection. The details of

an excessively harsh realism were carefully avoided. Everything was gay, for everything was amusing. And this atmosphere was emphasized even more by the extreme importance accorded to landscapes. In each of these paintings, the trees, flowers, the sky and the statues exist and are endowed with life not as decorations but as complementary beings. The charm of the Saint-Cloud festivities sprang from the fact that it was so easy to confuse the foliage, the fountains, the forest and the strollers. Never, even in Impressionist paintings, were the human beings to be caught up in the landscape as they are in these exceptional works. The women were flowers among so many others, and the roses took on a human expression. These slender and gracious taffeta dolls, as colourful as flowerbeds, were Marie Antoinette and her companions, who thought they could abandon themselves to the pleasure of no longer considering or thinking, but only of enjoying the present like a rose blossoming in the sun. Supreme pleasure was not to be sullied with any obligation, nor with the weight of material worries or useful work, nor even the torments of passion and still less the sight of another's misery. To be beautiful and gay, to abandon oneself to the impulse of the moment under a blue sky and in the midst of radiant nature, was the real happiness which Fragonard thought he could portray and Marie Antoinette thought she could experience. Did they dream it or did they really live it ? Painting has preserved its reflection and the Queen certainly desired to experience its sweetness.

But if it is natural that the ideal of a fortunate few should coincide with the vision of artists, a serious misunderstanding arises if one applies the same terms to the needs of the most deprived, or translates their converging desires into economic or political terms. A people still living in fear of famine did not know how to be carefree : they were preoccupied above all else with material concerns. True freedom existed perhaps for those in the seats of power; the bourgeoisie and even those artisans who were wealthy and comfortable were oppressed by the humiliation of not being able to share in the honours or the functions reserved for the nobility. Material progress for all and greater equality among individuals demanded the sacrifice of certain privileges and temporary hardship for everyone. How could they accept the fact that happiness can never be universal or everlasting, that life can never coincide exactly with one's dreams ?

The young king's first political decision, probably taken at the instigation of his aunt Adélaïde, was a wise one. He wrote to one of his grandfather's former ministers, Maurepas, who had been in office for about thirty years before being expelled by the Marchioness of Pompadour :

Sir, in the righteous sorrow which weighs me down and which I share with the whole kingdom, I have, however, duties to carry out. I am the King; this single word implies many obligations, but I am only twenty. I cannot have acquired all the necessary knowledge; moreover, I cannot see any of the ministers for they were all closeted with the King during his illness. I have always heard of your integrity and the reputation which your knowledge of state affairs has so justly earned. This is what urges me to ask you to have the goodness to help me with your advice and your understanding. I would be obliged to you, Sir, if you would come to Choisy as quickly as possible where I shall take the greatest pleasure in seeing you.

Although Maurepas was aged, he had a gay and undemanding nature, and had managed to change his years of exile with his wife and a few faithful friends into a happy period of his life. He succeeded in pleasing Louis XVI at once, he did not displease Marie Antoinette at all, and by the prudence of his simple good-heartedness and his experience, he increased the young couple's popularity.

Louis XV's ministers were hated. Maupéou, Terray and d'Aiguillon were not only responsible for reforms which were considered despotic during the last four years of the King's reign, they physically personified what France detested. D'Aiguillon had "a yellow face, and a character inclined to spying and unfeelingness"; the Chancellor was a "little, dark man, with the most repellent face on which one could spit" and Terray was sinister and frightening, with a gloomy face and haggard expression. "The abbé is laughing," went the saying, "has misfortune come to someone ?" Thus the French tried to ignore the agonizing realities of their time, which they preferred to dismiss with a laugh.

As soon as Louis XVI came to the throne, the dismissal of the ministers was decided upon. It was not that the King and Maurepas were not aware of their competence and their good qualities, but already public opinion

was all-powerful. "I appoint the ministers," Louis XV had already said jokingly, "but the nation dismisses them."

Louis XVI did not think at that time of achieving his people's happiness in any other way than by fulfilling their desires. In this respect, Marie Antoinette thought like the enormous majority of French. She detested d'Aiguillon and his colleagues. She would have liked to see Choiseul come back. But there was no question of this; the King remained faithful to his father's memory, and Louis XV's son had detested this mocking minister who was an enemy of religion. The Queen therefore refrained from interfering, but she was not excluded from the selection of a new cabinet. Maurepas had a highly intelligent friend and confidant, the Abbé de Véri, who himself was very close to Vermond. Both passionately admired a former fellow student who had had remarkable success as the administrator of Limousin, A. R. J. Turgot. In July, immediately after d'Aiguillon's departure which Marie Antoinette approved and his replacement in Foreign Affairs by the experienced diplomat, Vergennes, Turgot was promoted to Minister of the Navy. For a short time, Véri and Vermond considered him as a head minister; in August, Maurepas succeeded in overcoming Louis XVI's hesitation. Turgot replaced Terray and became both Secretary of State and the Inspector of Finance. A member of Parliament of narrow intellect, Miromesnil, succeeded Maupéou.

From then on in the space of a few months there was to take place between Turgot and Louis XVI the captivating adventure of a revolution to ensure the happiness of the French people. The King brimmed over with good intentions. Turgot was in the prime of life, and as one of his assistants noted, "he has the frank, ingenuous gaiety of a child, he bursts into peals of laughter at jokes or at a touch of craziness". He pleased the King and even the Queen. "We two are the only persons who wish to make the French happy," Louis XVI was to say to him one day. But Véri, who was always shrewd and who knew his friend's immoderate character, wrote to Turgot one day : "You believe that you have a love of the public welfare; not at all, you have a passion for it."

Turgot generously lowered his own salary and Louis XVI agreed to reduce the expenses of his house. Turgot's and the new cabinet's overriding principle was liberty. Without hesitation they brought back from exile the members of Parliament who had been expelled four years ago for opposing the royal will. In the eyes of public opinion, Parliament represented a guarantor of liberties, despite the fact that it was recruited from the aristocrats and the bourgeoisie. Turgot imagined, very wrongly, that this oligarchy would help him in his audacious reforms. The key to economic prosperity, in his opinion, lay in liberalism. Until then, the royal government had controlled the price of grain—which was the main source of food—and had regulated and taxed its transportation from one province to another. The abolition of price controls and of internal customs duties were to facilitate an increase in production and to ease shortages in provinces where the harvest had been poor by contributions from regions which had a surplus. From this point of view, Turgot already reasoned like a twentieth-century economist.

He also aimed at the improvement of transportation, developing connections between cities by reorganizing the stages, which was to save travellers several days over long distances. And he finally abolished all traces of bondage which had come down from the Middle Ages. The last signs of serfdom were to be suppressed in lands belonging to the crown; statute labour, the peasants' obligation to provide a few days' work free to build roads, was done away with and replaced by a tax to be paid by everyone; the guilds and wardenships which formed the compulsory framework of urban craftsmanship and guaranteed the quality of the work supplied, but which were so organized as often to exclude even gifted workmen from any really profitable career, were also abolished.

This vast programme was the subject of long discussions during which Turgot put into the King's mouth an account of the idea of a natural law and principles of liberty and equality, which the Revolutionaries were later to develop.

The right to work is the most inalienable of all rights; every law which prevents its exercise violates natural law and must be considered as null and void; the existing corporations are tyrannical institutions produced by egotism, greed and violence; the King will not suffer that one part of the population should be given over to the avidity of the other.

The declarations by the King or his ministers, which agreed on this point with the writings of contemporary philosophers, stated that a society based on traditions often going back thousands of years was bad in itself, and that it was possible to create an ideal city within a short time. In politics, the art of happiness consisted in finding the formula which could change the living conditions of the French, abolishing want and the most flagrant inequalities.

These prospects doubtless captivated public opinion. There was a period of confidence and enthusiasm. The people were less preoccupied by their actual problems than by the happiness which was close and promised by the King, the ministers and the writers. Henceforward no one could stop this leap of their hearts towards an inaccessible paradise.

Buffon, one of the most famous authors, noted: "The King shows a father's tenderness for his people" and the poorest people in the country and the towns sang popular refrains:

> I will no longer go to the road
> As if to the galleys,
> Everyone can live from his trade today
> Without paying a jury or mastership.

But neither Louis XVI, who was always slow to take a decision, nor Turgot, in spite of his talents as an economist and his qualities of a man of action, could make these promises instantly come true. And furthermore, Turgot's edicts menaced the fortune and the privileges of the nobles and the bourgeoisie.

Open or dramatic struggles were rarely to take place during this royal revolution, which was often as radical in the economic and social spheres as were the measures taken twenty years later after royalty's shipwreck. A series of legal skirmishes, brief riots and court intrigues were enough to destroy the promise of happiness for a time; but it still survived in thousands of frustrated hearts.

Parliament, set up again, dared not totally oppose a humanitarian policy which corresponded to such a great extent to the ideas

(continued on page 107)

In 1775, shortly after becoming Queen of France, Marie Antoinette ordered an official portrait from the painter Gautier-Dagoty. He painted the gouache on the opposite page as a souvenir of his work in the Queen's chamber.

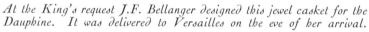

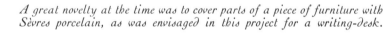

At the King's request J.F. Bellanger designed this jewel casket for the Dauphine. It was delivered to Versailles on the eve of her arrival.

A great novelty at the time was to cover parts of a piece of furniture with Sèvres porcelain, as was envisaged in this project for a writing-desk.

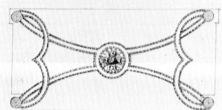

Marie Antoinette's taste inclined towards the small and elegant rather than the grandiose.

Light and practical furniture like this bonheur-du-jour satisfied all the requirements of an aristocracy with a refined taste.

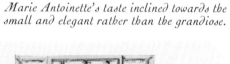

The most beautiful pieces of
furniture were often unique and
made of rare materials : exotic wood, precious metals, lacquer and bas-relief in porcelain,
very fashionable at the time.

The influence of antiquity,
rediscovered at Pompeii and
Herculaneum, appears in this
project for an incense-burner.

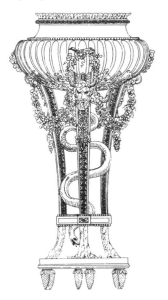

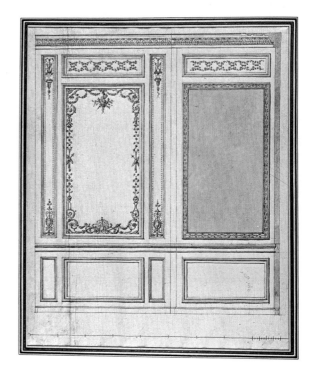

No effort was spared to enliven the atmosphere of the royal apartments. The weavers worked a miracle in creating this counterpane with its gay bunches of flowers.

To decorate her "petits appartments" the Queen had projects drawn up that combined wood, stucco, gold and colour in the most perfect harmony.

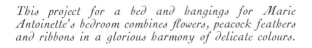

This project for a bed and hangings for Marie Antoinette's bedroom combines flowers, peacock feathers and ribbons in a glorious harmony of delicate colours.

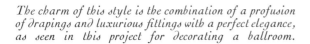

The charm of this style is the combination of a profusion of drapings and luxurious fittings with a perfect elegance, as seen in this project for decorating a ballroom.

Marie Antoinette was a great admirer of the geometric or antique style, as can be seen in her stucco room which was formerly a library belonging to one of her aunts, Sophie.

The young queen could no more bear monotony in the decoration of her apartments than she could in her life. In her stucco room the chimney face is a prodigious fantasy of detail.

Bibliotèque de Madame Sophie a Versailles
Face de la cheminée decorée en Stuc
et par le papier qui retombe face opposée a la cheminée

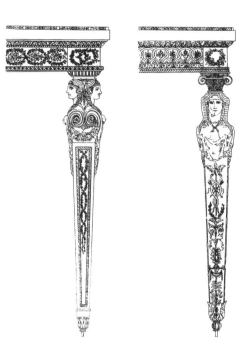

In these two drawings the tops, friezes and legs are, on the left, in green jasper and in red prophyry on the right : all the ornaments are of gilded bronze.

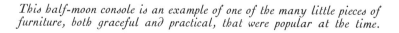

A two-tier table with four finely sculpted legs. The porcelain-decorated top picks up the same fine floral designs as can be seen in the frieze.

This half-moon console is an example of one of the many little pieces of furniture, both graceful and practical, that were popular at the time.

This bronze-decorated table, the legs of which remind one of caryatids, was bought by the Queen from the Duke of Aumont.

In spite of its geometric design this porcelain-decorated table manages to avoid monotonous symmetry.

Console-table with two marble trays. The bronze ornaments are applied with discretion and the legs continue into the frieze.

These small, flower-decorated tables carry two innovations: the gallery that encircles the tray and the legs on castors.

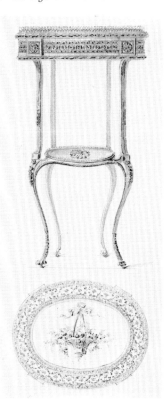

This study for part of the Queen's inner chamber at Versailles reflects Marie Antoinette's tastes and inclinations. Decoration is arranged with grace and delicacy within a geometrical plan. The painted panels represent the themes of music and dance. Gone are the once-popular allusions to mythology and war : pleasure and elegance reign supreme.

of the times. However it criticized each of Turgot's edicts, increased its admonishments to the King, and refused to register anything.

It was bad luck also that Turgot had adopted his first measures on the freeing of the prices of grain in a year when the harvest was bad and supplies difficult to obtain. On several markets, there were riots following a price increase or a scarcity of flour. Some people travelled from village to village to find this essential food. Bakeries were looted. The most violent affrays took place around the capital, and even at Versailles, where Louis XVI personally took charge of restoring order. In Paris, Turgot, who was on the spot, took energetic counter-measures. In all these riots, he saw an intrigue brewed by a few privileged persons, and wanted them to be put down rapidly and firmly. He had arrests carried out. Two men who were more or less convicted of looting were hung as examples. A few weeks later, an amnesty put an end to all criminal proceedings arising from the war on flour. Many people at that time, however, believed like Jean-Jacques Rousseau that "the blood of one man is worth more than the freedom of all mankind".

In the eyes of sensitive souls Turgot's humanitarianism had been irrevocably sullied. Nevertheless, he still remained in power for a few months, but a clique around the Queen now worked on her to obtain his departure. Marie Antoinette, who knew very little of politics, jealously guarded her authority and her influence on her husband. Choiseul's friends knew how to play skilfully on her weak points. One of their group, the Count of Guines, the French ambassador to England, had committed blunders and Turgot wished him to be recalled. Guines succeeded in worming his way into the circle of the Queen's friends, and from then on Marie Antoinette was bent on defending him. And Maurepas was not displeased at the prospect of ridding himself of a too enterprising minister without having to take the responsibility himself. Yet Turgot found staunch champions in Véri and Vermond. Under their influence, Mercy wrote to the Empress Maria Theresa and the Emperor Joseph II, asking them to encourage the Queen to abate her anger. In vain. On May 12th, 1776, Marie Antoinette obtained the dismissal of probably the only man capable of avoiding a violent revolution in France. Her con-

duct caused concern to her mother and brother and, too late, the Emperor Joseph wrote:

Why do you interfere in the dismissal of ministers? What studies have you carried out and what knowledge have you acquired to dare to imagine that your opinion must be good for something, particularly in affairs which require such extensive knowledge?

Unfortunately, the young queen only abandoned herself to her tastes and passions.

Marie Antoinette, no less dangerously, proposed to offer to all those who surrounded her the happiness very imprudently promised to twenty-five million Frenchmen, and to enjoy it herself. She had been curbed for four years by her fear of Louis XV, but now she plunged with a joyful heart into the adventure of reigning, which she thought meant behaving as she wished. "If I were the most powerful of men," Jean-Jacques Rousseau remarked one day, "I would have no difficulty in being just against my own interests, but I could not bring myself to do so against the interests of those who are close to me." Although the Queen was certainly guilty of excessive expenditure for herself, she did it even more for skilful friends who took advantage of her obliging nature.

In the eyes of the elderly persons at court, her first crime was to laugh and take a few liberties with etiquette. Surrounded by companions of her own age, she had a great deal of trouble in remaining serious during the long ceremonies to which her rôle of Queen condemned her. "The Marchioness of Clermont-Tonnerre" reported Madame Campan, the Queen's future chambermaid,

who was tired by the length of the session and obliged, by the duties of her position, to stand behing the Queen, found it more comfortable to sit on the ground, hiding behind the sort of wall formed by the hoops of the Queen and the palace ladies. There, to attract attention and feigning gaiety, she pulled the skirts of these ladies and played a thousand roguish tricks. The contrast between this childishness and the solemnity which reigned throughout the Queen's room disconcerted Her Majesty; several times she placed her fan before her face to hide her involuntary smile, and the severe aerophagia of the old ladies present made plain their opinion that the Queen had made fun of all the respectable persons who had hastened to pay their duty to her, that she only loved young people, that she had failed to observe the proprieties, and that none of them would ever go to court again...1

But apart from exceptional circumstances, she upheld her rank so earnestly, and her attitude was so majestic and royal that she was also reproached with being too haughty. With its splendour and its traditional customs, Versailles represented a social anachronism. The old proprieties among the nobles and the bourgeoisie of the eighteenth century stipulated that solitariness was unseemly and that in each home, family life should exist together with the children, visitors and servants. Rising, eating, and spending evenings socially were different actions of a religious rite whose importance is shown in the paintings of Le Nain and Chardin. At Versailles, many things were to change under Marie Antoinette's reign, and in Paris also, as was noted by Sebastian Mercier:

The mood of the century has shortened ceremonies and there is hardly a provincial man who stands on ceremony.... Meals are shorter, we have given up these foolish and ridiculous customs which were so familiar to our ancestors, the unfortunate proselytes of a cumbersome and constraining custom which they called seemly.... Of all the ancient and trivial traditions, that of giving one's good wishes when someone sneezes is the only one which still remains.... We let the shoemaker and the tailor give themselves a real or false knighthood which was still common in society forty years ago.... Only the lower middle-class still practises the tedious ceremonies and useless habits which they believe are courteous and which are extremely tiresome to those who know the ways of society....

The Queen's costly friendships were even more surprising. She really could not help trying to make those about her happy. The women in her service and the less important staff members never tired of praising her goodness, and at the time of their most terrible trials, they proved by their faithfulness and courage that this gratitude was not a pretence. The Queen also hoped to gratify the great ladies of her suite. And as the King could not bring himself to refuse his wife anything, this generosity took on the appearance of horrible wastefulness.

Marie Antoinette, who was very lonely during Louis XV's reign, had conceived an affection for the Princess of Lamballe, a stranger like herself for she was related to the Piedmont royal family. She was also a frustrated wife, for the Prince of Lamballe, Louis XIV's great-grandson, before leaving her a childless widow, had greatly neglected her and often deceived her. At the beginning of the new reign, the Princess of Lamballe accompanied the Queen everywhere, and from the month of June, 1774, it was whispered that she was to be appointed "chief lady-in-waiting of the Queen's household", a position which had been abolished a few decades earlier for reasons of economy.

It was probably the Count of Penthièvre, the rich and pious son of a bastard of Louis XIV, who conceived this idea, since he was very concerned about the honours due to the Princess, who was his daughter-in-law. But the matter was not arranged easily; the Countess of Noailles and the Queen's ladies strongly opposed this promotion which represented a danger to their authority. Mercy-Argenteau and Vermond, allied to the King's ministers, regarded this opportunity for new expense with a very unfavourable eye.

After several months of effort, however, the Princess of Lamballe was appointed chief lady-in-waiting. "Imagine my joy" Marie Antoinette wrote to one of Empress Marie Theresa's helpers, "I shall make my friend happy, and I will be able to enjoy her company even more." But the matter was not arranged without fresh discussion. Turgot, Maurepas and Vermond intervened to limit the emoluments and the powers of the intimate friend but Penthièvre refused to accept any compromise. Maurepas did not even dare to raise the question with Louis XVI and Turgot gave in. This cost the treasury one hundred and fifty thousand pounds per year, today about £84,000 (200,000 dollars).

Just after her marriage, Marie Antoinette had made the acquaintance of a young woman of her own age; Gabrielle Yolande de Polastron, the Countess of Polignac. She was an orphan and had been well brought up by an ambitious aunt, the Countess of Andlau, and she was Maurepas' great-niece. Very beautiful, with a cold and distant expression, she had married a person of very small means, descendant of one of the oldest families of the French nobility. A strange and ambitious personage was often seen with her, the Count of Vaudreuil, who had also been brought up by the Countess of Andlau; a brilliant lover of art and literature, certainly a childhood friend and, according to her enemies, the lover of the beautiful countess. A whole group of Choiseul's friends associated with the Countess of Polignac, and among them were Besenval, the lieutenant-colonel of the Swiss, a talented writer and a great intriguer, and the Count of Adhémar, ambitous and worldly, who had made a brilliant marriage.

This circle, with its frivolous gaiety, certainly did not displease the Queen. But she was particularly attracted by the Countess of Polignac's reserve, and the fact that the latter never asked a favour of her. Madame Campan wrote of her : "She sometimes spent several hours with me while waiting for the Queen, and talked frankly and ingenuously of all the honours and dangers that she saw in the kindness shown to her."

The Countess's reserve, unfortunately, did not last much longer than the number of months it took her to supplant the chief lady-in-waiting in her sovereign's heart. First of all, the Countess of Polignac asked for employment for her husband, for the couple actually had the greatest difficulty in supporting themselves while living at court. Marie Antoinette was delighted with the opportunity to satisfy her, and had Polignac appointed reversioner, i.e. the contingent successor of her first equerry, with an annual revenue of 80,000 pounds. Then, with no further ado, the father, "a person completely devoid of wit", as a contemporary said, was provided with a profitable ambassadorship to the Swiss cantons. Finally, a real scandal was unleashed when the Countess of Polignac married off her daughter to the Duke of Guiche; an unprecedented event took place when the King granted her the unheard-of dowry of 800,000 pounds (today about £500,000 or 1,200,000 dollars). By this time, the Queen's popularity had already greatly diminished compared with the honeymoon of the coronation.

At the beginning of 1775, the mourning following Louis XV's death came to an end. Louis XVI then left to the Queen the care of organizing life at court and of making it as brilliant as possible. This was playing with fire. After being deprived of balls and public amusements for a few months and prevented during Louis XV's lifetime from visiting Paris as much as she would have wished, this twenty-year-old Queen, who feared boredom above all else, increased the festivities and amusements. Marie Antoinette decided to organize two balls a week at Versailles and two theatrical productions, one by the French Comédie, and the other by the Italian Comédie. Once a week, the court was

to attend a production by the Opéra in Paris, for reasons of economy, to avoid the costly transport of the Opéra scenery to Versailles. On the other two days, gala banquets were to take place. Even for a young sovereign as brimming with health as the Queen was, it was an exhausting programme. Mercy did not cease complaining of this in his letters to Maria Theresa : ".... as a consequence of continual rehearsals for the ballets and through the resulting long waits, all the times for mass, dinner or supper or going to bed are disorganized". Papillon de la Ferté, the amusements steward, was, on the contrary, lost in wonderment at the splendid balls given to inaugurate the new reign. He noted, "From Sunday, January 15th, we were very busy with all the quadrille clothes ordered by the Queen for her ball which is to take place tomorrow, which makes quite considerable expense unavoidable, considering the amount of feathers and fine golden braiding ordered by Her Majesty."

The scandal, if there was one, resulted from the sums expended for the theatre, music, dancers and costume-makers and plays during a period of economic austerity. Was this a matter of taste, or was it a necessity ? For Marie Antoinette, art was limited to the ephemeral. Very few orders for paintings were given, no permanent constructions undertaken; it was chiefly costumes, concerts and plays. It would certainly have been impossible, with the state of public finances and in the face of the policy followed by Louis XVI and Turgot, to undertake anything more considerable. One hundred thousand pounds spent on festivities were enough to disorganize the very limited budget of the amusement administration.

And curiously enough, in this scene of varied and frivolous delights, architecture did not only appear to be an art, but also a game. Mercy again provides us with the strange story of how Bellanger built the exquisite Bagatelle Castle for the Count of Artois :

A short time before the departure from Fontainebleau His Highness the Count of Artois had the idea of knocking down a small house at the Bois de Boulogne, called Bagatelle, rebuilding it completely, and arranging and furnishing this house according to new plans to give a celebration in honour of Marie Antoinette when the court returned to Versailles. Everyone at first found it absurd to wish to try and achieve such an undertaking in six or seven weeks; this was, however, what was actually accomplished by nine hundred workmen of all kinds who were kept busy day and night with this work. The most striking fact was that material was lacking, particularly freestone, lime and plaster, and they did not wish to lose time in fetching them. His Highness the Count of Artois gave orders for the patrols of the Swiss guard regiments (of which he was colonel) to scout the highways and seize all the vehicles they might find loaded with such material; this method resulted in a sort of violence which revolted the public....

The Bagatelle, still admirable today in spite of unfortunate twentieth-century transformations, is an improvisation which is usually rather to be found in music, poetry, at the theatre or in ornamentation.

This example is enough in itself to show that the frenzy of enjoyment was not just another name for dissolute living; Marie Antoinette was rebelling against the monotonous remonstrances of Mercy-Argenteau or Vermond. But she suffered them and the Queen's efforts and progress in the arts which aroused her enthusiasm cannot be ignored. She perhaps went too often to the theatre, but not just as a simple spectator. She tried to learn to act better, and the long hours spent on elocution, her singing and harp-playing under exacting professors must not, in all fairness, be considered only as idle pastime.

Marie Antoinette had a rage for change and a passion for varying her activities and pleasures which gave a taste of ashes, a distressing aspect to this hectic and frantic life. How could the Queen's frequent presence at the Opéra's masked balls not arouse rather widespread disapproval among public opinion in Paris? Like the whole of the population, Marie Antoinette loved to watch the boatmen scenes which were sometimes organized at Versailles. The Count of Artois, who was always present, had even become a very skilful tightrope-dancer, and he was naturally imitated. Who was responsible for the introduction of horse-racing in France? Marie Antoinette, in any case, was present at the first meetings. On April 20th, 1776, at the Sablons plain at the gates of Paris, the first competitions took place. The Queen presided on a platform, surrounded by numerous attendants. The great lords had entered horses and chosen colours. The Duke of Chartres, who was the winner, had a black

helmet gallooned with red; the Duke of Lauzun had black decorated with green, and the Marquis de Voyer had puce. Mercy-Argenteau wrote severely:

Each week there have been several horse-races. The Queen, who has developed a taste for this type of spectacle, has not missed one. Each of these races takes up a whole day. On these occasions, the Queen either dines at the Muette or at the Count of Artois' at Bagatelle. Moreover, it happens that these races take place on Tuesday; then the Queen does not receive the ambassadors and foreign ministers, who recently found themselves deprived of the honour of paying court to Her Majesty for three weeks.

In fact, Marie Antoinette was only very much in advance on etiquette, for a few years later, horse-races were to be very fashionable throughout the whole of Europe, especially among sovereigns.

The Queen's excessive liking for card games was perhaps more typical of her instability. This, too, was an ancient and respectable custom at the Versailles court. But Louis XVI's edicts, as well as the morality of the times, placed a certain limit on betting. Mercy rightly complained about the Queen's behaviour from the summer of 1776 onwards:

Her game has become very expensive. She no longer plays the ordinary games in which losses are necessarily limited. Lansquenet has become her usual game, and sometimes faro if the game is not really public. The ladies and courtiers are frightened and afflicted at the losses to which they are exposed in order to pay court to the Queen.

Once, a card game at the Princess of Lamballe's even lasted thirty-six consecutive hours, until the very morning of All-Saints. Marie Antoinette, who was probably led on by dishonest partners, lost all the money allocated to her by the Treasury, and the King finally had to pay her debts from his personal funds. The losses were doubtless considerable.

Louis XVI probably tried blunderingly to make up for his failure in his marriage by a really boundless willingness to comply with his wife's whims. The sight of delightful bracelets and diamonds of rare quality were enough to make the Queen plunge into expenditures which were completely irreconcilable with her financial situation, but the King was always ready to pay for what she

Fighting side by side with American soldiers from Washington, the French troops captured Yorktown from the English on October 19th, 1781. The American War of Independence was over, but revolutions are contagious.

bought. In 1776, on impulse, she bought a pair of ear-rings from the jeweller Böhmer for 348,000 pounds. She admitted her rashness to her husband, who was to spend six years in paying this debt by successive instalments from his personal funds. Another time, the sovereign spent 162,000 pounds for diamond bracelets. But in all fairness, we must consider this taste for precious stones and the most beautiful jewels as being part of the Queen's passion for all artistic objects and for ornamentation.

Although Marie Antoinette rarely showed enthusiasm for architecture, and her taste in painting hardly led her to collect the paintings of the greatest artists of her time, she was the first Queen of France to show very strong preferences in interior decorating and the choice of furniture. This she did to such an extent that it is quite correct to speak of a Marie Antoinette style.

The correspondence concerning the administration of the buildings are full of very precise instructions given orally by Marie Antoinette, who was always in a hurry to see her orders carried out and who devoted extreme care to details. But one must naturally distinguish between the large suites at Versailles, where she was not free to change everything, and her private suites and homes at Versailles, Trianon, Fontainebleau, Saint-Cloud and Compiègne, where nothing was done without her approval. Similarly, certain sumptuous pieces of furniture which were a present from Louis XV, the city of Paris and other persons, were not chosen by her. Nor was she responsible for the festive halls or ball-rooms, which were temporary buildings giving the impression of having been created during the first half of the century, with their heavy, very rococo luxury.

When Marie Antoinette was responsible for decorating, she always proved to be an adept champion of the geometrical or antique style characteristic of Louis XVI's period. She did not like her furniture or decorations in an excessively tortuous style; her taste led

111

her to renew shapes, colours and materials constantly. She hated austerity and large, monotonous areas. Her curtains had to be decorated with a large number of trimmings, the woodwork enriched with skilful designs, and most of the furniture covered with bronze. And yet the effect was not at all heavy. The charm lay in allying an abundance of imagination and richness with perfect elegance.

Her activity in transforming her study at Versailles was very typical. First of all, she brought in mirrors to light up and enliven the room, and replaced the woodwork by gayer drapings. She ordered the pattern of a carpet from Bellanger, the painter; it had to be woven as soon as she had accepted it. The carpenter Babel made a new set of furniture whose design had been minutely studied by the Queen. The material and the pattern of the silks which were to be woven at Lyons were discussed with the upholsterer Capin. It was a very down-to-earth and gay scene with flowers, garlands and birds. Riesener, the best cabinet-maker of the time, and the Queens' accredited supplier, produced a table, a corner cupboard and a desk whose ornamentation matched. The only painting in this room was a canvas by Taraval, which was more a decoration than a painting. It showed cupids playing with flowers, thus matching the pattern of the silks.

Marie Antoinette, who was a capricious client, but skilful in discovering the slightest fault in taste, burdened her assistants with conflicting orders. On the whole, she proved to be faithful to the same men, the same ideas, and the same colours all her life. Thus in addition to the cabinet-maker Riesener, she singled out the carpenter Jacob, the watchmaker Robin, and the merchant and smallware dealer Daguerre, who were all among the greatest artists or decorators of the times. She was fond of a limited range of colours: first of all white, in satin or in coarse linen from Tours; then sometimes green, lilac and blue, but never in strong shades. Her menservants wore red livery bordered with silver, but she did not like these contrasting colours either for herself or in her apartments. On the other hand, she had a clear preference for articles from the factory of Sèvres and she chose plaques which were sometimes very large, with varied subjects and lively colours, to decorate furniture. Not only the architects, but also the cabinet-makers, upholsterers, and carpenters carried out plans which had been drawn and painted in water-colours, and sometimes even small models which enabled the Queen to decide and to make changes. A few examples which have miraculously been preserved, such as the Méridienne couch of the little suites at Versailles, or the intimate study at Fontainebleau with its mother-of-pearl table and the exquisite wall paintings, certainly help us to imagine the exaggerated and delicate luxury which Marie Antoinette loved to have about her. Only vestiges of the "lattice-work" room at Trianon remain, where this design was repeated on the walls, and the furniture in wood or gilded bronze, giving a curious impression of rusticity transferred and refined, and of which the armchairs or the wall-brackets, either in the palace of Versailles or the Gulbenkian collection, give us an idea.

The mechanical table supplied by Riesener in December, 1778 for the little suites, now preserved in the Metropolitan Museum in New York, helps us to imagine this constant harmony of comfort and beauty. The extremely fine legs conceal four hooks and a little bronze handle which enables the very thin top to fulfil another function and to be raised to a comfortable height for reading: a rectangle of wood with inlaid-work intended to bear a sheet of paper or a book is raised vertically from the upper part of the table-top.

The bounds of the Queen's dissipation are very evident in her taste for the arts. She had an impassioned but conscientious frivolity. She did not let herself be guided by chance. Her carefreeness prevented her from following a single line of conduct, and for her, art and morality were written without capital letters. But she was indifferent neither to the one nor to the other.

Why, if Marie Antoinette led a dissipated life, can she not be accused of licentiousness? She lived according to her whims, with a foolish unawareness of the scandal she created by innovations which were contrary to royal majesty, but her way of life was only very similar to the spirit which reigned in art at her time. Although she was placed in a very abnormal position, it is evident, in spite of calumny, that the Queen remained faithful to her husband. We would know nothing definite were it not for the fact that any unfaithfulness on the part of the Queen would have had the most important consequences for

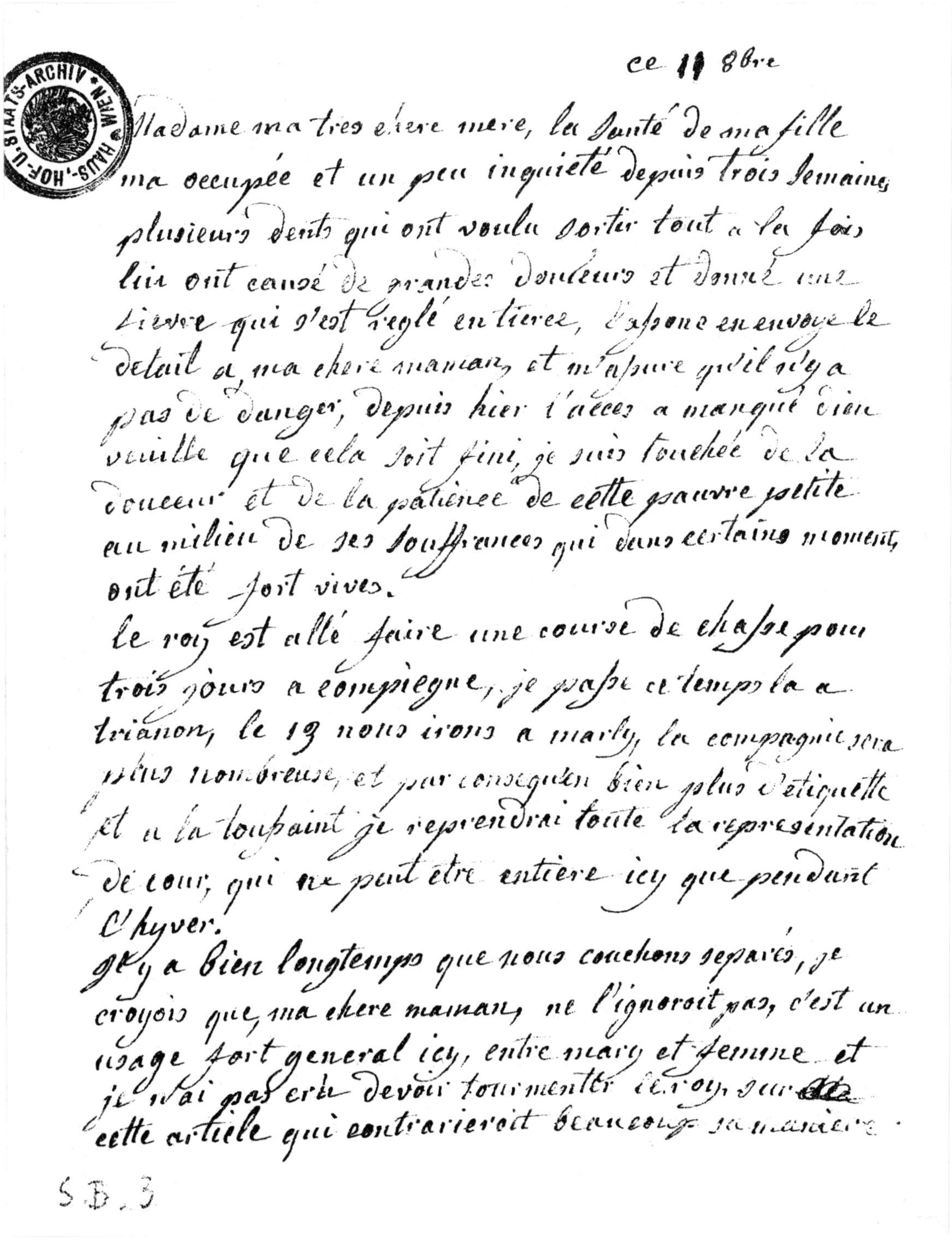

ce 11 8bre

Madame ma tres chere mere, la Santé de ma fille
ma occupée et un peu inquieté depuis trois Semaine,
plusieurs dents qui ont voulu sortir tout a la fois
lui ont causé de grandes douleurs et donné une
fievre qui s'est reglé entiere, d'apone en envoye le
detail a ma chere maman, et m'apure qu'il n'y a
pas de danger, depuis hier l'acces a manqué dieu
veuille que cela soit fini, je suis touchée de la
douceur et de la patience de cette pauvre petite
au milieu de ses souffrances qui dans certains moment,
ont été fort vives.

le roy est allé faire une course de chasse pour
trois jours a compiegne, je passe ce temps la a
trianon, le 19 nous irons a marly, la compagnie sera
plus nombreuse, et par consequent bien plus d'etiquette
et a la toussaint je reprendrai toute la representation
de cour, qui ne peut etre entiere icy que pendant
l'hyver.

il y a bien longtemps que nous couchons separés, je
croyois que ma chere maman, ne l'ignoroit pas, c'est un
usage fort general icy, entre mary et femme et
je n'ai pas cru devoir tourmenter le roy sur cet
cette article qui contrarieroit beaucoup sa maniere.

S.B.3

*In this letter of October 11th, 1780 to Maria Theresa, Marie Antoinette appears as an attentive mother
and an abandoned wife: "For a long while now we have slept apart...it is very common practice here...."*

international politics at that time. All the great powers were concerned with the possibility of Marie Antoinette becoming a mother. The Count of Artois was the only one of the three brothers who had children. As he was married to a princess of Savoy, the King of Sardinia could thus hope to see one of his grandchildren become King of France. The King of Spain, a descendant of Louis XIV, also remained a possible pretender. The Baron of Goltz, the ambassador of Prussia; the Count of Viry, the Savoy ambassador; and particularly the very remarkable Count of Aranda, ambassador of Spain or Salmour, and the envoy of the King of Saxony—all therefore had the Queen spied upon very carefully. Men-servants and servants of all kinds were in the pay of the foreign representatives, who collected pieces of gossip in their dispatches, on condition, naturally, that they did not risk giving false information. Yet all their accounts agree in the lack of any accusation that the Queen had a lover.

"It is said" wrote Viry, "that the Duke of Coigny can enter the Queen's suite at certain hours, which provides the basis for a great number of comments which I would, however, be led to consider as slander arising from the frivolousness of the Queen's conduct."

And Goltz, who was always very hostile to Marie Antoinette, who showed him her dislike of his master Frederick II a little too obviously, was forced to admit: "The Queen shows more than ever the desire to please everyone, and particularly young men. With ill-will, this could be interpreted unfavourably, although until now, it is true that no one in particular can be suspected."

Any lingering doubts would be diminished even further by the testimony of a severe witness who visited France at the beginning of summer in 1777. He was Joseph II, the Queen's elder brother, who wished to visit the most beautiful kingdom in Europe and to strengthen his alliance with France.

Before his arrival, he had been informed of his sister's bad conduct by Mercy, who in spite of his diplomatic style had denounced in a letter to the Empress "the complete forgetfulness which is becoming a habit with the Queen with regard to everything concerning her outward dignity, especially at Carnival time in 1777, when more frequently than ever before the Queen spent whole nights at the Opéra balls".

Joseph kept up a very assiduous correspondence with his younger brother Leopold, who was then the Grand Duke of Tuscany and the direct heir, as the Emperor had no children. It was a sort of private diary in which he expressed his impressions of everyone in complete confidence to a friend whom he thought more intelligent than himself. Yet in his letters to Leopold, Joseph was categorical: in spite of appearances, and in spite of the immorality of her attendants, their sister's virtue was saved "until now, at least":

She is a pleasant and honest woman a little young, and rather hasty, who has an honest and virtuous soul. She is very much under the sway of her desire for amusement, and as people know this taste, they take advantage of her weak point and those who give her the most pleasure are listened to....

It was a curious meeting between this brother and sister, who had both reached the pinnacle of honour, and were both sensitive, affectionate and full of goodwill; they were convinced that they were much more different from each other than they really were.

The Emperor had decided to travel incognito throughout Europe. He was only to be called Sir; he travelled under the name of the Count of Falkenstein. Refusing all the honours and hospitality of one of the French royal palaces, he entered Paris in a hired carriage and took up residence as a simple, private person at the hotel Tréville. At Versailles, in the same way, he lived at an inn. Joseph II, dressed with deliberate simplicity, did not at any time have the feeling of committing the basic mistake which was precisely that with which he reproached his sister: that of refusing to take on the high dignity in the eyes of the public to which fate had destined him. If their coquetry is shown in different ways, both suffered from an irresistible need to please their contemporaries, to take part in their life and not to reign by virtue of divine law. For Joseph, this took the form solely of efficiency in his work of governing; for Marie Antoinette, in the charm of her physical or moral being. Neither of them resigned themselves simply to enjoying their position as Emperor or Queen; both were to be the victims of the same ambiguity. They refused to inspire fear and respect alone; they wished to see a smile of happiness and liking on the faces around them which neither one nor the other was capable of making last.

114

Joseph was also particularly concerned with one aspect of happiness in France; the marital happiness of his sister and his brother-in-law. He had naturally been kept informed by Maria Theresa on the Dauphine's conjugal troubles, and later on those of the Queen of France. Louis XV had considered this difficulty very seriously and had had his grandson examined by his personal doctor, who failed to find any malformation. For her part, Maria Theresa had suggested to van Swieten, one of the most famous doctors of the time, whom she had summoned to her court, that he should prescribe aphrodisiacs for her son-in-law. But van Swieten had come to the conclusion that it was better to leave nature the time to do her work. Seven years had thus passed. Marie Antoinette felt humiliated and hurt at all the royal and princely births around her, and probably also at the ribald songs which did not fail to joke about her situation. Yet the King and Queen did not always have separate rooms. The servants in the pay of foreign ambassadors immediately reported to the Count of Aranda, for instance, what they had seen. But there was never any sign that the marriage had actually been consummated. Lassone, the French court doctor, had foreseen a surgical operation a little while after Louis XVI came to the throne. But without actually opposing this, the King preferred to put it off. The question was often brought up afterwards. In spite of the Empress's insistence in her letters to her daughter, it probably never took place.

Then on April 10th, 1776, Marie Antoinette wrote to her mother: "I am convinced that the operation is no longer necessary." What had happened? No one knows. In any case, Marie Antoinette explained to her mother a few months later "that there was not the slightest change in her condition".

In his letters, Joseph explained the problem to Leopold in great detail. Marie Antoinette had doubtless revealed the most intimate secrets of her married life to her brother on his arrival. It was only two months later that a man-to-man conversation took place between the head of the Holy Roman Empire of the German Nation and the King of France. It was followed by several others, and by consultations with Doctor Lassone; a last private meeting was organized on June 29th, the eve of the Emperor's departure.

Eight weeks later, the surprising news was spread that after seven years, the marriage between Louis XVI and Marie Antoinette had finally been consummated. On August 30th, the Queen wrote the following letter to the Empress Maria Theresa:

My dear Mother,
I am so deeply happy that it is the greatest moment of my life. My marriage was already perfectly consummated eight days ago; the test has been repeated and even more completely than the first time. I first thought of sending a messenger to my dear mother. But I was afraid that this would cause a stir and talk. I also admit that I wanted to be completely sure. I do not think I am already expecting, but at least, I hope to be from one moment to another. I feel so much tenderness for my dear mother, how great her joy will be! I experience it as though it were my own. Will she permit me to embrace her with all my heart?

The secret, which was of such importance, had been known to or suspected by the diplomatic envoys, thanks to their informers, a few days earlier. D'Aranda, the Spanish ambassador, who was always prudent and sure in his reports, even obtained a confirmation of this fact from Maurepas, the minister and confident of Louis XVI. Mercy, for once, was one of the last to know the truth, for the Queen had not wanted to reveal such a happy event to anyone except her mother.

Yet the months passed without the justified hopes taking shape. Louis XVI ingenuously told his aunts of his joy at discovering this new pleasure, but he was not very assiduous in his attentions to the Queen. Was it natural laziness or the excessive coldness of a woman who had long been frustrated? Marie Antoinette certainly ardently wished to become a mother. She considered the most extreme solutions and at one time imagined that if the King took a mistress, he would acquire more "energy". Mercy violently protested against this "bandying". But the Queen explained to her mother that the "King has no taste for sleeping two to a bed" and that she did not dare "to torment him to come more often". During the autumn and winter of 1778-1779, in the midst of worldly activities which were always brilliant, the news of the Queen's "hopes" was circulated several times, but each time the rumours were quickly denied.

On April 19th, Marie Antoinette finally wrote to Maria Theresa:

Madame my dear Mother,

Eight days ago, my first impulse was to write to my dear mother of my hopes. I was prevented by the fear of causing too much pain if my great hopes were to fade....

From the end of March, the doctors had noted the first signs of pregnancy, and Maria Theresa, who for a long time remained sceptical after being disappointed so often, was convinced in May by a formal letter from Mercy. The princes of the blood and the first in line for the succession to the throne, the Count of Provence, suffered a great disappointment: the most outrageous rumours were circulated at court and among the public to make them believe that Louis XVI was not the father of the expected child. But neither the songs nor the slander offered a possible alternative to a certainty recognized by objective witnesses, whether they were enemies or friends of Marie Antoinette.

By mid-summer, the approaching birth appeared to all of France like the proclamation of a rebirth for the country as a whole. The nation was incarnated in the King. The promise of offspring, particularly after such a long wait, took on the aspects of a religious symbol. In the month of December, during the weeks before Christmas, Te Deums were sung in the churches and good wishes expressed for the royal couple. People came to Versailles from all parts of France to be present at the birth or at least to keep more closely informed.

The delivery itself was public; it was the privilege of the great men of the kingdom to be present in the room itself during the Queen's labour. At the first pains, on December 20th at three o'clock in the morning, the state chamber began to fill with gentlemen who had been startled out of their sleep and who rushed from Versailles or Paris. During seven hours, the air in the room became foul with the windows closed, and the crowd in the neighbouring rooms was immense. At eleven o'clock the child was born; the disappointment was intense: it was a girl. The mother fainted in exhaustion; they thought she was close to death. The surgeon immediately bled her, and she regained consciousness. Louis XVI, who was very little affected by the disappointment of still not having a dauphin, was radiant with happiness at being a father. He had the whole country share this joy; prisoners were pardoned, money was distributed to the poor, and young couples were given dowries and married at the crown's expense. For her church reception after the birth, Marie Antoinette went to Notre Dame. It was one of the last times in her life that she was frankly and gaily cheered by the people of Paris along the way.

The Queen's popularity had, in fact, slowly diminished during the last four years. Her definite or relative responsibility in Turgot's disgrace, the end of a political experiment which had aroused great hopes, had completely alienated her admirers among the philosophers, and the enormous majority of intellectual youth, who were convinced of the need for rapid reforms. The abandoning of Turgot's most radical measures and the re-establishment of guilds and statute labour had aroused the people's anger. Necker, the new man responsible for finance, a Swiss banker who had rapidly made a fortune, was confronted with the same difficulties as Turgot when he sought to limit the Queen's spending. As he was particularly concerned with remaining popular, it was no deprivation to him to let her indiscretions pass.... But even more serious events were in the offing. The King and his Minister of Foreign Affairs, Vergennes, found themselves with contradictory obligations in international politics. Since the disastrous Treaty of Paris signed by Louis XV in 1763 in which France had lost its colonies, the government had built up a fleet again in the firm hope of one day capturing a part of England's empire across the seas. When the British colonies in North America revolted against their mother-country, the occasion seemed propitious. The united colonies called upon French help; the principles of independence proclaimed by the Americans from 1775 onwards fired French hearts: "We hold these truths to be self-evident, that all men are created equal, that they are endowed by their Creator with certain inalienable rights, that among these are Life, Liberty and the pursuit of happiness." And as if to give such an attractive proposal more strength and charm, America delegated an erudite man, Benjamin Franklin, as ambassador to France; his modest appearance and the simplicity of his words evoked a country which had remained at the happy and virtuous stage of primitive civilizations. Many young people, among them some of the Queen's close friends, enlisted in the American forces before France even took part in hostilities. Nationalistic and anti-English fervour, and the confused aspiring towards a simple world stripped of the artificial and exaggerated refinements of a civilization encumbered with its very advantages, and precisely the religion of happiness itself all contributed to an irresistable enthusiasm for freeing America from an unjust yoke.

At the same time, however, great international difficulties had developed in Europe. Joseph II, after sharing out Poland, would have liked to increase the size of his states still more at the expense of Turkey and Bavaria. France, Austria's ally, risked being drawn into another exhausting and useless continental war like that of twenty years earlier, at a time when all French efforts had to be concentrated on the seas. It was evident that it was not in France's interest to support Austria in her quarrels with her neighbours. Everyone was convinced of this: Louis XVI, Vergennes and French public opinion had little inclination to be indulgent towards Austria. Only Marie Antoinette, lectured by her mother, her brother, and the ambassador Mercy-Argenteau, attempted to convince the King and the cabinet not to go to war against England, but on the contrary, to support Austria's claims. She defended her family's interests to the King and Vergennes with fervour, sometimes with violence and always clumsily; although she still had no influence, the stand she took up made her unpopular. In Europe, France succeeded in remaining neutral and helping the cause of peace. At sea, however, Louis XVI's support of the American Revolution was considerable. After the first shipments of arms, the signing of a Friendship Treaty in 1778 resulted in England declaring war on France, and Spain's support

soon followed. The French and the English naval forces were too nearly equal to bring about a victory; but on the American battlefield the skilful handling of the French infantry under Rochambeau, combined with the American forces under Washington (of which one corps was under the orders of the Frenchman La Fayette) and a victory by the admiral de Grasse over an English squadron brought about the capitulation of a considerable British army at Yorktown on October 19th, 1781.

Two days later, on October 21st, 1781, Marie Antoinette gave birth to her second child. It was a son, a dauphin. Thus, at one and the same time, French royalty had their revenge for the military humiliations at the end of Louis XV's reign, and the perpetuation of the dynasty was assured.

The Queen, however, was not acclaimed at all as she had been earlier. This victory was not really hers and her son belonged in the first place to the whole French nation. For a year, Marie Antoinette had also learned to experience a new loneliness; her mother, Empress Maria Theresa, who had so ardently wished to see her daughter give birth to a son, had passed away. For all the fear which her mother had always inspired in her, the Queen was for a long time inconsolable. Marie Antoinette did not at all dislike being a child guided by her relations, and scolded for having disobeyed. How could she find peaceful freedom from care and complete happiness when her mother was no longer there to love and guide her? Henceforward, Marie Antoinette was responsible for herself, her children, and those near to her. But she took a long time to become mature. Cost what it would, she wished to find again and preserve, if only for an instant, the carefree happiness so incompatible with the real awareness of her duties and her very condition as Queen.

AUTUMN

This canvas by Madame Vigée-Lebrun was painted during the short period when Marie Antoinette was living with her four children : Marie Thérèse Charlotte (left), the Dauphin Louis Joseph (right), Louis Charles, the future King Louis XVII (on her knees) and (in the cot) Sophie Hélène Béatrice, destined to die early in her second year.

"You like flowers, well, I have a whole bouquet to give you, it is the Petit Trianon." It was with these words that the King gave Marie Antoinette her country retreat, seen here from the direction of the Temple of Love.

THE autumn of 1781 was an eventful one. The royal couple, henceforth certain of ensuring continuity of the dynasty, enjoyed the prestige of having wiped out the humiliating overseas defeats of Louis XV. The death of the aged Maurepas, in November 1781, further enhanced the prestige of Louis XVI, who, it was realized, would now have to reign by himself. The festivities in honour of the Dauphin lasted not for just a few days, but for several months, and took place throughout the whole of France, proof of the great enthusiasm for the monarchy at the time. Strasburg, Lyons and Limoges distinguished themselves by the extent of their celebrations. A sign of a new tolerance and cohesion in the kingdom was the fact that not only the Protestants but even the Jewish communities celebrated the birth of the heir to the throne.

Cannon salutes, illuminations and free distributions of food were organized in Paris, while the church bells pealed. Then the different corporations sent their representatives in their traditional costumes on foot to Versailles, often accompanied by bands, and performing symbolic dances or comic turns. The butchers brought the fatted ox right into the marble courtyard, the chimney-sweeps brought an enormous chimney on top of which the smallest of them did acrobatics, and the chairmen transported an enormous nurse carrying in her arms a tiny dauphin. The carpenters were followed in turn by the pastry-cooks, the locksmiths and even the grave-diggers, who were in costume too, with the attributes of their profession including a small coffin, finely worked : at the sight of it Madame Sophie, the King's aunt, had an attack and fainted. The Opéra, the Comédie Française and all the theatres gave performances entirely free of charge, and naturally many mediocre songs were composed :

La France à son Dauphin présente tous les cœurs
Et tous forcent l'Anglais à payer la layette....

(France to her Dauphin offers all hearts
And all will force the English to pay for
the layette....)

The celebrations reached their height with the festivities organized by the City of Paris for its sovereigns on the 21st, 22nd and 23rd of February 1782. On the Place de Grève and in the actual courtyard of the Hôtel de Ville, stands and a great ballroom had been erected. At the public dinner of Louis XVI and Marie Antoinette, the crush was so great that many of the guests were unable to reach their seats and had to leave without having eaten anything. The cold dry weather ensured success for the fireworks. At the costume ball, and then the masked ball, the King did not dance, but he good-humouredly took part in the rejoicings. Those festivities were to be the last at which Marie Antoinette was spontaneously acclaimed. Even then, unlike at the time of his first official visit to Paris, enthusiasm reached its peak when the King appeared, and seemed to die down somewhat when the Queen arrived. It was the beginning of a long period in which she was to meet, not with indifference, but with unpopularity, and later hatred. There are no doubt objective grounds for such a reversal of opinion : the time was to come when the agelong hatred of Austria would prevail over the charm and physical attraction of a young queen. Furthermore, the French have always been mysoginists. Since Blanche of Castille they have never had a lasting affection for any of their queens, and they have detested all those who, like Catherine or Marie de' Medici, or Anne of Austria, had to play a political role. In the case of Marie Antoinette a situation arose which was more serious, and from which there was practically no escape. She embodied, shared or influenced the taste of her contemporaries just at a time when the whole of society was questioning all the advantages she was enjoying and was dreaming of upheavals which would make it possible to attain for itself a happiness which appeared to be just around the corner but for which the headlong search always seemed to be in vain. Gay, coquettish, light and madly in love with the joy of living, Marie Antoinette was not only Queen of the French but the image of what they were and of that which no longer satisfied them. Had Marie Antoinette still a chance to escape from her fearful fate ? It does not seem so. She was much too fond of the atmosphere, the amusements and the art of France at the end of the Ancien Régime not to be the idol, both adored and hated, of a world which was rushing to its doom.

A coquette Marie Antoinette undoubtedly was, not only as a queen who loved display, but in her passion for elegant dresses and fine attire. She liked to dress and to do her hair according to her own taste, and with the same enthusiasm as she had for the arts which pleased her. She had, of course, an extensive wardrobe. We are acquainted, for instance, with the list drawn by the Countess d'Ossun, lady's maid to the Queen, when she took up her duties in November 1781; it contains no less than one hundred and seventy articles of apparel—that is to say dresses, or dresses and coats—varying according to the seasons and the circumstances in the life of the Queen. Thus, for the spring: "Two formal robes, four large pannier dresses, three informal dresses, fourteen Polonaises, twenty-eight *lévites* [gowns]."

Every year practically the whole of the Queen's wardrobe was changed—sold or given away, and then renewed. The cost was great. The funds allotted annually amounted to 120,000 pounds, about £84,000 (200,000 dollars). It always proved inadequate. But while at the beginning of the reign the deficit was only ten to fifteen per cent, it reached a hundred per cent in 1781, and by 1785 it was more than double the regular amount allocated.

The maintenance and daily choosing of apparel required quite an organization in itself, for every day the Queen, according to her engagements, had to change dresses several times. Madame Campan relates:

"Take him, he is the State," Marie Antoinette is supposed to have said when, on October 22nd, 1781 she gave birth to the Dauphin, Louis Joseph. The baby was immediately decorated with the blue ribbon of the Order of the Holy Ghost.

123

Every morning the wardrobe valet on duty presented to the principal *femme de chambre* a book, to which were attached samples of the dresses, formal robes, informal dresses, etc.... a small portion of the material showed of what kind it was. The principal *femme de chambre* presented that book to the Queen on her awakening, together with a pin-cushion. Her Majesty put pins in everything she wanted for the day: one in the formal robe she wished to wear, one in the informal dress for the afternoon, one in the decorated dress for the hours of play or for supper in the *petits appartements*. The book was taken back to the wardrobe, and there soon appeared, in large sheets of taffeta, everything that was necessary for the day.

Madame d'Ossun's books, or at any rate one of those books, for the year 1784, still exists, and glued on every page are samples of the material from which each of the Queen's dresses had been made. This enables us to get a better idea of Marie Antoinette's taste. Here, too, she liked soft harmonies, and fairly geometrical designs. Her preferences were for pale pinks, violets and especially white barely enlivened by discreet decoration.

In the field of feminine attire, thanks to her charm and also to her very personal tastes, Marie Antoinette, from shortly after her arrival at the French Court and right up to the time of her extreme unpopularity, exercised an influence which was hardly questioned. She was helped in her choice by a young woman dealer in fashions—we would today say couturier—whose talents and inventive turn of mind were an effective complement to the gifts of the Queen. That young woman, Rose Bertin, who came from a very simple background, started as a "fashion girl" with a dressmaker who was then all the rage, Mademoiselle Pagelle. Paris at that time enjoyed in the sphere of feminine costume a pre-eminence throughout the western world which no one dreamt of challenging. French dresses were to sell abroad even better under Louis XVI than under Louis XV, largely thanks to the Queen. Every year the principal couturiers used to send to Russia, to Germany, to Italy, to Spain and to England a "fashion doll", forerunner of today's flying mannequins. It was a doll, over twenty inches in height, clad in all the dresses devised by the French dressmakers, made to its measure. The customers, instead of watching a parade, looked at the doll, dressed in turn in a *polonaise*, a *robe à la française*, etc.

Rose Bertin had her first success at the age of twenty-two, on the eve of the arrival of Marie Antoinette, on the occasion of the marriage of Mademoiselle de Penthièvre, the sister-in-law of the Princess of Lamballe, to the Duke of Chartres, the future Philippe Egalité. She set up shop at the sign of the "Grand Mogol" in the Rue St. Honoré, where the Magasins du Louvre now stand, but before long she was to have as a workshop the centre of production in which were designed, made up and tried on the dresses of the Dauphine, soon to be Queen of France. Variations and imitations of these were to spread throughout Paris, and then, thanks to the fashion doll, throughout the whole world. Rose Bertin was for twenty years a regular supplier to Marie Antoinette. Her staff of thirty-six seamstresses shows that she also had an extensive clientele. Her proud ways were not well received by the Queen's ladies. She talked about her work with Her Majesty as if she were the "Minister of Fashion". Madame d'Oberkirch, who was always independent and seldom inclined to speak ill of people, in her memoirs considers "the jargon of this young person as very entertaining; it was a singular mixture of the haughty and the common which bordered on impertinence if she was not kept strictly in her place".

Rose Bertin was very often ushered into the inner apartment of the Queen, where—a signal favour—she remained alone with her sovereign for interminable discussions.

The term "mode" had a very general sense in the eighteenth century. In the dealers' almanach of 1772 it is said to be

the name given to certain goods of which the forms and uses are subject to the supreme but changeable decrees of caprice and taste: hats, *demi-négligés*, costumes of the court and the theatre, mittens, gloves, fans, cuffs, purses, workbags, mantlets, capes, shoes and slippers, etc.... in short everything connected with clothing, and the majority of frivolous objects.

The fashion for the *pouf*, a finely worked decoration in the middle of a coiffure skilfully built up to a height, dates from the end of the reign of Louis XV. The invention of the *pouf à la circonstance*, the happy circumstance in this case being the arrival of the young sovereigns, linked Rose Bertin more intimately with Marie Antoinette and made her fame secure. This *pouf* shows a rising sun on a field of corn being harvested by hope. Great numbers of *poufs* subsequently began to appear, illustrating the most varied events and sentiments. Not long afterwards, there was the "inoculation pouf" when Louis XVI was vaccinated against smallpox, and others to celebrate the victories in the American war or the birth of Madame Royale. Those coiffures finally became so inconvenient that, in order not to spoil the fragile structure, the ladies had to kneel on the floor of their carriage instead of sitting on the seat. Such uncomfortable constructions were given up soon after the birth of the first dauphin.

Marie Antoinette had brought the coiffeur Larseneur from Vienna, but from 1780 on she preferred, and at once made fashionable, the celebrated Leonard. As she had a very high forehead, Leonard invented a coiffure, very quickly imitated, which brought part of the hair to the front of the head.

In the first three-quarters of the eighteenth century, feminine fashion evolved slowly. The dress *à la française*, placed on panniers like crinolines, adjusted in front, with folds at the back and reaching to the ground, was, with variations, a dress for both Court and town. The genius or skill of Marie Antoinette and Rose Bertin was ceaselessly to invent new forms and to be inspired by the tastes of the time for antiquity or the less formal ways of English society.

The dress *à la française* remained the ceremonial costume, but all sorts of transformations were made in the corsages, which were sometimes cut low with a very fitted waist, and the bottom of the dress hitched up at the front or on the sides. Finally the pannier was abolished or greatly reduced.

Thus the *polonaise* is a convertible dress in which a system of slots makes it possible to pick up the folds of the skirt and then create a train and two wings. The sheath-gown, fashionable just before the Revolution, is in a single piece, without corset and without pannier. The *anglaise*, on the contrary, is very much fitted to the waist and adorned at the back with a bustle; it was often worn with a shawl. On these very general lines, Marie Antoinette and Rose Bertin gave free rein to their imagination, making use for a time of the parasol "recommended" by Dr. Tronchin for walks in the open air, or reducing the length of skirts *à la paysanne* (peasant style) and choosing new materials such as cottons. A portrait of Marie Antoinette dressed as a "Gaul", that is to say in a simple dress of white cotton, shown by Madame Vigée-Lebrun at the Salon of 1781, caused such a scandal that the royal authorities decided to withdraw it. The public, it was felt, should imagine a queen dressed only in sumptuous Lyons silks.

This effervescence, this need felt by Marie Antoinette and in turn by the Court and soon by the whole of the French bourgeoisie to change fashions so often, created a new movement which in fact has gone on ever since for two centuries. By contrast, in former times a mother would will her dresses for special occasions to her daughter.

It was not long before a specialized press came into being to serve a clientele avid to know what the current fashion was, and what the next fashion would be. Thus we find appearing in 1778 *La Galerie des Modes et Costumes français*, published by the print-sellers Esnauts and Rapilly, which boasted work by excellent artists like Augustin de St. Aubin, Desrais and Leclerc. Some of the pictures show coiffures, others costumes. The plates were first sold separately, then they were collected in volumes. Over four hundred plates appeared in ten years, some of them coloured in water-colours by a certain Madame Lebeau. There is no doubt that such a publication, and the atmosphere created by the changing fashions, helped to add to that extraordinary craving for movement and change that seized people's minds on the eve of the Revolution in this country which had always been accustomed to calm and to stable institutions.

Marie Antoinette and her contemporaries were subject to a veritable psychosis of upheaval which seemed very innocent when it attacked only fashion and the arts, but which was to prove very dangerous when political and social institutions, and then philosophical and religious ideals were in turn overthrown.

Véri, always objective and perceptive, noted in his diary:

The continual variations in taste in fashions are the true cause of the popular feeling against the Queen. The *petit bourgeois* claims he is ruined by the fancies of his wife and daughters, who want to imitate the Queen's changing tastes. The merchant and the manufacturer no longer have a fixed basis for foreseeing what will sell. As the same people know that the King has simpler tastes, he is loved for this contrast between his tastes and those of the Queen.

From the day when Marie Antoinette realized that she had become Queen, to the day on which she left Versailles for ever, her dreams, her tastes and her joys were all expressed in the tiny palace of the Trianon and its park of modest dimensions.

The Trianon is the true mirror of her innermost self. That is why, in spite of the fact that it was first of all the large pink marble construction of Louis XIV, and the Petit Trianon was built by Louis XV for Madame de Pompadour, and then lived in by him with Madame du Barry, the two names of Trianon and Marie Antoinette remain, rightly, indissolubly associated. Already on July 7th, 1774, well before the official funeral ceremonies for Louis XV, Mercy-Argenteau wrote to Maria Theresa:

When Madame the Archduchess was still Dauphine, she very much wanted to have a place of her own in the country. At the time of the King's death, the Count and Countess of Noailles suggested the Petit Trianon.... At the first word uttered by Her Majesty, the King replied that this country house was the Queen's, and that he was delighted to make her a present of it.

One chronicler puts into the mouth of the young Louis XVI a more gallant remark. "You like flowers," he is supposed to have said to his wife, "well, I have a whole bouquet to give you, it is the Petit Trianon."

Situated at a quarter of a league from the Château de Versailles, that is, near enough to reach on foot or in a few moments on horseback, the Trianon is sufficiently isolated to be a real retreat from the large palace, from its constant official restrictions, and from the austere and sumptuous beauty of the park with its vast vistas of trees, lawns, water and admirable statues. Julie, Jean-Jacques Rousseau's heroine in *La Nouvelle Héloïse* had her "Elyseum". Nobility and bourgeoisie also reserved for themselves a place where they could dream far from the world, in the bosom of nature. This French fashion was, moreover, in keeping with a tendency of the Austrian imperial family to disregard etiquette outside official ceremonies, and to live as much as possible in freedom in the country.

One June 6th, 1774, Marie Antoinette was in possession of the Petit Trianon. She received the King to dinner there, with her two brothers-in-law and their wives and her sister-in-law, Clotilde, who was soon to marry the eldest son of the King of Sardinia.

Marie Antoinette at once wanted to create a garden to her own taste. Already on July 2nd, 1774, Mercy reported to the Empress: "The Queen is now busy with an English garden she wishes to have at the Trianon."

Primarily interested in the so-called minor arts, Marie Antoinette was more preoccupied with gardening than buildings.

The architects—first Gabriel, the creator of the Petit Trianon itself as well as of some of the most famous buildings completed under Louis XV; and then, after his retirement, Richard Mique, a Lorranier, who had been the architect of the King of Poland, Stanislaus, when he reigned at Nancy—were entrusted not with plans for some new buildings, but with a garden of somewhat small dimensions.

Already under Louis XV the Petit Trianon had been conceived in terms of Nature aesthetically tamed. There was a garden *à la française* and also a remarkable kitchen-garden with hothouses where Antoine Richard, reputed to be the best gardener in France, grew flowers and vegetables for the King. There was also an area devoted to the rarest of foreign shrubs and plants. Marie Antoinette appreciated neither the stiff regularity of the French garden, nor scientific botanical research. On the other hand, she had seen at the property of the Duke of Chartres in the Monceau plain near Paris a "Chinese garden" where there were, collected within a limited space, the most unexpected creations of nature and man: rocks, a stream with an island where sheep were grazing and another planted with flowers, a Roman sanctuary in ruins, a Chinese *jeu de bague*, a Moorish minaret, and all sorts of signs of a wilderness skilfully arranged to please and surprise.

It was a similar "Chinese garden" that Marie Antoinette ordered from her architects and Richard. A plan was quickly submitted to the Queen in which were assembled an incredible number of "natural accidents"; two rivers, several islands, many rocks and thickets, a temple, a pagoda, an aviary. These preserved Louis XV's hothouses and the vistas *à la française* before the façades of

To celebrate the birth of the Dauphin, Paris gave a lavish banquet for the King and Queen and the Court on January 21st, 1782. It was an extravagant gesture in view of the grave food shortage in the town that winter.

the château. Marie Antoinette turned it down. In July she went to the home of an officer who was an extremely keen agriculturalist, the Count of Caraman, who had designed a charming "Chinese garden" for his house in the Rue St. Dominique. The Queen was very pleased with it, and the gentleman-gardener was instructed to devise a scheme for the Trianon. It was infinitely more simple, and less overladen, than the plan of Richard or the garden of Monceau. Above all, it was much better suited to the landscape and much more natural. A river wound its way among flower-beds, lawns and thickets, and there were few rocks or ruins; the artificial devices would come later. Delighted, the Queen at once wanted Monsieur de Caraman's plan to be carried out. But although the rare plants of Louis XV's botanical garden condemned by the new projects were rapidly transported to the royal garden, directed by Buffon in Paris, it was very difficult for the Queen to obtain the necessary credits to get the work started. And yet they were relatively small: an expediture of 8,000 pounds —about £4,000 (10,000 dollars)—was refused or delayed through Turgot's intransigeance for nearly two years. Such an attitude may perhaps have contributed to the Queen's dislike of that reforming minister and hastened the fall of a ministry which might have saved the monarchy.

In 1777 the Queen's "English garden" was far from finished. Mique transformed and completed the drawings of 1774, and had a model in relief made so that the Queen might form an opinion more easily. It was planned to have a river, a lake, a spring, waterfalls and islands; also a circular temple, a hermitage with its bell, and finally a belvedere from which it would be possible to admire the landscape. The Queen caused this new project to be simplified still further; but the cost already amounted to some 300,000 pounds. The work was then accelerated. On September 7th, 1778, Marie Antoinette gave a big party at the Trianon in honour of her husband. The park presented a fair, at which the ladies of the Court were vendors, and the Queen a "lemonade-seller". It was considered at that date that the "Chinese garden" was beginning to take on its final appearance.

The Chinese *jeu de bague*, which has now disappeared, had already been in existence for some time. The charming Temple of Love,

which we still admire today, already stood on its island in the summer of 1778. It was then that Marie Antoinette decided to put up a little theatre where she could act on a tiny stage before a very limited number of guests. The Queen supervised its completion down to the smallest detail. Preserved almost intact, it remains one of the best witnesses to the preferences of Marie Antoinette .On the outer surface, only the entrance is decorated, for all the rest of the building had to be concealed between an artificial mountain and the hedgerows of the French garden. The door appears at the end of an avenue of trees which make a natural frame. At the top of a few steps, two Ionic columns support a triangular pediment adorned with stone sculpture showing *Apollo as a child surrounded by the attributes of Comedy and Tragedy*, by a good artist of second class, Deschamps.

The stage is provided with the best of everything. The hall and the proscenium are very richly adorned with sculptures and hangings. Particular attention was given by the Queen to the choice of materials, and the way in which they were draped. Lagrenée completed the painting of the ceiling in July 1779. This little building, reserved for the entertainments of a Queen and unusable by even a moderately numerous company, seems, in its search for perfection and its adaptation to the tastes of a single person, a more surprising luxury than the ostentatious display of a large theatre which a vast audience could enjoy. In this connection one can better understand how the intimate buildings of Marie Antoinette can both move one more profoundly and shock one more gravely than the alarming extravagances of Louis XIV, who was building for posterity as well as himself. Yet the caprice of a moment has survived as long as the dream of eternity.

It was in this little theatre that Marie Antoinette no doubt experienced the greatest pleasure in acting. Her family and a few close friends normally constituted the company, and were often advised by famous actors. The repertory was that which was fashionable in Paris at the time. The Queen played and sang in the *Devin du village* by Jean-Jacques Rousseau, and the plays—much appreciated then but now completely forgotten—of Sedaine. Melchior Grimm, in his diary entry of October 20th, 1780, refers to these entertainments :

The performances given in the past few days in the pretty hall of the Trianon concern too closely the honour and glory of Monsieur Sedaine for us not to permit ourselves to preserve their memory in our literary annals. One has never seen, and doubtless never will, *Le Roi et le Fermier*, nor the *Gageure imprévu* played by more august actors, nor before a more imposing or well selected audience. The Queen, to whom none of the graces are foreign, and who knows how to adopt them all without ever losing that which is natural to her, played in the first the part of Jenny, and in the second that of the *soubrette*. All the other parts were taken by persons in the intimate circle of Their Majesties and the Royal Family. The Count d'Artois played the part of a game-keeper in the first play and a valet in the second. It was Caillau and Richer who had the honour of coaching this illustrious company. The Count of Vaudreuil, who is perhaps the best society actor in Paris, did the part of Richard; the Duchess of Guiche, the daughter of Countess Jules de Polignac, of whom Horace might have said "Matre pulchra filia pulchrior" [a daughter even more charming than her charming mother] that of little Betsi, Countess Diane de Polignac that of the mother and the Count Adhémar that of the King.

The last show put on by the Queen at the Trianon in August 1785 was typical of the rapid evolution in the political situation. It was *The Barber of Seville* by Beaumarchais, the author of lampoons against Marie Antoinette who had been imprisoned in Vienna in 1774. His second comedy, the *Marriage of Figaro*, played on the stage of the Théâtre Français, was to shake the very foundations of society of the Ancien Régime. In the course of the rehearsals, the Queen was informed of the first developments in the sinister affair of the necklace. The Count of Artois was Figaro, Vaudreuil played Almavira, and Marie Antoinette Rosine. It was indeed a far cry from the carefree happiness of the pretty Spanish fiancée to the anxieties of a woman defamed, attacked and frightened. An excellent Rosine, according to witnesses, Marie Antoinette in the years which followed no longer felt the courage to appear again on the stage of a theatre.

As the periods spent at the Trianon became longer or more frequent, Marie Antoinette was anxious to have a library. We find Mique, her architect, working out the alterations necessary in order to make a room suitable for books. The little dauphine certainly had changed; she could not now do

without reading, though she may well not have read the hundreds of works in her rural retreat, most of them bound in calf bearing the Queen's arms with the letters "C.T." (Château de Trianon) surmounted by a crown on the back of the book. But it was clearly a matter of personal choice. Of the two thousand volumes in the Trianon, contrary to the wise advice of the Empress Maria Theresa who was thinking mainly of the education of a sovereign, more than half were novels or plays. Among the others were to be found many historical tales.

The Queen of France read Voltaire, Rousseau, Montesquieu, Marivaux, Diderot and even Restif de la Bretonne, and also Cervantes, Goldoni, Fielding, Swift, and Goethe. Her tastes strangely resemble the enthusiasms of those passionate women who were to have such an important rôle in the revolutionary saga. At the Court as in the city, sensitive souls were swayed by the same philosophical ideas, and moved by the same heroes.

Meanwhile, work was being continued in the garden. The making of the grotto, which had always been planned, was particularly laborious. Mique finished it only in 1782, and he altered it again several times later. It was romantic and mysterious. The Count of Hézecques, who was at the time a young page at the Court, relates:

This grotto was so dark that the eyes required time to discover what objects it contained. It was all carpeted with moss and freshened by the stream that flowed through it. A bed of moss too was an invitation to repose. But, whether by chance or by intentional arrangement, a crevice, opening at the head of the bed, made it possible to survey the whole of the meadow and to spot in the distance anyone who might approach this refuge...while a dark stairway led up to the top of the rock.

At about the same time the Belvedere was completed, on the shores of the lake; this was a small octagonal *salon* of intentionally restrained architecture adorned with sculpture in lead on the outside and stucco on the inside. The ceiling painted by Lagrenée represented simply a blue sky in which some cupids frolicked. The tripods and tables were in keeping with the architecture. All around were flowers; it was a sanctuary of freshness, and of an extremely refined luxury, which the Queen imagined to be of Roman simplicity.

As in the Salon of the Louvre where the scenes of Roman history painted by Vien, David and Germain Drouais are to be found side by side with the peasant studies of Greuze, Lépicié and Aubry, the adornments of the Trianon ranged from the Temple of Love and the Belvedere to the rustic cottages of the Hameau. In point of fact, those themes of inspiration, apparently opposed, really complemented and harmonized with each other. Rousseau was not the only one of his day to extol the virtues of antiquity. The Greeks and Romans were held to be peasant nations which had not yet been contaminated by the evils of luxury and civilization, and people took pleasure in rediscovering among the shepherds and tillers of the soil round Paris the simplicity and merits of those who lived in the days when Rome was founded.

The Trianon was both a dream and a rejection. It was the expression, on pretexts which were in no way immoral, of a flight from the obligations, inconsistencies, excessive ease, and boredom of a jaded society.

In the first plans for the "Chinese garden" provision had been made for a ruin. Rather than the roofless columns of a Greek temple, the Queen preferred a kind of dilapidated keep, of the kind one sees in the French countryside; that was the "Tower of Marlborough". There was a twofold reason why the song, composed at the beginning of the century when the Duke of Marlborough was victoriously attacking the armies of Louis XIV, was fashionable. Geneviève, known as "Madame Poitrine", the Dauphin's wet-nurse, was in the habit of humming the ditty, which she had learnt in her village. The Queen, the King, and the whole Court had learned it, and then Beaumarchais had given the simple tune other words for his very subversive comedy, the *Marriage of Figaro*, so that the name of Marlborough was full of ambiguous associations.

Mique began to build a farm, for which he had had the plans approved some time before. Tiles and flooring were put in it as in a real, well-kept house of a peasant. In 1785 a herdsman and his oxen were put on the farm, and then a few cows. Soon there was a water-mill, the wheel turned by an artificial river; a barn; a dovecote; the gardener's dwelling, and then a more spacious house for the Queen; a dairy, and a second smaller house where one could be more completely isolated. From outside, all the buildings looked alike with their thatched roofs and the front painted to imitate old bricks, worm-eaten wood, and cracked stone covered with Virginia creeper. But inside, while the farm and the mill were neatly arranged, everything in the Queen's house was of refined comfort. There was a dining-room, a backgammon room, and on the first floor a large drawing-room preceded by a Chinese room and another apartment called the Hall of the Nobles. Nearby, hidden in a clump of bushy shrubs, were the service quarters: kitchen, laundry, shed, larder, and even a special house for the footmen.

The Queen, in her hamlet, lived in the midst of fields which were, it is true, small, but were tilled and cultivated by real peasants with real herds of cows and flocks of sheep. Contrary to a persistent legend, Marie Antoinette did not disguise herself as a farmer's wife and never took part in the work in the fields, but she maintained simple and familiar relationships with the peasants on her estate and thus became imbued with country life.

The many parties given at the Petit Trianon reflected the same trend as the successive transformations of the surroundings of the little château. Marie Antoinette liked to be hostess to the eminent visitors to Versailles, such as her brother the Emperor Joseph II, the Czarevitch of Russia who travelled incognito under the name of the Count of the North, and King Gustavus III of Sweden who had chosen for a tour round Europe the title of Count of Haga. The last entertainment, and without any doubt the most sumptuous, was given on June 21st, 1784 in honour of the King of Sweden, who was passionately fond of art, the theatre and festivities.

The monarch wrote next day to his brother:

There was a performance in the little theatre of the *Dormeur éveillé* of Marmontel, with music by Gretry, done with the whole apparatus of the ballets of the opera and the Italian Players. Supper was served in the garden pavilions, and after supper the English garden was illuminated: it was quite enchanting. The Queen had given permission to walk in the grounds to worthy people who were not invited to the supper, and the word had gone out that all were to be dressed in white, which really gave the place the appearance of the Elysian Fields. The Queen did not wish to sit down at the table, but did the honours just as the most worthy mistress of the house might have done....

The Dauphin's nurse, "Madame Poitrine", was fond of humming this popular song about the death of Marlborough. Beaumarchais was later to adapt the tune for his comedy "The Marriage of Figaro".

Marie Antoinette received the gift of the Petit Trianon with great joy and immediately set about rearranging the garden. She wanted one that was neither too severe in the Le Nôtre style, nor too complex, and was completely taken up with the idea of an English garden. She rejected a first project by Antoine Richard and finally accepted a plan proposed by M. de Caraman : the garden would have a wooded hillock covered with yew and box trees, a grotto with a water-fall, rock arrangements and a belvedere surmounting a lake and a river. Turgot, however, managed to hold up the work for two years. In 1777 Mique took up the 1774 plans and transformed them : he envisaged a spring, a river, a lake, islands, a circular temple, a hermitage with a bell and finally a belvedere from which it would be possible to admire the entire landscape. The project was realized very quickly, for the Queen hurried the work so that she could have a place in which to escape the obligations of the Court. This garden, which reproduced the accidents and picturesque views of the country, was greeted as a symbol of the advent of truth. Can the influence of "La Nouvelle Héloïse" be felt or is it merely necessary to remember that Marie Antoinette had lived all her childhood in a family that ignored etiquette outside of official ceremonies and that lived, as far as possible, freely in the country? The Queen was happy to be able to relax at the Trianon, out of the public sight. From 1777 to 1779 she had a small theatre built where she could act out plays with her friends ; the King, Monsieur and the Princesses did not act but were content to provide an audience. The last performance at the Trianon was of "The Barber of Seville", in the summer of 1785.

RECEUIL
des Plans du Petit
Trianon

Par le Sr Mique Chevalier
de L'ordre de St Michel
Premier Architecte
honoraire Intendant
Général des Batimens
du Roy et de la
Reine.
1786.

Jacques-Ange Gabriel began to build the Petit Trianon in 1762.

View of the Queen's Hamlet from the other side of the pond.

The Trianon on the gallery and the "jeu de bague" side.

The Temple of Love emerging from amidst a mass of foliage.

The Belvedere rising above a romantic landscape.

A picturesque grotto hidden beneath the greenery.

The theatre of the Petit Trianon remains one of the best testimonies to Marie Antoinette's tastes and preferences. The stage was perfectly fitted out and the Queen herself kept a careful watch on everything, down to the finest detail.

136

Marie Antoinette can be identified as the figure in the centre of these drawings by Boquet of persons in theatrical costume; on the left is the Count of Artois and below him Elisabeth, one of the King's sisters.

The 1785 Salon - Extract from the "Mercure de France" of Saturday October Ist, 1785

VIEN—Return of Priam with the Body of Hector: "the beauty of the arrangement, the purety of the draughtsmanship, the truthfulness of the colour, such are the qualities that strike one on first seeing this painting. An examination of its details only serves to add to the esteem it initially inspires...."

SUVÉE—Death of Cleopatra: "The colour tone is too white and the attitudes of the figures are cold".

DAVID—The Oath of the Horatii in the Hands of their Father: "The composition of this painting is in a new style; it is the sign of a brilliant and courageous imagination. Few painters would have dared position the three brothers on the same line, for fear of becoming dry and harsh....

The character and action of the Horatii show pride. One can see in the face of the father a patriotic ferocity which is reminiscent of the murderous valour of the first Romans. The correctness of the drawing; the faithfulness of the details that indicates a great knowledge of anatomy; the beautiful colour tones; the intelligent and felicitous arrangement of the light; the simple but sublime composition of this picture lead us to consider it as the most distinguished production to come for a long time from the brush of a Frenchman."

RENAUD—Death of Priam: "More of affectation than truth in its effects, a very mediocre colour tone, a disconnected style and on the faces either feeble or unnatural expressions...."

Arrangement of paintings
in the Louvre "Salon,"
in 1785

At the end of the eighteenth century the Salon was much frequented and it was not unusual for a hundred thousand people to have been there in one month. Visitors to the 1785 Salon noticed how often blood and death figured on the canvases and how beauty emerged from horror. To be aware of this new artistic climate one has only to look at the titles of the pictures : David's "The Oath of the Horatii", Renaud's "Death of Priam", "Arria Exhorts her Husband Paetus to Kill Himself" by Vincent and so on. The carefreeness and elegance of a short while back have already been forgotten.

Peintures au Salon du Louvre, en 1785.

...rant le temps de l'exposition

Coup d'œil exact de l'arrangement des ...

Gravé de mémoire, et terminé du ...

The tables of honour were in the Petit Trianon itself. But in the outbuildings and in the Grand Trianon, hospitality was offered to the rest of the King of Sweden's suite, the officers of the bodyguard, the guards themselves, the Queen's maids, the actors, the dancers, the musicians, the personnel responsible for the revels, and indeed the whole staff of the Grand and the Petit Trianon including doorkeepers and gardeners, not to mention a vast number of workmen and stable lads. It was evident that the Queen's prejudices had softened considerably already. All the trees had been decorated with lanterns which threw on to the lake reflections so soft and "shadows so light that the water, the trees and the people all appeared to be of air". Behind the Temple of Love, for the purpose of illuminating it, a trench had been dug in which a fire consumed the prodigious number of 6,400 faggots—an electric illumination could have given no more vivid light nor one that was so moving.

Marie Antoinette received at the Trianon every week during her last years at Versailles, although she gave no great festivities. The Count of Vaublanc relates :

The Queen gave a ball in the gardens of the Trianon every Sunday in the summer. Everyone who was decently dressed was received, in particular nursemaids with their children. She danced a quadrille to show that she took part in the pleasure to which she invited the others. She called the nursemaids to her, got them to introduce the children, spoke to the latter about their parents, and showered kindnesses on them. As a rule nearly all the Royal Family were with her.... I observed with one of my friends that a small number of persons of high society were present at these rural gatherings. Rather more of a mixture would have made a better impression.

A tent was often put up on the lawn to give shelter to these very innocent rejoicings. No political calculation entered into the planning of the very simple festivities. Marie Antoinette really enjoyed being among the servants and country people, far from the thankless burdens of royalty. This attitude, so contrary to the traditions of the monarchy, was frequently misunderstood : to many Frenchmen, this woman who no longer fulfilled all the duties of her office, was no longer entirely their Queen.

Curiously enough, one of the most characteristic and moving aspects of the personality of Marie Antoinette has almost entirely escaped the attention of her biographers. All through her brief existence she retained the spontaneity of childhood, and a poignant longing for freedom and the affection which had been showered on her from her earliest days. A frustrated wife, she felt the need to be surrounded by children. An attentive and devoted mother, she took a very special interest in the young around her, and endeavoured to arrange for her daughter, and then her son, a way of living among children of their own age, not only to complete their education but also to develop in them the natural feelings of sympathy and affection which an excess of deference, honours and material advantages might diminish or cause to disappear. From the time of her arrival at Versailles, as the Count of Mercy often complained, the Dauphine had as her inseparable companion a child then five years old, the son of her chief *femme de chambre*, Madame de Misery. The following year the eldest daughter, aged twelve, also came to live with Marie Antoinette. Games became more and more noisy, and there were complaints of broken furniture and torn clothes. With sorrow the Dauphine finally resigned herself to being separated from her two companions.

Some years later, when she had become queen, Marie Antoinette adopted little Armand. But she did not merely take François Michel Gagné, known as Armand, away from his background; the whole of his family was placed under royal protection. Denis Toussaint, the elder brother, who showed even greater musical talent than Armand, joined the *Musique du Roi* as a page. This farmer's son not only received the same education as the pages who were children of noble families, but also completed his musical training. In 1787 he was appointed cellist to the King; and it was the Queen who paid the entire cost of his keep up to that date. Even at the time when the monarchy fell, she thought of the young musician; and to enable him to embark alone on a career which was to turn out brilliantly she sent him the sum of 2,000 pounds in 1792. Armand stayed with the Queen up to the time of the birth of her first child. Subsequently Marie Antoinette continued to concern herself with his education and paid for all his studies. At the time of the Revolution, Armand, although still very young, became passionately devoted to the new ideas, entirely forgot his benefactress, bravely enrolled in the armies of the Republic, and met a hero's death. Finally, the remaining two Gagné children, Marie Madeleine and Louis Marie, while remaining with their grandmother, received from Marie Antoinette regular allowances for their food and education. When Marie Madeleine got married, the notary entered in the contract among her assets "3,000 pounds from the benefits she received from the deceased, at that time the wife of Louis Capet, who took care of her maintenance until the Revolution of the 10th August".

Even before her terrible ordeals Madame Royale, Marie Antoinette's eldest daughter, never had an easy character. She was an authoritarian, selfish and not very amiable child. No doubt her mother thought it was good for her upbringing to arrange to have a companion with her all day. Marie Antoinette chose Marie Philippine Lambriquet, the daughter of one of Madame Royale's maids and a valet. Marie Philippine's name was changed and at Court she became Ernestine, for that was the christian name of the heroine of a sentimental novel of Madame Ricoboni, very fashionable at the time. Every morning the chairmen of the royal children went to fetch Ernestine, who was the same age as Madame Royale, and they took her back every evening to her parents. But in April 1788 Madame Lambriquet died; the Queen then decided to bring up Ernestine entirely with her daughter. A room was arranged for her with Madame de Polignac, the royal children's governess, identical with that of Madame Royale, and the life of the two companions was from then on similar in all respects. The same kind of clothes were bought for the Princess and for Ernestine, who had lessons from the same teachers. They had their meals together, and by Marie Antoinette's order one of the girls was served first on alternate days. Together Ernestine and Madame Royale moved into the main part of the Château near the Queen's apartment, together they lived at St. Cloud, and then at the Tuileries, to which the little Lambriquet followed the royal family on October 6th, 1789. In March 1790, Ernestine and Madame Royale, who had received the same outfit, went, on the same day, from the Tuileries to the church of St. Germain l'Auxerrois, their parish, to take part in the ceremony of their first communion.

The second dauphin, the future Louis XVII, also had a companion, the youngest daughter of a gentleman usher of Louis XVI. Her father and mother, who died within a few months of each other, left three orphan girls. Marie Antoinette, told of their tragic situation by Hüe, one of the King's valets, at once declared "I adopt them". The two eldest were placed in the Convent of the Visitation, in the Rue St. Jacques. Jeanne Louise Victoire, who in 1790 was three years old like the Dauphin, was installed in the apartments of the royal family. In accordance with custom, she was given a different name: Marie Antoinette called her Zoë. She was the Dauphin's playmate in the Tuileries between 1790 and 1792 when the children passed much of the time with the Queen.

No doubt Marie Antoinette had occasion to help and love many other children, the memory of whom is lost for ever. We find her, for example, arranging at her own expense for the care of the three children of the Swiss Bersy, one of the attendants at the Petit Trianon, when they got smallpox. The accounts reveal that the Queen even paid for a convalescence recommended by the doctors, on which their mother accompanied them. In 1787, Chevalier de Boufflers, a great traveller, brought back to the Queen from Senegal a parrot...and a young negro child. Instead of treating the black child as a little blackamoor, as was customary, and taking him into her service, Marie Antoinette had him baptized at Notre Dame de Versailles and gave him the christian names of Jean Amilcar. Müller, one of the Queen's houseboys, was instructed to look after him. After the days of October, when revolutionary conditions made it difficult to find a lodging for him at the Tuileries, Marie Antoinette had him placed in an institution for children at St. Cloud and made monthly payments for him up to August 10th through Monsieur de Salvert. When the monarchy fell and Marie Antoinette was made a prisoner in the Temple, nobody had the charity to look after the black child. Driven from the place where he boarded, he died of cold and hunger.

At the time of the flight to Varennes, Marie Antoinette had of course to take great precautions to place Ernestine and Zoë in safety. The former was entrusted to her father who was then living at Versailles, and to her father's home were even taken the toys, furniture, books and piano which Ernestine had received at the same time as her companion. Zoë went back to her sisters at the Visitation Convent in June 1791, where she was to remain even after the return from Varennes. Ernestine, on the other hand, came back to the Tuileries in July 1791, only to experience a new ordeal on the morning of August 10th, 1792 when the royal family left the palace for the Assembly. Providentially it was possible for her to be taken away from the palace by Madame de Mackau, the under-governess of the royal children.

In the Temple, Marie Antoinette was anxious about her adopted children. She managed to ascertain from an obliging guard that Zoë and her two sisters had been taken to their father's family at Brives la Gaillarde. But she knew nothing of what became of Ernestine, whose father was guillotined during the Terror. In vain did Madame Royale, when she was allowed to depart from France, ask to leave with her adopted sister. Ernestine was then living at her grandmother's and the Directory's investigators never found her.

Madame Royale, who became Duchess of Angoulême when she returned to Paris in 1814, again tried to find Ernestine at that time. But it was to no avail. Her childhood companion had died some months earlier, and all she could find was the site of her tomb.

It is impossible to over-emphasize the wit and the art of Marie Antoinette in the mixture of refinement and simplicity which characterized the existence of the royal family in its daily home life. One basked in the "virtuous" or rather benevolent atmosphere depicted by Greuze and Rousseau. Some of the most interesting evidence in this connection is that of one of the valets of Madame Royale, the young Hanet Cléry, whose brother was to accompany Louis XVI to the tower of the Temple. Hanet shows the extent to which the Queen and the King concerned themselves personally and every day with their children. He tells us how Marie Antoinette and Louis XVI refused to leave by day or by night the bedside of their sick daughter. Always keen on his children's education, Louis XVI used a new way of drawing maps to show his daughter the shape of each country and thus enable her to "reconstruct" the world like a game of patience; and the Queen taught her embroidery. Hanet tells touchingly naive stories:

One day the Queen, opening the last door of the corridor leading to her daughter's apartment with a lively movement, broke in the lock the pass-key which served to open all the other doors, so that, having closed the previous one, Her Majesty found herself imprisoned in a dark corridor. The Queen saw me through the window; she knocked, and raising her voice somewhat, ordered me to run and fetch her another pass-key. There was quite a long way to go round, and it was precisely in order to avoid it that the corridors had been made. I made such haste to carry out her orders, that, not imagining that it could be me arriving already, she was somewhat alarmed. The piece of her first pass-key, having remained in the lock, prevented the one I brought from being used. Thus the Queen, being unable to get to her daughter's apartment that way, must needs return to her own. She did me the honour of leaning on my arm, and I took her back to her own quarters. The Queen hastened to tell the King the story of the pass-key, stressing the extreme promptness with which I had liberated her. "That does not surprise me at all," said the King, "he is the best lady's man at Versailles." A moment later, Louis XVI, equipped with locksmith's tools, said to the Queen "Come, Madame, we are going to repair the accident of the pass-key. Hanet, take a torch, and give us light." We arrived; the lock was soon dismantled; and the Queen went through to her daughter's apartment. But the King wished to complete the repairs. Having remained to give him light, I was soon the witness of a very funny scene. The King had put the lock together again, and in order to see whether the key turned properly, he left that part of the corridor. My light did not light up the other part, so that he was in the dark. It so happened that Delmas, a valet, was in fact expecting a locksmith to work in Madame's apartment. Seeing a man with his back to him who was turning a key in all directions, he took him for the workman in question, came up, slapped him rather roughly on the shoulder, and said "Well, old fellow, you do keep one waiting"! The King opened the door and turned round; and Delmas recognizing his master, gave a cry of alarm. The Queen, who heard it, came running out from Madame's apartment, and saw on one side a horror-struck Delmas, and on the other the King laughing heartily and rubbing his shoulder.

In order to choose her gowns for the day Marie Antoinette made use of books in which samples of dress materials were attached. Reproduced here are three pages from a book for the years 1782-4, which was at that time in the keeping of Madame d'Ossun.

Madame La Comtesse D'Ossun

Garde Robe des Atours
De La Reine

Gazette Pour L'année 1782

Gazette de la Reine

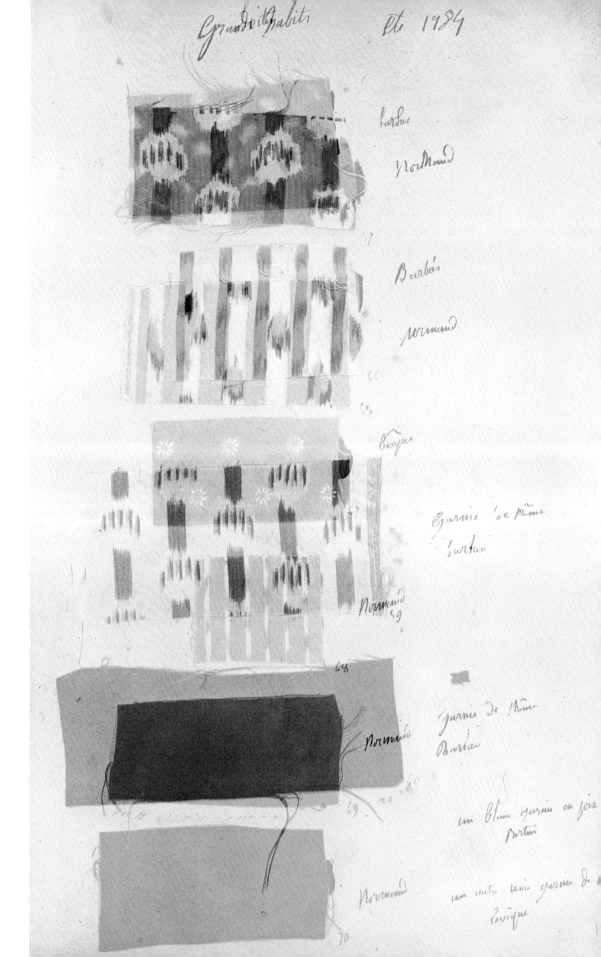

barbes

Normand

Barbés

normand

évêques

Garnie de même barbés

Normand

Normandie   Garnie de même Barbés

un Blanc garni en foin barbés

Normand   un autre uni garni de évêque

Robes vuo de petit d'anne

Robe brodé dno fond
Tricolité par Mlle Le normand

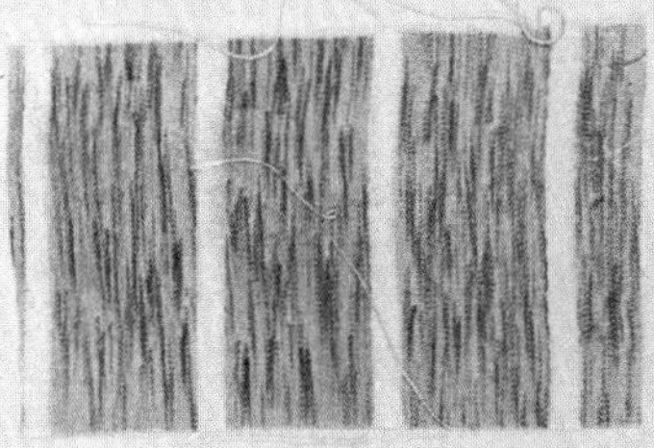

Robe par Mlle Le normand

Robe impériale en fournie
en pouls de soie par
Mlle de normand

Robe garnie par Mlle Bertin

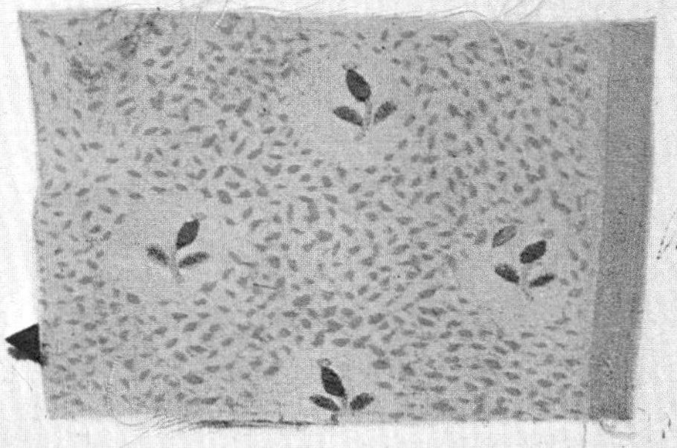

Mme de normand

An Austrian archduchess, of course, could not fail to love music. Marie Antoinette had the same tastes as all her family; but as she did nothing by halves, she showed in that field a passion and conviction that were infectious. Although the Queen of France did not have a good voice and only played music in mediocre fashion, she persisted in taking lessons so as to improve her talents, particularly in order to be able to perform better on the harp, which was her favourite musical instrument.

But the main role of Marie Antoinette in this field was to guide the taste of her day. She liked the French music of Lully, of J.P. Rameau...or of Jean-Jacques Rousseau enough to listen to it with pleasure or even to sing to it in her theatre, but she did not regard it as a great art. Many composers whom we admire were, to her, persons almost totally unknown—for example Bach, Händel, even Haydn in spite of his connections with the Court of Vienna, or Mozart whom she had met several times. For Marie Antoinette, the best composer, whose music carried her away and enthused her, was Gluck. It is true that he first found success in Vienna. But he was not a very likeable musician, or someone with whom it was easy to converse, even for a queen. It is difficult to imagine Marie Antoinette forsaking the balls and lawns of the Trianon to go and listen to *Orfeo* or *Iphigénie*. Here is an interesting contradiction in Marie Antoinette's character. She liked facile pleasures yet dreamed of a difficult, wonderful and exalting world.

It was only thanks to the Dauphine's personal intervention with Louis XV that *Iphigénie en Aulide*, Gluck's first opera to be produced in France, could be put into rehearsal at the Paris Opéra at the beginning of 1774. It was an arduous battle. Gluck was dissatisfied with his singers, his orchestra, and his chorus. He struggled long to persuade them to play his opera as he himself saw it. The first performance took place on Tuesday April 19th. By eleven in the morning, curiosity had already attracted huge crowds to the Opéra. A plot was feared. At half-past five the Dauphine, determined to put up a fight, arrived accompanied by her husband and a large part of the royal family. Princes, ministers, great nobles and all the Court were gathered to be present at the discomfiture or the triumph of Chevalier Gluck, whose music

was so surprising to French ears. Grimm, like the whole band of the philosophers, was enthusiastic. Mademoiselle Arnould, according to him, played the part of Iphigenia as it had never been played at the Comédie Française, and he was loud in his praise of Larrivée, Legros and Mademoiselle Duplan. Jean-Jacques Rousseau, who was nearly crushed in his efforts to attend the performance, emerged enthusiastic.

But the majority of the audience gave the performance an icy reception. A correspondent of the *Nouvelles à la Main* noted that "The applause which was given can largely be attributed to the public's wish to please Madame la Dauphine."

Some days later, Marie Antoinette wrote to her sister, Maria Christina:

We have had the first performance of Gluck's "Iphigénie". I was carried away by it; people can talk of nothing else. People are divided and attack each other as though it were a matter of religion; at the Court, although I spoke out publicly in favour of this work of genius, people take sides and there are singularly lively discussions. Apparently it is much worse in the town. Monsieur Gluck himself had explained to me the scheme he had in mind for fixing, as he calls it, the true character of the music of the theatre, and making it harmonize with what is natural. To judge by its effect on me, his success has even surpassed his hopes. The Dauphin himself was moved. He found much to applaud; but, as I expected, while people were carried away by certain passages, the general reaction appeared to be one of hesitancy. One has to get used to this new system; and today everyone wants to go and see the work, which is a good sign.

This young girl, full of feeling, was already capable of fighting ardently for an art in which she was able to recognize something new, and for an artist whose genius she admired.

Gluck's *Orfeo*, some months later, of a pathos perhaps easier to grasp, aroused more unanimous admiration. Sophie de Lespinasse, the friend of Diderot, proclaimed: "I felt the perturbation, and the happiness, of passion.... I wish I could hear ten times a day that tune which rends me and makes me enjoy all I regret: 'I Have Lost My Eurydice'."

Taken from a contemporary book of French costumes for the year 1779, this picture shows a young bride in her gown of pekin trimmed with gauze, ribbons and flowers.

On these two pages can be seen some of the gowns fashionable during the reign of Marie Antoinette. These dresses were described variously as "à la Reine", "à la Polonaise", "à la Créole", "à la Circassienne" or merely as a "ceremonial gown" for special occasions.

And Voltaire, the patriarch in his distant country retreat, proclaimed: "We are all for Gluck at Ferney."

For Marie Antoinette it was a personal triumph and thenceforth she remained unshakeably faithful to her favourite musician. The Parisian public, however, showed itself fickle. It again showed enthusiasm for the music of Rameau and gave a triumphant reception to *Castor et Pollux*, which Gluck and Marie Antoinette despised as a pleasant but superficial musical work. It also provided a prodigious success for a young Italian composer, Piccini. Gluck, in spite of these vexations and backed by the Queen's support, persisted in producing his works in Paris, and even spoke of ending his days in France.

Quarrels and difficulties, however, were not lacking for this musician who was so accustomed to adulation in Vienna. The musical enthusiasts of Paris were in 1781 invited to hear two operas on the theme of *Iphigénie en Tauride*, one by Gluck, and the other by Piccini. The battle was violent. Marie Antoinette was, of course, at the head of the "Gluckists", but the "Piccinists" for a time seemed to carry the day in France. Great rivalry was shown in comparing the numbers of performances, the size of the audience, and the box-office figures. Finally, a fire at the Opéra put an end to this musical tournament at a time when the general attitude of the public appeared definitely to give preference to Gluck—a verdict confirmed by posterity.

In 1784, Gluck, very old and tired, was unable to attend the performance of the last opera he composed for the Parisian public. But the Queen was still there to watch over the success of the great composer, who was no longer strong enough to leave Vienna. Tactlessly she left it to Mercy-Argenteau, the Austrian ambassador, to negotiate officially with the management of the Opéra for a change of date in the programmes; this seemed an unwarranted interference by a foreign power in the artistic affairs of France. On the day in April 1784 when the Paris Opéra finally put on *Les Danaïdes* by Gluck, the Queen was only moderately applauded on entering. When the Bailli de Suffren, the hero of the war against England in India, took his seat, there was thunderous acclaim.

Marie Antoinette was humiliated, but nevertheless she had the joy of being present at the final triumph of Gluck, who was by now universally admired. Piccini, whose admirers became increasingly less numerous, found himself in 1786 in a difficult situation. The Queen intervened personally to see that he received a substantial gratuity. Marie Antoinette had a deep love for the art of music. She fought with the passionate feeling characteristic of her for the success of the works that she preferred. But she felt a natural sympathy with all sincere musicians, whether composers, singers, or instrumentalists. During the last years of her life, she was often to get support from them.

The tastes of Marie Antoinette in architecture are to be judged by her achievements at Versailles. That is where she lived most, and most often thought of new projects. Louis XIV, and more recently Louis XV, had left their personal mark on the old château just as much as any of the great architects. Now, for the first time, a queen was taking a real interest in what was built at Versailles, and she completely eclipsed in that field the modest actions of her husband. It was not that Louis XVI did not intend to busy himself with such problems, at least through an intermediary. He had chosen, as superintendent of his buildings, one of the intimate friends of his father, the Count of Angivillers. That enlightened man, a friend of the philosophers in spite of his unswerving royalist allegiance, supported the painter Jacques Louis David from the latter's earliest days, disregarding his difficult character. He also supported, despite criticism and attacks, the most brilliant architect of the eighteenth century, Nicolas Ledoux. Thus David and Ledoux, the two most revolutionary artists of Louis XVI's reign, found in the last minister of the arts of the Ancien Régime their best defender. Marie Antoinette did not like d'Angivillers, and she ignored him. She had her own architect, Mique, and always worked with him. The department of the Superintendent of Buildings was responsible only for paying expenses, and never for proposing plans or supervising their implementation.

Did the Queen like Versailles? Certainly not as much as the Trianon. She accepted the need to live there like her obligation to take up her duties as a queen; but she sought to create in the great château a domain of her very own, where she would have more freedom and could increasingly transform her austere official apartments and enlarge the area of her own private suites. We can see, or shall be able to see, nearly all that Marie Antoinette did, thanks to the restoration which has been going on at Versailles for the past twenty-five years. Soon the Room of the Queens of France is again to have the appearance Marie Antoinette wanted it to have, in its "summer furnishings", the fruit of carefully thought out transformations in 1782, 1786 and 1787, with silks on the walls and on the bed, chosen by the Queen and re-woven in our own day on the same looms as were used for the original materials. Here Marie Antoinette did not in the least bother about having things in the antique style. Her furniture was rich, but slender and elegant, and her silks beautiful and gay. Much of the *chicorée moderne*, the showy decoration which was in fashion at the beginning of Louis XV's reign, was done away with by Marie Antoinette.

In the *Cabinet des Nobles*, where the Queen's ladies slept on the terrible night of the 5th to the 6th of October 1789, Marie Antoinette had caused tapestries and marbles which dated from Louis XIV to be removed in 1785. Mique replaced them with white and gold pannelling, high mirrors, and woodwork of soft green with three fine chests-of-drawers by Riesener. The antechamber of the great dining-hall retained much of its Louis XIV character, but in 1786 Marie Antoinette had hangings put up in it which were to her taste, more pleasing and closer to life and to the world of her dreams. Instead of the "Fruits of War" the Queen, with a fine sense of what was fitting, chose the admirable tapestries of Mignard representing the four seasons, of which the paintings had been done in the gallery of Monsieur, the brother of Louis XIV, at St. Cloud. In the guardroom, a little farther on, nothing was changed.

On the other hand, in the *Salon de la Paix* at the other end of the apartments, which was really a continuation of the Hall of Mirrors, Marie Antoinette kept on making changes. Was it not her Games Room, adjacent to her own room, and in which she received the visitors who came to Versailles every day? Generally temporary constructions which could be taken down were put up there. However, in 1786 Marie Antoinette asked, in spite of the austere appearance which Louis XIV had wished that room to have, "that an endeavour be made by all possible means to give her Games Room neatness and

gaiety". A radical step was proposed, to abolish the marbles and all "the heavy and shabby ornaments of bronze and lead, and also the celebrated ceiling by Lebrun". D'Angivillers manœuvered, prevaricated and procrastinated in order not to damage one of the most prestigious ensembles of Versailles; and finally the Queen contented with a few changes in furnishings.

However, she was able to give full play to her taste for light, nature, fantasy and gaiety in her interior apartments. Here everything is marvellously worked, and the *Cabinet doré* or the *Méridienne*, visited only by the privileged, give one the extraordinary impression of discovering a human being through the architecture and decoration which she wished to have, and, in part, designed. Nor was the Queen happy with the private apartment which had belonged to the wife of Louis XV. She extended her domain towards the ground floor of the château where the rooms gave on to the marble courtyard. The death of Madame Sophie, her aunt, enabled her to make her first incursion into this area. In 1783 a new room was built there, with a bed covered in green damask. Then Madame Sophie's library, fitted out with some furniture by Riesener, became that of the Queen. The ground floor apartment was greatly enlarged when Marie Antoinette decided to have her daughter Madame Royale with her, with her ladies and her young companion; and here she also installed the Duke of Normandy, her second son, the future Louis XVII.

The oddest and most interesting products of Marie Antoinette's architectural tastes have, however, disappeared for ever. It was a prevailing fashion in the eighteenth century, and even at earlier periods, to construct rooms and buildings that could be taken to pieces. The last Queen of France turned that taste for "pre-fabricated" houses into a veritable institution. At Compiègne, in 1774, Marie Antoinette had a wooden house brought to make a billiard room; and five years later she set up at St. Cloud a theatre which could be dismantled. At the end of her reign the Queen had all sorts of "houses" that could be transformed and displaced, and in which skilled work with tapestries over specially made wooden framework made it possible to produce the illusion of real palace halls.

These settings were rather costly. The carpenters', locksmiths' and painters' bills for

The decorations of the Royal Manufactures at Sèvres were inspired by themes dear to Marie Antoinette.

In this service, called "Masson arabesque" after the architect, the influence of finds at Pompeii and Herculaneum can be recognized.

Another pattern for a decoration under the direction of Masson.

In 1783 the painter Legay the Elder proposed this Three Graces decoration for the royal service.

For the borders of the pieces Legay drew masks and goats, a transposition of classical themes.

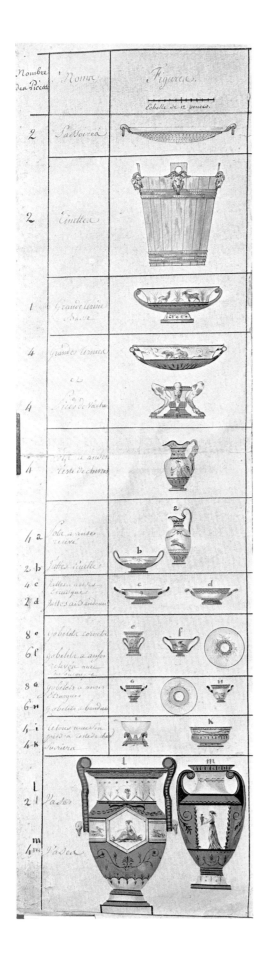

the Queen's houses in 1785 amounted to 100,000 pounds (today about £63,000, or 150,000 dollars). For the Carnival, wooden houses were set up against the walls of the Château of Versailles, either in the royal courtyard or on the terrace towards the park. The façades were thus completely disfigured. In 1787 there were to be found in the South Park a lobby or covered walk, a billiard room, a games room, a ballroom and a buffet. It was quite a palace, put up in front of the Château of Louis XIV, of which it covered, at first floor level, five windows in the main building and three in the south wing. This device of wooden houses, which in fact were sumptuous, was so ingenious that three of them could be transformed into a vast theatre capable of holding five hundred spectators.

This fine group of apartments designed by Marie Antoinette for balls and shows was to serve from May to October 1789 as the premises for the sessions of the States General, which was soon to proclaim itself the National Assembly.

Under Marie Antoinette, however, there was also another kind of architecture—that of the de Waillys, the Ledoux and the Antoines — with which the Queen was acquainted and to which she was by no means indifferent. It is true that it was not she who ordered from Ledoux those admirable constructions of the Gates of Paris, of which so few remain in our day, at La Nation, the Parc Monceau, and Denfert-Rochereau; and of course she never knew the achievements of Boullée. But it was in the new Comédie Française, designed by Peyre and de Wailly, which we today know as the Odéon, that Marie Antoinette listened with intense feeling to Monsieur de Beaumarchais' comedy, the *Marriage of Figaro*, which appears to us today as an infernal machine designed to blow up the Ancien Régime. That same Queen had also envisaged a complete transformation of Versailles, which would have become a classical palace in the sober style of an antiquity. In such ambitious projects Marie Antoinette was a child of her age : she dreamed of Greek architecture rising on the ruins of two centuries of traditional art.

155

In that respect, it was the Revolution which saved the Ancien Régime.

Marie Antoinette, treated variously as a saint and dissolute woman by her contemporaries and posterity, showed the true measure of her surprising lack of moral prejudices and the extreme delicacy of which she was capable in human relationships in the sentimental adventure of her life, her liaison with the handsome Swede, Count Fersen. This story is established beyond controversy and conjecture. It is possible to reconstruct with certainty at least as regards its main features, the course of an affair so closely akin to the plots of the eighteenth-century novels but in which, strange to say, the irresistible impulses of passion go with a sang-froid, a prudence and an intelligence which seem incompatible with such strong sentiments.

Axel de Fersen was the tall, handsome and rich son of one of Sweden's most powerful men, who had served for a long time in the French army. He was just Marie Antoinette's age. In the course of a tour through Europe to complete his education, he spent some months in Paris at the beginning of 1774. He was received, as his rank entitled him to be, at the Court of France, and he danced with the Dauphine on the occasion of the Carnival. Perhaps he was picked out then by Marie Antoinette. The Swedish Ambassador in Paris, the Count of Creutz, wrote to the King after his departure: "Young Count Fersen has just left for London. Of all the Swedes who have been here during my time, he is the one who has been best received in high society. He was extremely well treated by the Royal family. It is not possible to be more seemly or becoming in one's behaviour." After spending some four years in Sweden, Fersen decided to return to France. That was quite natural. He had liked it there, and the war with England might enable him to distinguish himself. On August 25th, 1778, he was again at the Court of France: "It was last Tuesday," he observed in a letter to his father, "that I was at Versailles to be presented to the royal family. The Queen, who is charming, said on seeing me: 'Ah, it is an old acquaintance!' The rest of the family did not say a word to me." Then, some days later, "The Queen, who is the prettiest and most amiable princess I know, had the kindness to enquire after me often; she asked Creutz [the Swedish Ambassador]

why I did not come to her card parties on Sundays, and having learnt that I had come one day when none had taken place, she made me some kind of excuse. Her pregnancy is progressing and is very obvious." And again, "The Queen always treats me with kindness.... She had heard talk of my uniform and expressed considerable desire to see it.... I am to go there on Tuesday wearing it.... She is the most amiable princess I know...."

Thus discern the beginnings of an idyll—very decorous as yet, as otherwise Fersen would have refrained from mentioning it to his father. But in the first months of 1779, Marie Antoinette showed a penchant for the Swedish officer. Her intimates, Vaudreuil, Besenval and Madame de Polignac noticed it. Fersen then courageously decided to join the French army which was setting forth to support the Americans. Separation would enable him to avoid giving in to passion. That at any rate was what Creutz thought. He wrote to the King of Sweden in April 1780:

I must confess to Your Majesty that young Count Fersen found such favour with the Queen that it gave umbrage to a number of persons. I confess that I cannot refrain from thinking that she had a fondness for him; I saw too positive signs of it to doubt it. Young Count Fersen behaved admirably, both by his reserve and, more especially, by his decision to go to America. By going away, he removed all danger.

It seems highly unlikely that during the American campaign Fersen and Marie Antoinette ceased to correspond. In the first place, the young officer was the subject of such flattering promotions that one cannot doubt that there was influential patronage. Then, when he got back to France in 1783, Fersen showed complete opposition to all marriage projects suggested by his father, and announced his firm intention to settle in Paris. No doubt his friend de Staël, the future husband of Mademoiselle Necker who was soon to become Swedish ambassador in Paris, was the secret go-between. In any case, in July 1783, Fersen was no longer in doubt as to Marie Antoinette's love. He wrote secretly to his sister: "I cannot belong to the only person I would wish to, the only person who really loves me, and so I do not wish to belong to anyone." Moreover, when in November 1783 he was appointed Colonel Commandant of the Royal Swedish Regiment he thanked the Queen for that promotion.

From then on Fersen, in his correspondence, took precautions in order not to compromise the Queen. He kept a register of his letters. All the missives sent to Marie Antoinette were under the name of "Joséphine". And those letters, published in the nineteenth century by an heir of Fersen's at a time when it was not customary to make light of adultery, were cut and mutilated, and to a large extent destroyed, with the obvious purpose of concealing an inadmissible secret. In spite of that *auto-da-fé*, a copy in Fersen's hand of a letter from Marie Antoinette survives, and ends with these sufficiently explicit words: "Goodbye, most loving and most loved of all men."

Further, Fersen took good care to conceal, as far as possible, his presence at Versailles. He wrote as follows to his sister: "It is eight in the evening, and I must take my leave of you. I have been at Versailles since yesterday. Do not say I am writing from here, for I date my other letters from Paris." Fersen did in fact have a rather large house in Paris, situated at the corner of the Avenue Matignon and the Faubourg St. Honoré; part of it is still there. It was primarily for appearances' sake; for in all probability Fersen often lived in the interior apartments of the Queen at Versailles.

Two facts hitherto unknown strongly support that theory. Marie Antoinette, in a move unusual for those days, had had installed in her official bedroom an ingenious locking system which enabled her, by merely pulling on a cord, to lock all four doors of the room and then unlock them at will. It still exists.

More convincing yet is the link between a passage in Fersen's correspondence book and certain projects carried out at Versailles. In April 1787 he noted:

April 7th: Plan for lodging upstairs; let her send her answer to me at the regiment; I shall be there on May 15th. April 20th: What she has to find me for living upstairs; I leave on 29th or 30th; I expect to be in Paris on 20th or 21st. 8th October: by M. de Valois; that she should have an alcove made for the stove; that I shall leave on 18th to be on 19th in Paris, and at her place in the evening; let her send me a letter at 3 or 4 to tell me what I should do.

Now at this same time, Marie Antoinette had alterations made in her interior apartments which corresponded exactly to Fersen's requests. On October 9th the mirrors were removed from a room in the Queen's small apartment on the second floor; they were replaced on October 23rd; on October 18th arrived "marble slabs to make a place for a stove in the Queen's small apartments".

In the surviving archives of the Service of the Royal Buildings, there is a hitherto unpublished letter, dated October 14th, 1787, which confirms that this work was done:

I have the honour to report to the Director-General of Buildings, that the Queen sent for the Swedish stove-maker who made the stoves in the apartment of Madame, and that Her Majesty ordered him to make one in one of her inner rooms, with heating pipes to heat a small neighbouring room; the Queen also orderer me to get ready the place where the stove was to be put, which meant the removal of two pieces of panelling, the demolition of part of a partition and re-making it in bricks, and the removal of part of the floor in order to make a brick hearth there.

It is thus quite clear that in accordance with Fersen's requests Marie Antoinette altered the room in her Versailles apartments in which her lover was to live.

Those close to the Queen had no doubt about the relationship between Marie Antoinette and Fersen. Saint Priest, the minister of Louis XVI, whose wife had a great liking for the handsome Swede, wrote in his memoirs: "Fersen used to go riding in the park in the direction of the Trianon three or four times a week; the Queen, on her own, did so too; and these rendez-vous caused a public scandal, in spite of the modesty and reserve of the favourite, who was never outwardly remiss in any respect."

Today it is scarcely possible to doubt that a liaison did in fact exist between Marie Antoinette and Fersen. One would have to ignore all such testimony, overlook all the evidence which points in this direction, and to disregard as well the particular characteristics of a time when custom was extremely tolerant of such things. Nor is it possible to confirm or invalidate the hypothesis that the Duke of Normandy, born at a time when Marie Antoinette and Fersen were seeing a great deal of each other, and when the King was paying markedly little attention to the Queen, was the son of the Swede. Yet it is interesting and curious to speculate how, in that strange period, so obvious a liaison could have been concealed. For even after two centuries its existence is not universally accepted.

157

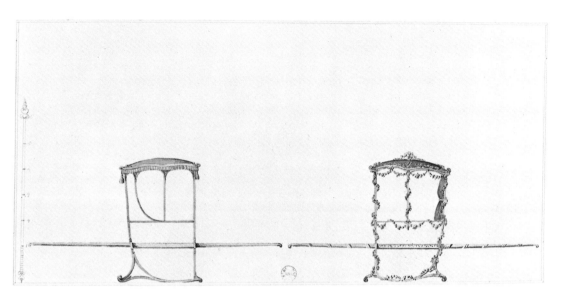

Under Louis XVI the use of sedan chairs almost died out.   Landau designed for excursions in fine-weather conditions.

Fantasy landau designed to be used for children's outings.

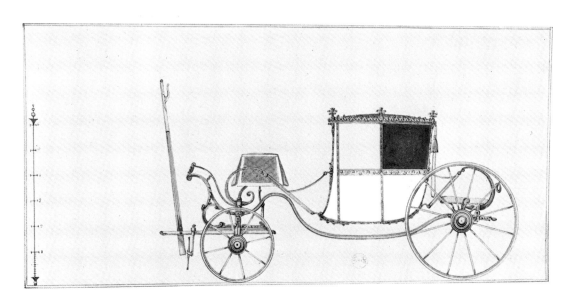

Delicate, fairy-tale-like landau with sunshade.   *Town landau with places for a coachman and valets.*

Two-seated landau designed to be pulled by lacqueys.

Never once did Fersen appear in public at the side of Marie Antoinette. Even more surprising for us, if not for his contemporaries, was the attitude of Louis XVI. Was he ignorant of the relationship between Fersen and his wife? That seems very unlikely.

"Marie Antoinette," alleges Saint Priest, "had found the means of getting him to accept her liaison with Count of Fersen." That of course is by no means certain, for no document will ever reveal the secret thoughts of the King. But at any rate Louis XVI's diary at the time of the birth of the Queen's second son, in refraining from any mention of his own paternity, is disturbing: "The Queen delivered of the Duke of Normandy," he notes on March 27th, 1783; "everything went off as in the case of my son." One finds in the diary only one occasion on which, in referring to the third of his children, he uses the term "my son", and that is in a part of the text drafted in the solitude of the prison of the Temple. However that may be, Marie Antoinette, either by a sincere confession, or by skilful discretion, seems to have retained her husband's affection and even his confidence: the period of the liaison between Marie Antoinette and Fersen was also that during which the Queen's influence on her husband was most marked, particularly in the field of politics. It seems then that the King did not suffer at all from the situation. Was not discretion, in the view of people of that day, what counted the most?

Marie Antoinette did not deprive herself of loving nor of being loved by the attractive and handsome man for whom she felt, not just a passing inclination, but an emotion which was very strong—it lasted nearly twenty years. Nevertheless, this woman who was supposed to be frivolous was sufficiently prudent in a difficult situation not to impair the harmony of her home and not to make her husband unhappy. Fersen, who was always so reserved that it is difficult to judge his feelings exactly, never married. After the Queen's death he had a brilliant career at the Court of Sweden, where he became the leader of a monarchist party hated by the masses whom he himself detested and despised. On June 20th, 1810, the anniversary of the flight to Varennes, the Grand Marshal of Sweden, Count Axel de Fersen, aged fifty-five, was following the funeral procession of the heir to the kingdom, alone in his carriage.

The crowd shouted insults. The troops made no move. The mob then rushed to the carriage of the man they hated, and in the heart of the city, with sticks and stones, massacred the friend of the guillotined queen.

How many writers, philosophers, historians, learned men and poets have tried to define the causes of the French Revolution! That search, both fascinating and vain, leads one back to the reflexions of so many remarkably clear-sighted witnesses who wrote before, during or after the last decade of the eighteenth century. Abbé de Véri foresaw with calm certainty at the beginning of Louis XVI's reign the radical upheavals which he hoped only not to live long enough to witness. To the enormous amount of material connected with the study of the origins of the Revolution it seems necessary to add an account of the Salons where the painters showed their works during the final years of the Ancien Régime. For nowhere can the evolution of opinion be better seen than in the works of the painters and sculptors. By 1781, they were mixing sentimentalism and war-like courage. At a time when everyone was seeking pleasure, heart-rending or heroic paintings were what the artists were offering and patrons were buying. Twenty years before David, Vincent showed the Sabine women stopping the fight between their Roman husbands and their Sabine brothers. Vien, that same year, showed the tender Briseis in the tent of the ardent Achilles. Van Loo was weeping over the deserted Lover, Aubry was pitying Coriolan's wife bidding farewell to her husband, and Debucourt showed a wretched peasant family being helped by a "benevolent gentleman" whose features strangely resembled those of King Louis XVI. Van Spaendonck painted flowers and fruit as was his wont, de Machy views of Paris, Hubert Robert the fire at the Opéra seen from a casement window of the Academy of Painting, and Lépicié an old man reading, while Boizot sculptured a bust of the Queen.

The atmosphere remained much the same at the Salon of 1783. It was the period of greatest glory for Greuze; the engraver Levasseur showed a reproduction of *La Cruche cassée* (The Broken Pitcher) under the modest title *La Laitière* (The Milkmaid). Lépicié, with sensitivity, showed the *Déjeuner des Elèves* (The Pupils' Luncheon), Vien another of his Greek subjects *Priam partant*

The jewellers Böhmer and Bassenge collected 540 diamonds to make this multi-tiered necklace. They sunk all their capital into it but at the time there was not one sovereign or lord who could permit himself to buy a piece of jewellery at the exorbitant price demanded. Marie Antoinette herself had refused it in 1778 when the King had wanted to give it to her on the occasion of the birth of Madame Royale.

Madame de la Motte assured Rohan that the Queen wished to buy the necklace through his intermediary.

Monsieur de la Motte acted as his wife's commissary: he fled to England to auction some of the diamonds.

Mademoiselle Oliva unknowingly played the part of the Queen when she received Rohan in the Trianon garden.

Cagliostro, the Cardinal's confidant, was falsely accused by Madame de la Motte and was sent into exile.

Louis-René-Edouard, Prince of Rohan, Cardinal and Grand Almoner of France, was seriously compromised in the Affair of the Necklace as a result of his credulity. His arrest, trial and acquittal resounded like a thunderclap throughout contempory France.

supplier Achille (Priam Leaving to Entreat Achilles) and his disciple David *La Douleur et les regrets d'Andromaque* (The Grief and Regrets of Andromache). Ménageot painted an allegory for the Dauphin's birth, and Guérin a more realistic scene: *La naissance de Monseigneur le Dauphin annoncée à l'Hôtel de Ville de Paris aussitôt que la reddition de l'armée anglaise aux ordres du Général Cornwallis* (The Birth of His Royal Highness the Dauphin Announced at the Town Hall of Paris at the Same Time as the Surrender of the English Army under General Cornwallis). In a picture by Barthélemy, Maillard was shown killing Etienne Marcel and thus saving the authority of the future King Charles V over Paris in revolt. Lecomte sculptured a bust of the Queen; and Madame Vigée-Lebrun painted her *Portrait en gaule* in a cotton dress.

If one is to judge by the subjects chosen by the artists, the Revolution and even the Terror did not start in 1789 or in 1793, but rather with the Salon of 1785. At that exhibition there appeared the manifesto picture by Jacques Louis David, the *Serment des Horaces* (The Oath of the Horatii) which immediately had a prodigious success: Horace is swearing to kill his brother-in-law, Curiace; Camilla, his sister, weeps; from the horror of that Cornelian situation beauty emerges.

But blood and death already filled the Salon. Bardin showed *L'Extrême Onction* (Extreme Unction), the younger Wille *Les Derniers Moments d'une épouse chérie* (The Last Moments of a Beloved Wife), Renaud *La Mort de Priam* (The Death of Priam), Suvée *La Mort de Cléopâtre* (The Death of Cleopatra), and Vien *Le Retour de Priam avec le Corps d'Hector* (The Return of Priam with the Body of Hector). Vincent even painted two canvases which outdid in horror all the others: *Arrie exhorte son mari Poetus à se donner la mort* (Arria Exhorts her Husband Paetus to Kill Himself) and *Arrie s'enfonce un poignard dans le sein* (Arria Plunges a Dagger into her Breast) —an example to her husband who, of course, imitates her. In the midst of these, the pleasant picture by Wertmuller *La Reine, le Dauphin et Madame Royale se promenant dans le jardin anglais du Petit Trianon* (The Queen, the Dauphin and Madame Royale Walking in the English Garden of the Petit Trianon) seems a strange anachronism.

It was no better in 1787. There were two deaths of Socrates, one by David, the other by Peyron; the death of Cato the Younger and the death of Phocion by Monsian; the death of the Duke of Brunswick by Wille,

163

Uniforms at Versailles (left to right) : the Queen's Regiment, Lord Dillon's foot-soldiers, Count Esterhazy's hussars.

Amiral de Coligny et ses assassins (Admiral de Coligny and his Assassins) by Suvée; *La Mort de Cyanippe, roi de Syracuse et de sa fille* (The Death of Cyanippos, King of Syracuse and his Daughter) by Perrin; several shipwrecks by Vernet, and *Le Courage des Femmes de Sparte* (The Courage of the Women of Sparta) by Le Barbier. But one also finds touching scenes like *Les Adieux d'Hector et d'Andromaque* (The Farewells of Hector and Andromaque) by Vien, and *Priam demandant à Achille le corps d'Hector* (Priam Asking Achilles for the Body of Hector) by Doyen, and also *L'Instruction Villageoise* (The Village School) by Bilcoq. Houdon, with eclecticism, showed the busts of the King, of Lafayette and of Washington, while Madame Vigée-Lebrun showed a large picture entitled *La Reine, Monseigneur le Dauphin, Madame et le Duc de Normandie*. Just before sending it to the exhibition, the artist had to paint out from the cradle, now shown empty, the face of Marie Antoinette's last child, the little Sophie, who had died a few days earlier.

People thronged to the Salon at the end of the eighteenth century, and it was by no means rare for 100,000 visitors to be expected

in a month—an enormous number at a time when Paris had only 300,000 inhabitants in all. Few exhibitions of contemporary painting have recorded such admission figures in the second half of the twentieth century in Paris, London, New York or Tokyo. Must one not therefore assume that the painters were reflecting the general, if still secret, state of mind? The love of life and of all its fruits concealed a while longer the dangerous, unhealthy, dreadful fascination of death.

On a warm and cheerful sunny day, suddenly and without warning, a storm breaks out. In the midst of the most perfect happiness and the most ardently desired pleasures, sometimes, like a bitter taste, we feel a wish to obliterate ourselves, not to be there, to exist no more. This terrible suicidal complex afflicts not only individuals; it can also afflict peoples or an entire social class.

So it was that in 1785 this insidious poison laid hold of high society in France, the Court, the nobility and the middle classes of Paris, and the provinces. That dreadful disease, which caused the royal couple, the Catholic Church, the princes and the rich to revile and throw mud at each other, sometimes appeared

The Count de la Mark's foot-soldiers, Fersen's Royal Swedish Regiment and the Duke of Coigny's dragoons.

like an operetta and sometimes like a medieval farce. The episode is known to history as "the Affair of the Queen's Necklace".

Slowly and insidiously, the successes of the war in America, the justified fury of the French at the aggressive policy of Joseph II in Europe, the waste and the disordered state of the finances of the Court, and the frequent indiscretions of the Queen at her public appearances, had all greatly increased the unpopularity of Marie Antoinette. The number of insulting lampoons increased. When she made her entry into Paris after the birth of her second son, the crowd remained silent; at the theatre applause for her was rare.

Yet in 1785 no one had an inkling of the power of the hatred which was brewing. The fact is that Marie Antoinette had the great misfortune to embody at that moment of history that happiness which is the dream and the very life of the French. Like them, she was frivolous, generous, superficial, a good mother according to the ideas in vogue, with just enough disregard of the conventions to make her existence full of charm. All the women would have liked to be her. Men dreamed of a companion like her.

But more or less consciously, people also wearied of a life so gay, so hectic, and so empty, for they had at the same time the painful feeling that they had tasted all its joys, even the most unforeseen. It was themselves, their ideals, their happiness and their pleasures which the rich French people, at the end of the eighteenth century, were to have occasion to hate in the person of a queen whom nobody, either at the time or since, could regard, in the sinister affair of the necklace, as a possible guilty party. But in the existing circumstances she had been outrageously herself, and that was her crime.

It was a matter of a fantastic intrigue which only the confusions of life at Court and of the royal government could have set off. Marie Antoinette, as was common knowledge, adored jewels. Her main supplier, who was later to be appointed Court Jeweller, was called Böhmer. To tempt the Queen he thought it wiser to use intermediaries, and to start by having the jewels, which he intended to recommend and sell himself, shown by friends of the Queen.

He did so in the case of a bracelet and ear-rings. The most important item he possessed was a necklace—one could call it a river of diamonds of incomparable quality—made at the very end of the reign of Louis XV in the hope of getting the ageing monarch to give it to the Countess du Barry. As long as Louis XVI had not finished paying off the Queen's debts by successive instalments, Böhmer kept quiet. In 1784 he thought the time had come for Marie Antoinette to be offered the necklace, and he sought a suitable intermediary. As ill-luck would have it, he got into touch with a dangerous intriguer, who called herself the Countess de la Motte-Valois and had been able to win the confidence of Cardinal de Rohan.

As all the regular frequenters of Versailles knew, Rohan, a member of the Académie Française, Grand Almoner of France, a prelate more interested in festivities than in his archbishopric of Strasburg, had been hated by Marie Antoinette ever since the time when, as Louis XV's ambassador to the Austrian Court, he had scandalized the Empress by his dissipated life. The Queen also wrongly believed that he had informed her mother of the smallest details of her life at Versailles (which in fact had really been done by Mercy-Argenteau). The Countess de la Motte succeeded, as if in a well-staged theatrical imbroglio, in organizing a twofold piece of trickery. She made Rohan believe that the Queen was prepared to forget her old grudge if he would help her to gain possession of the wonderful necklace. Then she gave Böhmer to understand that Rohan was the man most likely to persuade Marie Antoinette to buy a piece of jewellery which she knew but whose enormous price—one

Jean-Jacques Rousseau, painted here by de la Tour, was prominent among those who in the eighteenth century favoured a return to nature and sincerity of feeling.

166

About Greuze, who painted this "Return of the Hunter", Diderot wrote : "Here is the first painter among us to venture to bring morality to art. A little vain, but his vanity is that of a child ; it is the giddiness of talent."

million six hundred thousand pounds—had prevented her from acquiring it.

Rohan had therefore to be persuaded to help, first by an exchange of letters with Marie Antoinette, then by a fleeting encounter at night in the park of Versailles with a young person whose silhouette more or less resembled that of the Queen and who was capable, for such a brief meeting, of impersonating her. Rohan, while not much of a believer as a priest, was extremely credulous : he believed in the charlatan's tricks of an adventurer called Cagliostro, and in the so-called "magnetic box" of a certain Anton Mesmer, who was credited with miraculous cures. With equal ease he imagined that

Marie Antoinette's attitude was changing towards him, although she still never spoke to him. He was thus quite ready to persuade Böhmer to entrust the necklace to him in exchange for a contract to purchase it by instalments. This contract bore the forged signature of the Queen.

So it was that in January 1785 Cardinal de Rohan secretly bought in Marie Antoinette's name and on her behalf a necklace worth one million six hundred thousand francs (over £835,000 or two million dollars). Payment was to be made over two years, a first payment on the following August 15th. The river of diamonds was handed over to the Countess de la Motte-Valois who, instead of taking it

Et qu'est-ce donc qui a couché avec ma femme?

*The Queen was known to read the new form of literature,
the novel of manners, that was becoming popular among
the upper classes. The above engraving is taken from
"The Loves of the Chevalier de Faublas" by de Couvray.*

payment of the first instalment was near,
Böhmer, who had occasion to see the Queen,
alluded to the purchase. A problem, forever
insoluble, concerns the time when Marie
Antoinette was informed of the swindle: was
it in July or not until August? If the former,
she knowingly let the scandal break to ensure
that the Cardinal was ignominiously condemned; if the latter, she took a very foolish
decision on a sudden impulse.

However that may be, on August 9th,
1785, Böhmer explained the affair verbally
and in detail to Marie Antoinette, who at the
time was very busy at the Trianon with
rehearsals of the *Barber of Seville*, in which she
was playing the part of Rosine. She asked for
a written report, which she received on the
12th, and communicated to the King on the 14th.

For Marie Antoinette there was no doubt
possible: duke or no, Cardinal de Rohan had
committed lese-majesty. The honour of a
queen required that the Grand Almoner of
France be arrested next day, the feast of
Corpus Christi, even though he was to

*Louvet de Couvray cleverly mixed sensibility in the
Jean-Jacques Rousseau sense with erotic romanticism.*

to Marie Antoinette—whom she did not
even know—had the stones taken from their
settings. She sold some of them in Paris and
sent her husband to negotiate the sale of the
majority on the London market.

The swindle could not fail to come to light.
The Paris police were first informed that the
diamonds were being sold at abnormally low
prices. But that track was not pursued,
because it soon led to the Countess de la
Motte and her important connections and
patronage. When the first time for the

celebrate it with great pomp at Versailles. Louis XVI, with the approval of at any rate one of his ministers, Breteuil, who had long been the declared enemy of the Cardinal, complied with the Queen's wishes.

The scandal was unprecedented: before an immense gathering of courtiers, Rohan was arrested in all his priestly robes and taken off to the Bastille. The King could have himself sentenced Rohan to imprisonment or exile. At the Queen's instigation, he committed the supreme error of having the Cardinal tried by the Parliament of Paris.

If the King, the Queen and Breteuil did everything wrong, even allowing Rohan time before he was imprisoned to send a secretary to destroy compromising papers at his home, the French authorities on the other hand were excellent, and the investigation was carried out efficiently, speedily and successfully. First of all, the departure for London of the Count de la Motte, who refused to appear in court, then the disappearance of the necklace itself, incriminated Madame de la Motte-Valois, who, in turn and to divert suspicion, claimed to have given it to Cagliostro, Rohan's friend. Immediately the "magician" was also arrested, while to justify her sudden and unexpected prosperity the Countess de la Motte-Valois claimed to be the mistress of the Grand Almoner of France. The interrogation of the witnesses, however, threw light on the plot.

A former convict, crook and forger, named Pétaux, confessed that he had fabricated the alleged letters from Marie Antoinette to the Cardinal; and the little modiste, who had been made to play the part of the Queen of France one evening in the park of Versailles, recounted her adventure with amusing candour. In fact, everything was becoming clear: the diabolical schemings of the Countess de la Motte-Valois had deceived the naive Cardinal, whose fault, serious it is true, was to have been lacking in respect for his Queen.

But then the affair took on an entirely new turn. By this time the whole of France, nobility, middle classes and masses, were fascinated by this fantastic story in which so many powerful personalities had been hoaxed. Rare were those who regarded the Queen as entirely innocent. Had she not taken advantage of Rohan's naivety to try to secure for herself a long-coveted piece of jewellery? Why had Marie Antoinette not taken action immediately after Böhmer's first revelations?

In "The Perverted Peasant" Restif de la Bretonne real-istically portrayed the corrupt customs in Paris.

Moreover, it was very soon no longer a question of knowing the whole truth. What Parliament was to judge was not a crime of lese-majesty or a swindle, but a series of trials of an entirely different order. First of all the Church of France found itself affected as a whole by the public affront to the Grand Almoner. Was it not possible to have had him arrested more discreetly? Great efforts were made to get the Pope to act, and to convince Parliament that a cardinal was only responsible to an ecclesiastical court. The

169

When building the Church of St. Genevieve Germain Soufflot had roman models in mind : the Pantheon of Agrippa and St. Peter Basilica. The church's name was changed to the Pantheon under the Revolution.

French nobility, indifferent, frivolous and divided, suddenly felt an entirely new feeling of solidarity with Rohan, who was related to the greatest families of France, the Soubises, the Marsans, and the Condés. The highest dignitaries of the country closed their ranks around the threatened prince.

The Parliament of Paris itself consisted of magistrates who were largely of a more or less recent nobility, or related—thanks to their wealth—to princes or dukes. Very strong pressure was now brought to bear on the magistrates by their relations and friends. Finally, the immense mass of tax-payers was revolted at the idea that money collected for taxes might be used to buy jewels for a coquette queen. All of their anger was fused, not against the Cardinal, but against the scandalous practices which made it possible to have the crown jewels paid for by peasants who could not even feed their families.

The acquittal of the Cardinal soon appeared certain. But there were two possible solutions : Marie Antoinette's partisans demanded that Rohan be reprimanded for the "excessive temerity" he had shown in coming to greet the make-believe Queen secretly in the woods of Versailles, and for purchasing outside normal channels a river of diamonds for his queen. In this case he would lose his positions and would have to make a humble apology.

The other side wanted a complete acquittal, on the grounds that Rohan had been duped and was entirely innocent. But in that case

In spite of the ruin of the State, the architect Boullée conceived a project for transforming the Château of Versailles.

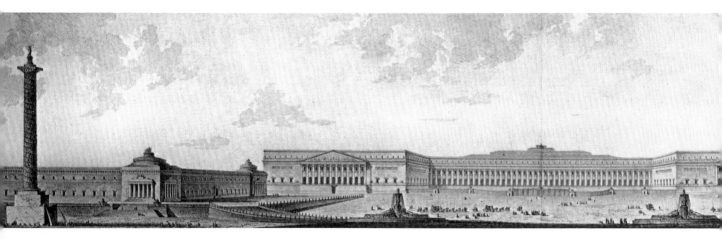

Marie Antoinette would indirectly be condemned, for Parliament would then be implicitly recognizing that the Cardinal had good reason for thinking that the Queen used unorthodox means to obtain her jewellery.

In the weeks and days preceding the magistrates' decision, Paris afforded a spectacle which was little in keeping with the serenity of justice or the minimum of public spirit necessary for the stability of a State. A prodigious amount of tracts, journals and lampoons were published throughout France about various shades of meaning in a pronouncement by the Parliament. As the fateful date approached, professional activity was all but suspended: everyone was discussing the indiscretions of a queen and the follies of a cardinal. The two sides, that of Rohan and that of Marie Antoinette, intensified their approaches to all members of the Parliament. These gentlemen were cajoled, visited and overwhelmed with gifts. Everyone was humming the verse:

> If this decree of Parliament
> Seemed to you too illegal
> Know that high finance....
> Governs all in France
> Hearken to me well!

On May 31st, 1786, the day on which the judgment was to be delivered, the whole of Paris had been out in the streets since dawn.

The architect François-Joseph Bélanger proposed this entrance for the pavilion of the Count of Lauraguais.

Boullée's imagination swelled to outrageous proportions.

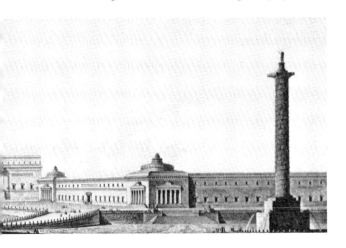

By five in the morning the streets surrounding the Palace of Justice were black with people. The crowd overflowed into neighbouring streets, on to the Pont-Neuf, and even on to part of the right bank. As the police with difficulty opened a way through the crowd towards the old Palace of St. Louis, the sixty-four members of Parliament were quite conscious of the importance of the decision they were to deliver on the singular question of the jewels, and thereby the fate of the French monarchy. Nineteen representatives of the high nobility related to the Cardinal, all dressed in mourning, had taken up positions before the entrance to the great Hall of Parliament where the magistrates were to deliberate. None spoke when a judge arrived, but all approached together and bowed in a sign of humble supplication.

The incredibly long hearing lasted for sixteen hours. After the Advocate-General's

171

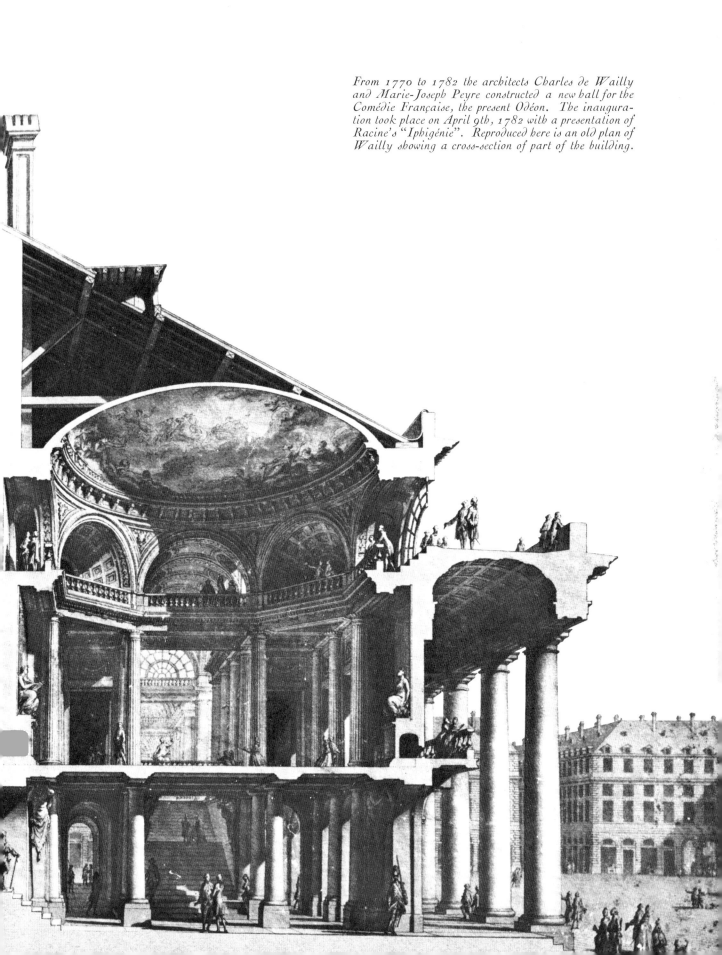

From 1770 to 1782 the architects Charles de Wailly and Marie-Joseph Peyre constructed a new hall for the Comédie Française, the present Odéon. The inauguration took place on April 9th, 1782 with a presentation of Racine's "Iphigénie". Reproduced here is an old plan of Wailly showing a cross-section of part of the building.

In 1777 the Baron de Breteuil decided to build a hotel in the new Rue de Provence. Above can be seen a cross-section of the buildings together with the decorations for the main courtyard.

On the garden side, the hotel's façade expresses simplicity and airiness, in spite of the rather heavy draughtsmanship.

Marie Antoinette was never to see the completion of work on her apartments at Compiègne which were finished in 1789.

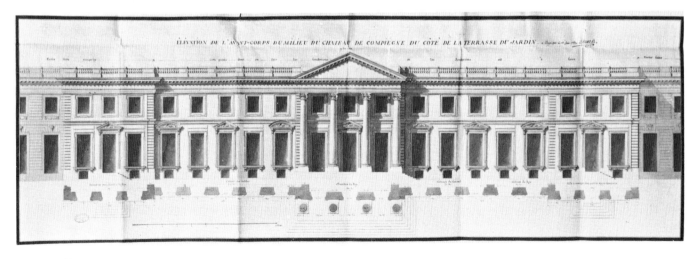

address, the admonishments of the President, and the explanations of each judge, the verdict, a very close one (25 votes to 22), came at ten o'clock at night. Rohan was completely acquitted. The little modiste Oliva, too, was pardoned. Only Madame de la Motte-Valois was sentenced to the horrible punishment of being lashed by whips, branded on her shoulder as a thief with a red-hot iron in the shape of a V, and shut up for the rest of her days in the prison of the Salpétrière. The outcome recalls both the plays of Beaumarchais and the stories of the Marquis de Sade. It produced an extraordinary outburst of enthusiasm. All night long, the Parisians expressed their joy. There were repeated shouts of "Long live Parliament!"; the cry of "Long live the King!", as natural on all occasions in those days as "Hooray!" is today, was totally forgotten. Rohan in his cardinal's scarlet left the Palace of Justice in the midst of a noisy crowd which accompanied him to the Bastille where he was officially set free.

Assassinated in her reputation, her dignity as Queen and her honour as a woman, Marie Antoinette received these news as a totally unforeseeable blow. With a shock she became aware of the gravity of the situation. In a letter to her brother, and her avowals to those close to her, the depths of her despair appear. Marie Antoinette, frivolous but sensitive, understood in a confused sort of way that her own death-warrant had been signed.

Nevertheless she put up a fight. She asked for and obtained from her husband penalties, not against the judges who had indirectly accused her, but against Rohan and his friends. The Cardinal was banished, and Cagliostro exiled. The Countess de la Motte-Valois was indeed soundly punished by the lash and then branded with a red-hot iron by fourteen executioners who had the greatest difficulty in overcoming this roaring lioness. She fought to such effect that she was burnt on the breast and not on the shoulder, underscoring the odious cruelty of the punishment. Imprisoned, she received visits from ladies of the highest society who came to sympathize with her "misfortune". The Duke of Orleans started a public collection on her behalf.

In 1777 the Count of Artois purchased the property of Bagatelle and Marie Antoinette challenged her brother-in-law to have a building constructed there in less than three months. The architect Bélanger finished the work in fifty days.

After a few weeks, thanks to mysterious influences, she actually managed to escape and get to England. From there, she published memoir after memoir. She explained how Marie Antoinette had in fact ordered the necklace, and she claimed that Rohan had already been the lover of the very young archduchess in Austria, and that she herself, physically, had been the Queen's friend. Torrents of mud were hurled across the Channel. In spite of the most incredible improbabilities, absurdities and contradictions, the French regaled themselves for years with these appalling slanders.

The dominant passion for politics of Maria Theresa doubtless helped to turn her husband, the Emperor Francis of Lorraine, from this aspect of governing, and it must also have disillusioned most of her children with such a difficult art. Only two devoted themselves to it with any success, and fate decreed that they should become emperor one after the other. While Leopold II was cool and skilful like his mother, Joseph II took things less seriously, considering his profession as sovereign a fascinating game which he preferred to all others. Maria Theresa's daughters and her younger sons were very mediocre at politics, and yet they were far from lacking in intelligence or other necessary qualities such as a stately bearing and a sense of authority. But they were not capable of the constant application and patience essential for keeping oneself well informed and bringing difficult affairs of State to a successful conclusion.

In the field of politics, Marie Antoinette deserved neither the praises of her rare supporters in the past century, nor the horrible accusations made against her and renewed in our own time. The reason is very simple : she had no head for politics. Mercy was constantly complaining about this. The Queen was interested in details, or in great issues such as international alliances, peace and war, and the defence of the monarchical system ; but anything between those two extremes, such as a decision of foreign policy, the choice of a minister, or the adoption of economic and social measures bored her, and appeared to her (as to many of our contemporaries) to be abstract and tedious. It needed a real drama directly affecting herself to bring her to engage in serious correspondence or devote herself to true political problems. Marie Antoinette was not interested and never would be interested in any new law. One finds her violently berating a minister, and then neglecting to request his resignation from the King, and even more quickly forgetting all resentment.

Thus, in spite of the extreme indecision of Louis XVI and his inexhaustible complaisance towards his wife, Marie Antoinette for a long time had no share in the responsibility for the choice of his chief advisors. Maurepas, Turgot, Vergennes, and Necker were chosen through the influence of Madame Adélaide, and sometimes that of Vermond, but in no case that of the Quenn. Her candidate for minister, Choiseul, very quickly learned that he could expect nothing from so unstable a patroness. "It is a fact," Mercy wrote one day to Joseph II, "that the Queen's feelings guide those of her august husband, but it is equally a fact that this influence has very little effect on the way things go." She candidly and mischievously confessed to her brother : "I let the public believe that I count for more than I really do, because if they did not believe me, I would count for still less."

Nevertheless, on various occasions, Marie Antoinette did play a political role. At such times she was an instrument in the hands of intriguers or a political faction. This was the case at the time of the fall of Turgot, when Choiseul's supporters rubbed salt in the wound caused by the severe repression of the "flour war" and made use of the personal charm of the Count de Guines. A similar intrigue, conducted this time by a master at manœuvering, Baron de Besenval, in 1780 made the Marquis de Ségur the Minister of War. The choice was a good one ; but it was piquant for those "in the know" to reflect that the Baron, a talented novelist and connoisseur of art, had long been the friend of the Marquise de Ségur and the father of her second son, the Chevalier de Ségur, who was also to achieve literary distinction.

Promotions in the army depended on the Minister of War. All the young noblemen who frequented Court and surrounded the Queen were serving as officers ; hence her interest in that department. One day Count

It was the fashion at Court for the Queen to have favourites among her ladies. The Duchess of Polignac, painted here by Mme Vigée-Lebrun, soon supplanted the Princess of Lamballe in Marie Antoinette's heart.

Montbarrey, who was at the time chief assistant to the Minister, chose as second-in-command of the Royal Regiment of Dragoons a certain Count Laval Montmorency, a first-rate officer whose father had been killed in action. Montbarrey, as he writes in his memoirs, was unaware that Marie Antoinette had a candidate for the post:

The next day, Quasimodo Sunday (the first Sunday after Easter), I received orders to go to the Queen at half-past four. This princess having had me called into the bedroom, I perceived a lively change in all her features and an air which made me think she was agitated by a violent passion…. She led me to the first window in her room nearest the entrance to her apartment, and there she began in a most animated tone to reproach me bitterly for having ignored the favour she had desired for a protégé…. It was in vain that I protested that I had not known of the interest with which she honoured her protégé…. Nothing could calm the anger to which she continued to give vent with such force that I found myself compelled to reply to Her Majesty that I had at pains not to forget that I was in the presence of the wife of my Master and sovereign in order to contain and repress all the feelings which afflicted and constricted my heart.

Louis XVI did his best to pacify Montbarrey, but asked him to avoid, as far as possible, meeting the Queen. It was good advice. Some time later Montbarrey became Minister of War and Marie Antoinette raised no objection to his promotion.

It so happened that both of Louis XVI's principal ministers were skilled at manœuvering. Maurepas, and Vergennes to an even greater extent, knew the art of appearing to give way at the time while in fact conceding nothing essential.

In 1784, Joseph II, with an irresponsibility worthy of his sister's character, embarked on a diplomatic struggle which could at any time have degenerated into an armed conflict with the Dutch Republic, the neighbour to the Austrian Low Countries. There was a danger that the Franco-Austrian Treaty of 1755, which was still in force, might drag the kingdom into an absurd war. Vergennes tried to explain this to his Queen. Marie Antoinette merely replied: "One would be failing in all proprieties if one did not oblige the Emperor in this matter."

Vergennes then retreated. He gave the Queen to understand that he agreed that France should send Holland a totally unacceptable ultimatum. Then in the Council of Ministers he persuaded Louis XVI to do nothing of the kind but to reply to Joseph II that he disapproved of his bellicose policy. The furious emperor did not even complain to his sister; he wrote slyly to his ambassador, the aged Mercy-Argenteau: "There is no doubt that Vergennes tricked the Queen and you as well, my dear Count…."

That was not the end of the matter. There were many repercussions and further violent scenes between Vergennes and Marie Antoinette. Nevertheless, that excellent diplomat managed not only to preserve peace, but also the friendship of the Dutch Republic which was so important for France, always anxious about England's progress.

To restore the state of public finances, Marie Antoinette in 1783 suggested the appointment of a new controller-general who, like Turgot, was the administrator of a province. He was a friend of the Count of Vaudreuil, the Count of Artois, the Duchess of Polignac, and the lover, it was said, of Madame Vigée-Lebrun, official portrait painter to the Queen. These were strong claims on the Queen's patronage. The choice of Calonne, to all appearances excellent, proved under the difficult circumstances which France was going through to be deplorable. To revive confidence and credit, Calonne embarked on lavish expenditure; he bought for the King Rambouillet in the heart of a forest abounding in game; and for the Queen, St. Cloud, half-way between Versailles and Paris.

Finally Calonne, having run out of expedients, discovered too late that the country's salvation lay in the political and fiscal measures advocated ten years earlier by Turgot, and in particular in the establishment of a certain equality in respect of taxation. He believed that he could secure the adoption of measures which were highly unpopular with the privileged through an Assembly of Notables carefully chosen from among those most in favour of such a policy. This became the occasion for an outburst of extremely violent criticism of the royal government and also of the Queen. Rather than vote for tax reform, the Notables, at the instigation of Monsieur, the King's brother, attempted to obtain political measures to limit the absolute power of the King. This factious Assembly had to be dissolved. Calonne's policy had failed. He had to retire in 1787.

These miniatures, decorations on a snuff-box, show scenes from various plays acted by Marie Antoinette at the little theatre of the Trianon. Among the pieces chosen for performance were Rousseau's "The Village Soothsayer", Beaumarchais's "The Barber of Seville" and "Rose and Colas" by Sedaine. The actors, according to Madame Campan, were good for amateurs; the audience would applaud them heartily and then make adverse comments on the way out.

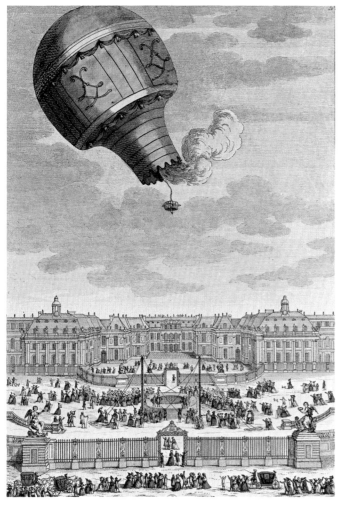

The first Mongolfière balloon ascent took place at Versailles in 1783 in the presence of the royal family. It carried a cock, a duck and a sheep which, to the admiration of all, came back safe and sound.

Then it was that the Queen, conscious at last of the danger threatening the country, the royal dynasty and perhaps even the civilization she loved, attempted to deal herself with matters of State. Nobody knew better than she the inadequacies of the King and the abuses of the favourites. She showed some courage in choosing as her principal minister a man who was supposed to have been won over to the new ideas, but whom her brother Joseph II, and Vermond and Turgot, her friends, looked on as the best political brain in France. He was Loménie

de Brienne, who although an unbeliever was Archbishop of Sens.

Louis XVI had accepted him with repugnance. Marie Antoinette tried to help him all she could. She braved the resignations of two ministers who did not wish to have over them a real prime minister. In implementing the Archbishop's first measures, she obliged her favourites to give up most of their financial privileges. Marie Antoinette was quite happy to fall out with the Duke and Duchess of Polignac. The Count of Vaudreuil, who had been brought up with the former favourite and benefited from many royal favours, was ruined in a few weeks, and had to auction off his magnificent collection of paintings.

Unfortunately, Loménie de Brienne's reputation proved entirely unfounded. Furthermore, the economic, political and psychological situation worsened so rapidly that the most justified of his measures proved, at that stage, ineffective. Brienne exhausted himself in a sterile struggle with the Parliaments in an effort to get them to pass the most essential and most urgent tax laws. It was also the period when the Dauphin, the Queen's eldest son, had fallen seriously ill.

Marie Antoinette thought no more of balls, of buildings, or of dresses. She concerned herself with the education of her children, and belatedly tried to learn about political problems. She got her obliging husband to allow her occasionally to attend the Council. But what could such a woman understand about the terribly difficult questions that she never had the patience to analyse?

The inconsistencies and unpopularity of Brienne, and his blunders, rebounded on to the Queen. When Marie Antoinette went abroad in Paris people shouted: "There goes the deficit!" And right in front of the royal couple at the Comédie Française, the audience frantically applauded a passage from Racine's *Athalie*:

Confonds dans ses desseins cette reine cruelle!
Daigne, Daigne, mon Dieu, sur Nathan et sur elle
Répande cet esprit d'imprudence et d'erreur,
De la chute des rois funeste avant-coureur.

(Confound in her designs this cruel queen!
Deign, deign, my God, on Nathan and on her
To shed that spirit of imprudence and error
Which is the fatal forerunner of the fall
of kings.)

From then on it seemed necessary to Marie Antoinette to call on the only minister who

180

was popular, even though he had speeded public finances to their ruin through his loans and favours. Necker won the support of the French by having the effrontery to denounce the extravagances of the Court and the blunders of the Government. Marie Antoinette resigned herself to that solution nevertheless, although she found it loathsome. She demanded the resignation of Loménie de Brienne and accepted Necker's humiliating conditions.

"A brake must be applied," she noted. "The personage above me," she continued with clear-sightedness, "is not in a state to do so; and I, whatever people say and whatever happens, always have to take second place."

It was the autumn of 1788. After Loménie de Brienne's departure, Marie Antoinette kept entirely out of politics and confined herself more and more to her children and a small circle of real friends who did not belong to the group of her former favourites. She read, painted, embroidered and played music. The news of the grave decision to convene the States General, and to double the representation of the third estate, reached her as a faint echo. Her brief incursion into affairs of State simply afforded her the opportunity of realizing how serious was the tragedy which loomed ahead. The insults as she passed in public, and the diminishing number of people who attended the Court festivities, were a constant reminder. In the anxious expectation of events which everyone felt would be decisive for the future of France and of the Monarchy, Marie Antoinette sought refuge in her friends and above all else in art. She devoted much time to it, and perhaps she found here some serenity or consolation.

Pierre-Joseph-Victor de Besenval was a colonel in the Swiss guards, a lieutenant-general and one of the Queen's intimate friends.

WINTER

Circumstances prevented Kucharski from finishing this portrait of Marie Antoinette at the age of thirty-six. According to the governess, the Countess de Tourzel, the likeness was perfect.

The Place de la Concorde was originally designed by Gabriel to show to advantage the equestrian statue of Louis XV. In 1792 the statue was removed and the square, formely dedicated to Louis the Beloved, became the Place de la Révolution.

For Marie Antoinette, the Revolutionary period began with frightening omens. Her eldest son lay at death's door, still conscious, his pain-wracked body deformed by an incurable illness. An outburst of scurrilous satire, a real tidal wave of hatred throughout the country, answered her need for popularity.

And yet, apart from her sorrows as a mother, Marie Antoinette appeared to have no inkling of the approaching tragedy, but rather felt that she was plunging into an enthralling adventure. The quintessence of her character, her passion for movement, her taste for new things, her desire to please and particularly the hunger for her own happiness and that of others, had not changed. But circumstances had, as it were, refined them. She was no longer coquettish with the gallants at court, instead, she flirted dangerously in the Woods of St. Cloud where she succeeded in secretly rallying Mirabeau, the most influential Revolutionary leader, to the cause of the monarchy. Later, in the coach bringing her back from Varennes, she managed to beguile the austere Barnave amidst hostile cries and threats of death by the crowd.

Worn down by suffering, and with her hair almost white, Marie Antoinette was even more beautiful, more womanly, after her fall from glory than she had been when she was queen. Trapped in the Tuileries Palace, confined to the Temple prison, isolated and guarded night and day in a dungeon of the Conciergerie; heaped with frightful accusations, and a hair's breadth removed from being condemned to death, she still aroused extraordinary devotion. Her love of life, people and objects remained intact, as did her unshakeable confidence in the future. She never gave up. Before going to the scaffold, she still gave evidence of coquetry, and her last dress was of dignified, elegant simplicity. During the time she was a prisoner, she continued to carry on her children's education, wove, embroidered, played music, and wrote until her strength was exhausted. Flowers and animals surrounded her. Right until the end, she made plans to escape; before the Revolutionary tribunal, she still hoped to be acquitted. But in particular, her despair never incited her at any time to abjure the good-will towards everyone that was so much a part of her nature. The royal couple never used force against their enemies, unless it were to put down a revolt or to defend themselves.

In the awe-inspiring continuation of her whole life's dream, the image of Marie Antoinette became purified, although basically unchanged. Fragonard's shepherdess appeared as David's heroine, and this progression helps us to understand the relationship between these artists, whose inspiration seems so contradictory. These two painters portray an ideal of universal happiness in the surrender to sensitivity and the senses. David schematized, simplified and emphasized the heroic aspect of the conquest of the Garden of Eden, but the bodies of his men and women, which are beautiful and desirable in the *Serment des Horaces* or *Les Sabines* are of a more audacious sensuality than the flower women of the *Escarpolette* or the *Fête à Saint-Cloud*. This is how Marie Antoinette appeared in the midst of the riots or under the Reign of Terror. During the evening of December 5th, 1789, a hostile crowd besieged the Palace of Versailles; the Queen did not demand that the troops disperse these dangerous attackers. The next day, after the palace had been occupied, and in spite of the threats of death, Marie Antoinette appeared on the balcony before the armed rabble. Yet the night before Count Fersen had occupied the chamber which had been secretly reserved for him in the Queen's suite.

Such is the paradox of happiness. To believe that one need sacrifice neither one's own pleasure, nor that of others, is perhaps idealistic, for the two are often irreconcilable. But this passionate quest for an impossible happiness, a quest in which were to be lost Marie Antoinette, the artists, the men of politics and all the witnesses of this extraordinary period, immoral and virtuous, selfish and generous—this has the grandiose beauty of a tragic fate foreseen and freely accepted.

At the beginning of May, the States General met at Versailles. On May 4th, a long procession passed through the town and a Te Deum was sung at St. Louis Church. Marie Antoinette courageously upheld her position during the ceremonies, although, as Jefferson, the future president of the United States, wrote: "She knew that she was detested and that an explosion was not impossible."

A witness, Miot de Mélito, accurately described the atmosphere during these days when the storm was brewing:

Out of curiosity, I attended the ceremony which preceded the eve of the opening of the States General. In this long procession which passed along the wide streets of Versailles, the public noted with pain the differences of rank and clothing which distinguished between these men who were supposed to have equal rights. They were hurt at seeing the gold flaunted on the deputies' and nobility's shoulders, while a humble, black woollen cloak protected the deputies of the third estate. Yet the latter's firm expressions drew warm cheers which were not granted to the other ranks. The King walked forward in his usual way, without dignity, and seemed to fulfil a simple duty prescribed by etiquette. The Queen, her forehead lined with worry, and her lips pressed tightly together, vainly tried to hide her uneasiness and give her noble and majestic face an expression of satisfaction which the flutter of her heart, oppressed with worry and dissembled thoughts, promptly dispelled.

During that day, Marie Antoinette was continually humiliated by the crowd whose "Fie, away with you!" drowned out the rarely favourable cries; and by the Duchess of Orleans, the first princess of the blood, who snubbed her by refusing to accompany her in the carriage, and even by the silence of the Court and the royal family, who triumphantly witnessed her abasement.

On the next day, May 5th, the first session of the States General took place at the Hôtel des Menus Plaisirs. An armchair, two steps below the royal throne, was intended for Marie Antoinette. There was an icy silence at her entrance. Madame de Staël, Necker's daughter, noted that Marie Antoinette was "very moved" and that "she changed colour". During Louis XVI's speech, the Queen remained standing, her eyes lowered. Then Necker spoke, interminably, and insistently. It was then that the atmosphere changed.

"At the end of this speech," the American Gouverneur Morris noted in his diary, "the King rose to leave; he was greeted with a long and touching cheer of 'Long live the King'. The Queen rose, and for the first time for months, the cheer of 'Long live the Queen' was heard. She made an extremely gracious curtsy, and the cheers redoubled; she acknowledged them even more graciously." But this brief success was not to last.

In the course of forty days, during May and June, 1789, decisive events were to take place under the appearances of tedious procedural disputes. The States General formed by the nobility, the clergy and the third estate, who were called together in council by an absolute monarch, were changed into a parliamentary assembly whose rôle was to check the government and then to lead the country. This was to throw all the traditional structures in France into confusion. The decisive sessions took place on June 17th, when several hundreds of deputies formed the National Assembly; and on June 20th, when they took refuge in the Jeu de Paume and the deputies took an oath not to separate until they had given France a new constitution.

The position of the monarchy now deteriorated with lightning speed. Louis XVI was incapable of appreciating the significance of the deputies' daily discussions, which understandably seemed trifling to him. Very wrongly, he considered them to be scarcely dangerous. Meanwhile, as their fate was thus being decided, Louis XVI and Marie Antoinette were preoccupied with family problems which distracted them from politics. At the castle of Meudon, a few leagues from Versailles, Marie Antoinette watched over her eldest son who died on June 14th at one o'clock in the morning. And during a week of major importance, the King and Queen hid their unconsolable grief in solitude at Marly. When they tore themselves away from their despair, it was already too late. The Revolution was not a coherent series of political, economic and social events. What actually changed during the summer of 1789 was the state of mind of a country, the heart of the French. To feel how the rhythm of its beat progressed, it is useless to consult historical accounts which only skim the surface of the facts; the literary, and particularly the artistic works of this period help us to understand the processes of thought and the revolution of feeling. During 1789, theatrical and literary production sank into a very characteristic mediocrity. There were great writers, but these men—Chénier, Sade, Restif, and Laclos did not publish anything, and Beaumarchais did not put on any new plays. The authors who carried off a great success were brilliant journalists such as Chamfort and Rivarol, Camille Desmoulins and Marat and orators like Barnave and Robespierre. At the theatre, the general public only acclaimed imitations of former works in which it found allusions to contemporary events. A keen observer of the France of 1789, the bookseller Campe of Brunswick, noted during that summer:

Amidst the thousands of persons swarming on the Pont-Neuf, in the Tuileries, or along the

OPENING
OF THE STATES-GENERAL
AT VERSAILLES,
MAY 5TH, 1789

On May 5th, 1789 representatives of the nobility, the clergy and the third estate met together as a States General in the Hôtel des Menus Plaisirs at Versailles. During the opening ceremony Marie Antoinette was extremely moved and according to Madame de Staël her face changed colour. Another witness, the American Gouverneur Morris, noted that for the first time for many months shouts of "Long Live the Queen" could be heard.

boulevards, there is hardly anyone who walks slowly and phlegmatically and whose features are not in constant agitation. This gives the Parisian crowd an originality not found elsewhere; it is livelier and noisier than any other. Everyone talks, sings, shouts or whistles instead of remaining silent like our people at home.

Perpetual agitation, superficial excitement, a frenetic need to drug themselves with words, new decisions, changes which were or were not real, characterized this extraordinary period in history. At the Salon of 1789, in the Louvre, despite the presence of very great painters and sculptors, current events occupied the position of importance. Houdon exhibited exclusively busts of famous men in favour, and Pajou those of his friends. In the pictures, although the subjects were still for the most part religious, mythological or historical, many allusions to the current circumstances were to be found. Vien painted Cupid "fleeing slavery"; Hubert Robert devoted himself to the *Demolition of the Bastille*; and Durameau, as well as Jean-Michel Moreau and several others, portrayed the inauguration of the States General. The number of portraits, flowers and landscapes increased. But David's contribution offered a fearsome warning. One of his paintings bore the title of *Brutus, the first consul, back in his house after condemning to death his two sons who had conspired against Roman liberty ; the lictors bring back the bodies....* On the right, Brutus' wife and daughters shriek with grief at the sight of the corpses. On the left, the pensive consul indulges in the bitter satisfaction of having done his duty. Brutus' philosophy announced and summed up all the Revolutionary excesses. In the eyes of the greatest painter of the period, the hope of establishing a better world, the importance given to the words "happiness" and "liberty" justified a father sacrificing the life of his only two sons.

The brutal intrusion of politics into the choice of subjects in painting heralded changes much more profound. Indeed, during the Revolution, the daily life of all men was so deeply involved with the events in which they took part, and reality was confused to such an extent with a dream or an ideal that the relationship between the public and the artists changed radically. Because material circumstances, the lack of commissions for paintings and the disappearance of any peaceful surroundings in which to work; and also simply

because of changes in the way people thought, great works became increasingly rare. Artists who before had been more ambitious now rushed to portray the most recent event and illustrate and flatter the rapid changes in public opinion. For a time, great art remained in suspense, as it were, and was replaced by a literary or artistic journalism. Many painters even stopped exhibiting or working altogether. Madame Vigée-Lebrun went into voluntary exile. Fragonard apparently refrained from painting from 1790 onwards. Hubert Robert produced only works of minor importance. Although David painted some extraordinary canvases, he devoted most of his time to political activities. He was not alone in this; many painters whose work had been commissioned by Marie Antoinette enthusiastically enlisted in the ranks of the Revolutionaries. Confronted with the awe-inspiring range of the Revolutionary scene, the artists, with their imagination and sensitivity, sensed the futility of individual works and transformed their rapturous artistic emotion into political passion. This is why it is not proper to speak of Revolutionary art. During this period, artistic production wilted; it was either a relic of times past or was limited to a few exceptional works. For the real work of art of this age was the Revolution itself, in which not only the great thinkers, writers and artists took part, but a whole nation. The doors of creative inspiration, imagination and freedom, which were normally reserved for a very small minority, were suddenly thrown open to all. Each individual, rich or poor, brilliant or less gifted, shared in an extraordinary collective work. From the months of June 1789 onwards, every Frenchman found himself in the same situation as a painter before his canvas, a writer before his paper, or a sculptor before his clay; everything seemed attainable. The deputies, the electors and the people not only practised the art of governing or reforming, but also the business of challenging all or part of the established order and of thinking out a completely new state of affairs. Louis XVI and Marie Antoinette, powerless and for a long time unbelieving witnesses of the events taking place around them, experienced and were subjected to these brusque changes.

The dramatic clash between the traditional government and a society which was already in a state of perpetual transformation, came

On October 5th Saint Priest suggested that the Queen should take the children to Rambouillet while the King gave himself up to the Parisians. The Queen refused and everyone stayed at Versailles.

The royal family managed to pass the summer of 1790 at the Palace of St. Cloud. It is there that Marie Antoinette received the Count Mirabeau, who promised her he would save the toppling monarchy.

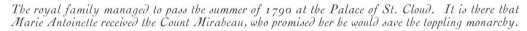

at the end of June. A royal session had been planned for June 22nd, during which the King was to ratify or denounce the decisions taken by the Assembly. Necker, the most influential minister, was in favour of giving in. Prompted by her brothers-in-law, the Queen brusquely interrupted a very long discussion at Marly during which Necker had almost convinced Louis XVI, and succeeded in persuading the King to disavow the Assembly's decisions.

Louis XVI's interference was received even less kindly by the deputies since Necker, demonstrating his disapproval of his sovereign's attitude, refrained from accompanying him. The majority refused to give in, so the King capitulated, partly out of an unwillingness to fight, no doubt, but also to gain time.

During the last days of June, Louis XVI brought back to Paris the troops which had been stationed in the country. They were mostly foreign regiments, German or Swiss. The language barrier had probably prevented them being infected by Revolutionary ideas.

At the beginning of July, the Maréchal de Broglie, a famous soldier, was appointed commander of the Palace of Versailles; under his orders, Besenval, the Queen's friend and colonel of the Swiss guards, was charged with the supervision of Paris. Far from calming public opinion, these energetic measures stirred up the people. From June 30th onwards, Paris seethed with emotion. The electors' Assembly, which had chosen the city's deputies in the States General, met illegally. The French guards regiment and the Paris Police Force no longer obeyed its officers. The revolt against discipline spread throughout the French and foreign troops who had begun to arrive at the outskirts of the capital. There were many desertions among the Swiss and Germans, who were lodged, as was customary, in private houses, and most of the soldiers swore that they would neither take up arms against the Assembly nor against the population. Even the companies of body-guards consisting of members of the nobility and responsible for the defence of the Palace of Versailles could no longer be relied on; it seemed impossible any longer to impose any rules or discipline.

In its blindness, the royal couple chose this moment to restore the sovereign's authority. Necker and three other ministers were brusquely dismissed. On Saturday, July 2nd, a new government was set up under the Baron de Breteuil, the former ambassador to Vienna and a protégé of the Queen. This measure met with practically unanimous disapproval. Even the royalists became anxious. With the dismissal of the minister who had initiated the most beneficial policies the men of independent means and the bankers feared at least partial bankruptcy. In Paris, the announcement of the change in the ministry immediately released sporadic agitations which rapidly became uncontrollable. On Sunday, July 12th, a detachment of the Royal German Cavalry, led by its colonel the Prince of Lambesc, was stoned by the crowd in the garden of the Tuileries. Lambesc ordered a charge to escape the mob. The incident was magnified, and provoked riots during the evening. The crowd looted, searched for arms, and burned the tax-levy posts at the city gates. The royal troops stationed at the Champ de Mars were no longer to be relied upon, and their leader, Besenval, took good care not to interfere. In the capital, order was restored only gradually. On July 13th, the Assembly asked the King to dismiss the troops and to recall Necker. He refused. On the same day, a town council committee, then a popular militia, were formed of their own initiative at the Paris Town Hall.

On the 14th, before the eyes of Besenval's soldiers, who still watched passively, the crowd stocked up with arms at the Hôtel des Invalides. In the afternoon, a few columns of this people's militia made for Paris' oldest fortress, the Bastille, which was supposed to be impregnable. It was a former State jail in which only four prisoners remained : Launay the governor, at the head of thirty Swiss soldiers, did not know whether to capitulate or resist. Shots were exchanged, and several of the attackers were wounded before the fortress surrendered. Launay was massacred; then, a little later, the provost of the merchants of Paris, Flesselles.

The King learned of this on July 15th when he awoke. Besenval and Broglie admitted that they could no longer make their troops obey them. The soldiers had lost all hope.

Louis XVI then went to the Assembly on foot and announced that the regiments grouped near Paris were to be disbanded. Immediately afterwards, he reinstated Necker. The members of the high society of the Ancien Régime, knowing their unpopularity, now took steps to leave France. Most of the Queen's friends

In the 1785 Salon Louis David exhibited "The Oath of the Horatii". The picture caused a sensation and everything seemed to indicate that the public had the more or less confused presentiment that it would one day be necessary to abandon old-world elegance and grace and follow the masculine example of the Roman Republic. David was a leader in the revolution against the old school of painting and himself sought simple forms and serious subjects.

195

left with the Count of Artois and the Prince of Condé. The departures took place at night, secretly and in precipitous haste. Marie Antoinette did not even have time to see the Duchess of Polignac. She could only have a note taken to her: "Farewell, most tenderly loved friend," wrote the Queen, "this word is frightful, but it must be so. Here is the order for the horses; I have only the strength to embrace you."

When Louis XVI in an attempt to regain the people's affection, went to Paris alone and unguarded on July 17th, the situation was terrifying. Madame Campan wrote:

His departure caused as much pain as alarm in spite of the calmness which the King showed; the Queen held back her tears and closed herself in her study with all her family. A deathly silence reigned throughout the palace, everyone was extremely afraid. The King's return in the early evening filled all his family with inexpressible joy; in the arms of the Queen, his sister and his children, he gave free reign to his satisfaction that no accident had happened, and he then repeated several times: "Fortunately, no blood has been shed, and I swear that no drop of French blood will ever be shed by my orders."

To replace Madame de Polignac, her children's governess, Marie Antoinette chose the Duchess of Tourzel. The suites of the Queen and her children were redecorated during the summer at the Palace of Versailles as if nothing had changed.

"On the morning of October 5th, 1789," Madame Royale was to note a few years later, "everyone was still calm. We had just finished dinner when it was announced that Madame Elisabeth requested to speak to the Queen. She went into another room, and came back almost immediately, very agitated by what she had just learned."

Thus began the climatic phase of the royal tragedy. During the summer, life at Versailles had been painfully quiet. News of the looting of lordly mansions and sometimes of massacres arrived from the provinces. The National Assembly had multiplied the radical decisions to which the King refused to give his consent. Marie Antoinette was not unaware of any of the threats which weighed upon her. And Fersen, who was obliged to remain at the head of his soldiers in the north of France, had only been able to join his friend in September.

At the end of the month, in order better to protect the castle, the eleven hundred soldiers belonging to the Flanders regiment had arrived at Versailles. To ensure their loyalty, a banquet was arranged for their officers on October 1st by the bodyguards in the magnificent opera hall built by Gabriel. There were cries of "Long live the King", "Long live the Queen", "Down with the Assembly", and Marie Antoinette, touched by these unaccustomed cheers, agreed to attend the banquet with her husband and children. The enthusiasm was then delirious. Having heard nothing but derogatory cries and songs for five months, the Queen believed that she was now witnessing a change in public opinion, and she was delighted with her afternoon.

In Paris, however, the Versailles celebration was portrayed as an anti-Revolutionary orgy and provocation. On Sunday, the crowd filled the streets in a state of seething excitement, and on the next day, October 5th, roaring troops of several thousands, among them many women who were probably also embittered by the lack of food, headed for Sèvres and Versailles, armed with a miscellaneous assortment of weapons including pike-stuffs and parade guns and marching to the roll of drums. The assault of these Amazons was less ridiculous than it might seem. According to the philosophy of 1789, no one thought in fact of using force against women; and other battalions, those of the French guards and the National Guard, followed this advance party and swept along willy-nilly their highly-respected leader, General Marquis de la Fayette.

Arrived at the palace, they pushed against the ornate iron gates. The locks, unused for a century, did not close properly. The troops were uncertain of what to do. The first women to reach Versailles made no secret of their intention "to cut off the Queen's head". Fine rain had been falling since morning. Wet and tired and in an ugly mood, the women provoked incidents with the soldiers.

La Fayette arrived in the evening. "I have come, Sire" he said with insistence, "to offer my head to save your Majesty's."

"But what *do* they want?" asked Louis XVI.

"The regiment of French guards desires to take up its former positions again in your Majesty's service."

"Well," said the King, "let them do so!"

The soldiers who had mutinied thus found they were now assigned in the middle of the night, to the principal defence positions of a palace besieged by the crowd. La Fayette, the King, the Ministers and the crowd talked of battles, but no one really believed this. It was a fascinating scene which, as at the theatre, should have had a happy ending. When, that evening, Marie Antoinette declared, "I know they have come to Paris to demand my head, but I have learned from my mother not to fear death. I will wait for it," she, too, was reciting a part.

Then, on La Fayette's advice, towards midnight, everyone went to bed. That night, Fersen occupied his secret apartment above the Queen's bedroom.

Marie Antoinette only slept a few hours. The noise of hurried steps beneath her windows woke her at dawn. Two of her chambermaids, Madame Thibault and Madame Auguié, who had slept in her antechamber, rushed to the encounter, but saw nothing suspicious.

A few minutes later, the three women, their hearts in their mouths, distinctly heard cries and the sounds of a struggle. Madame Thibault rushed to see what was happening. Just then, a bodyguard half-opened the opposite door of the large antechamber and cried, "Madame, save the Queen. Her life is in danger. I am alone against two thousand tigers!"

Madame Thibault and Madame Auguié threw a cape over the Queen's shoulders, and whisked her along the shortest corridor to the Oeil de Boeuf lounge, the first room of the King's suite. Soon all the royal family was assembled in the King's chamber.

The situation in the palace was very confused. A few detachments of the Paris National Guard, alerted by the noise, came to lend their assistance to the bodyguards. It was high time. About a hundred rioters had slipped inside the iron gates towards four o'clock in the morning, and had headed directly for the Queen's suite. Two of them had been killed. The sacrifice of their lives gave the Queen time to flee.

But the disorder in the courtyards was frightening, with the crowds of the curious, the rioters and the soldiers rushing hither and yon. They naturally demanded that the King

Philippe Egalité, cousin and enemy of Louis XVI, was part of the Convention that voted for the King's death but was soon to suffer the same fate. Here Bouilly portrays him in the uniform of the National Guard.

197

July 12th : an angry crowd bars the doors of the Opéra.

The bust of Necker is taken to the Place Louis XV.

The Royal-German enters the Tuileries garden.

July 12th-13th : one of the toll gates is set on fire.

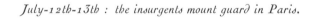

July-12th-13th : the insurgents mount guard in Paris.

July 13th : St. Lazare convent attacked and pillaged.

July 13th : Revolutionaries pillage the Garde Meuble.

July 14th : the citizens take over the Invalides.

July 14th : the taking of the Bastille by the people.

July 14th-15th : the popular militia is put on the alert.

July 15th : the cannon are transported to Montmartre.

July 17th : the King gives himself up at the Town Hall.

come out on to the balcony. He appeared, accompanied by the Queen, his children, Necker and La Fayette. Their appearance was greeted with cries of "Long live the King", "Long live the Royal Family". Louis XVI then asked the crowd to spare the palace's defenders, and in the midst of cries, the bodyguards exchanged their white cockades, the King's colour, for the tricolour cockades of the National Guard. Gradually, voices were raised asking the King to go and live in Paris. The sovereigns took council, then Necker announced that Louis XVI consented to go to Paris and to take up residence there. Now the joy became indescribable. The noisy and fervent cheers of the crowd created a kind of general intoxication. How could one refuse anything in answer to this untamed love? Louis XVI and Marie Antoinette gave up their palace which they were never to see again, and renounced their liberty which they would never find again, in an impulsive gesture. At the beginning of the afternoon, an enormous procession got under way on the road to Paris. The court carriages rolled along very slowly in the midst of a widely assorted mob of women, idlers, and soldiers of all ranks and regiments; it was a rowdy folk-dance, which was both gay and tragic. Some of them cried "Long live the Queen", and others shouted insults at Marie Antoinette, threatening to hang her from the nearest lamp-post. The journey seemed endless. They took six and a half hours to reach the Tuileries, where nothing had been made ready for their arrival.

"People will never be able to believe what has happened," declared the Queen to Mercy. "In spite of all they may say, they will not be able to exaggerate; on the contrary, everything will be milder than what we have seen and experienced."

When the tide has swept away the first dykes, one lets oneself relax in the hope that everything is over, and fearing to disturb the relative peace which one savours, one omits to take the necessary precautions. To some extent, this is what happened after the days of October 5th and 6th.... Of its own initiative, the Assembly appeared at the Tuileries palace, where it was not expected.

The chemist de Lavoisier, portrayed here with his wife by David, was assistant deputy at the Assembly. His position as a farmer general cost him his life.

The King showed himself to be very responsive to this step. On leaving his suite, the Assembly visited that of the Queen. The President made a speech to her which was imbued with the feelings of old French loyalty, and which ended with the wish to see the Dauphin in the Queen's arms.... Deeply touched, she presented him to the Assembly which continued to give resounding cheers of "Long live the Queen, Long live the Dauphin!"

These lines, which were written by Pauline, Madame de Tourzel's daughter, who lived among the Queen's attendants at the Tuileries, exactly portrayed the situation at the end of 1789. Temporary stability seemed to have been restored. Even hatred seemed to have lost its cutting edge.

On the morning of October 8th, a group of women from the poorest classes of Paris gathered in the Tuileries garden below the room in which Madame Elisabeth had breakfast. One of them asked to see the Queen. As soon as she was ready, Marie Antoinette came to the window and conversed for hours with "the common people and the lower classes". She answered all kinds of questions, discussed her behaviour and her feelings, and to mitigate the misery of the poorest Parisians, promised to make the pawnshop of the Mont-de-Piété return the underclothes and winter garments pawned there to buy bread.

Marie Antoinette was always prone to actions of simple, human generosity. Was she not, above all, an impassioned wife and mother? During this period, she noted, "When I am sad, I take my little boy with me" and again, "I am alone all day in my suite. My children are my sole salvation; I have them with me as much as possible."

Yet the Queen had a physical fear of the crowd, whose uncontrollable outbursts she had witnessed several times, and she could not prevent herself from considering as an absurd game of ill-omen the Assembly's debates and decisions. To understand her feelings, we must imagine the peculiar scene afforded by the deputies. During the winter of 1789-1790, more than half the deputies elected to sit in the States General had either left the country or returned to their provinces. The opposition fled in fear of riots or simply gave up, overwhelmed by the uselessness of its efforts. This improvised democracy, in spite of its impressive legislative work, was reeling like a vessel guided by drunkards.

In a letter written in October 1789, the future United States ambassador to Paris, Gouverneur Morris, gave an account which reflected the Queen's feelings:

Everything here has, so to speak, gone to pieces. The army is undisciplined and no longer obeys, the civil magistrates have been done away with, and the finances are in a deplorable state; there is no guide-line laid down for confronting problems, but the people live by their wits and are at the mercy of inventors of plans. It is impossible to imagine greater disorder in an Assembly; no reasoning, no examination, no discussion. We see a speaker stand up in the middle of another discussion and make a fine speech which ends with a good little motion, which is adopted with cheers of "Hurrah!" For instance, they were debating a plan for a national bank put forward by Mr. Necker; a deputy had the idea of suggesting that all his colleagues should make a gift of their silver buckles: this motion was immediately adopted; the honourable deputy placed his own on the table, and then the members reverted to the original point in question.... The anarchy which reigns is inconceivable.

The sentimental, unreasonable nature of the Revolutionary impulse is particularly noticeable in the attitude of the artists. Their embrace of a movement of which they would in any case be the first victims because of the ruin of the princes and the Church, their main clients, was at first unanimous. It was a common sight to see the wives of the greatest painters, sculptors and architects place their jewels on the Assembly's table as patriotic gifts. Amidst the members of the bloodthirsty Revolutionary tribunal, several artists were to be found, such as Châtelet, the painter of the Trianon whose romantic landscapes seemed to be inspired by Rousseau, and the sketcher Prieur, who were to be guillotined with Robespierre; but the future Baron Gérard and Topino-Lebrun also sat in it. David the painter, and Sergent Marceau, the sketcher, were to belong to the influential members of the Convention. Even Fragonard or Hubert Robert, who were afterwards so moderate, adopted the new ideas in 1789.

Indeed, art seemed to inspire the first Revolutionaries who were fond of referring to ancient sculpture and philosophy, and suggested popularizing the work of artists to stir up Revolutionary enthusiasm. They wrote that "the statue of a hero is a lesson in courage; the statue of a wise man a moral treatise". And they also proclaimed that "the arts must be popularized even in cottages, and spread like a fertile river over the whole territory of the kingdom".

Such were the principles. But in practice, the Revolution delivered blows of such severity to the arts that some of them were never to recover completely. The writers and dramatists were the first to suffer. With the suppression of all the royal privileges, the rights of authors ceased to be protected, editors could—and they did not fail to—publish and sell works, and theatre managers could have plays acted, without paying royalties to the authors. It was proclaimed that "the essential freedom of art, since the characteristic of genius is independence, must be the luxury and the religion of free nations". Between 1789 and 1793, however, the number of art patrons continually declined in spite of the increase in public liberties. When the Duke of Orleans sold his collection of paintings, he had to have it sent to England. The auction galleries abandoned Paris for London. The situation of the artisans deteriorated even more rapidly than that of the artists. The trade guilds were suppressed which threw into confusion or wiped out the frameworks of the traditional trades; luxury disappeared in the Revolutionary society. Consigned to unemployment and abandoned by their clients and patrons, many craftsmen —cabinet-markers, goldsmiths, gilders, tailors or milliners—lost their professional skills. "I may be wrong," wrote the Republican Marat in alarm one day, "but I would not be surprised if in twenty years there were not a single craftsman in Paris who even knew how to make a hat or a pair of shoes."

Marat was not wrong; the perfection which certain trades, such as cabinet-making, had succeeded in attaining at the end of the eighteenth century has never been achieved again. The confusion and inactivity of the Revolutionary years were fatal.

In the arts, the confusion of ideas was general. The artists announced that they were "tired of being dictated to by ignorant amateurs" just at a time when orders for paintings were becoming increasingly rare. In the name of liberty and under David's influence, the Academy was suppressed; now everyone could exhibit at the Salon, but so much servile conformity had never before been seen among artists, and artistic sectarianism had never been so narrow in the government's attitude.

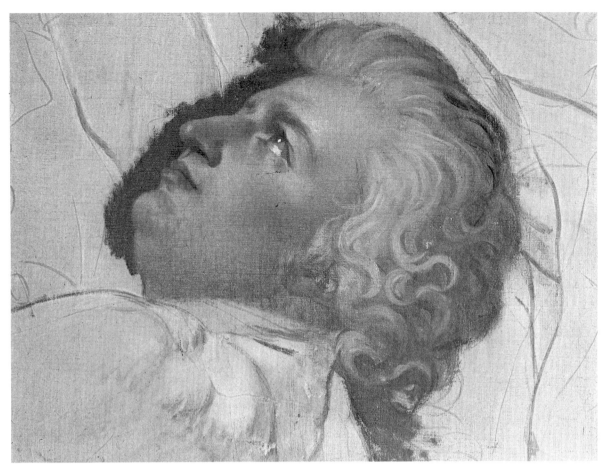

In this study of Mirabeau David flattered his model, who was ugly and pitted by smallpox. "His sentiments led him to love liberty," commented a contemporary, "his reason to love the monarchy and his vanity to love the nobility."

This confused situation also had its positive aspects. First of all, the public was admirable; unstable, it is true, but more impassioned in its love of art than it had ever been. "What a detestable crowd," protested a critic, referring to the Salon. "Dockers, fishwives, valets, and a swarm of children, pushing, shouting, stepping on everyone's toes. The dust sometimes prevents us from seeing anything, and certain rooms can only be visited at the risk of being smothered." The number of visitors to the contemporary art exhibitions was higher, in a city with a much lower population, than it is in twentieth-century Paris. At the theatre, the same enthusiasm reigned, in spite of the mediocre quality of the plays, which caused a disillusioned journalist to reflect:

"It seems that Pitt and Coburg [the Prussian minister] have conspired together to make French theatre fall into degradation, to snatch away its glory, and deprive dramatic art of the powerful means which it possessed of strengthening the Revolution."

The theatres multiplied, however, and were almost always full. One day, four thousand spectators climbed at the same time on to their seats and benches, and linking hands in a human chain, sang and danced in chorus.

If there were hardly any art collectors, there were still numerous enterprises to fill this lack. In 1789, the architect de Wailly founded the Society of the Friends of the Arts. It issued a thousand shares at 69 francs each (about £40, a hundred dollars) each year, and

These rather naïve medallions represent scenes of October 5th, 1789: when the drum sounded the King left Versailles.

bought about thirty paintings and four thousand prints from contemporary artists, sharing them out among the Society members by drawing lots. This association developed with complete success, in spite of the financial difficulties of the times.

Revolutionary art was characterized by the fact that it became less and less the business of professionals. Art became popularized on a scale as immense as it was brutal. The public no longer consisted of a small number of discerning and cultivated collectors, readers or spectators; it was made up of an enthusiastic, impatient and changeable crowd. There were also countless men and women who considered themselves gifted in writing, painting or composing music. Amateurism, heralded by Marie Antoinette's taste and attitude, reigned supreme. If David still dominated the times, he was an isolated figure. The authors of Revolutionary songs, such as Rouget de Lisle, Marie-Joseph Chénier, and Fabre d'Eglantine were inspired amateurs. For the Revolutionaries, the passion for art entailed the need which Marie Antoinette also felt, not only to be a spectator, but also an actor. In the improvised celebrations, all

kinds of art, painting, music, architecture, and literature, were combined. The most popular works, such as the famous song *Ça Ira*, were continuous creations; everyone added couplets at will, or illustrated, completed and published it according to his fancy.

The most typical example of this art was the festival of the Federation during the summer of 1790: on a very large scale, it was what we would call today a "happening". Improvization and careful preparation were closely intermingled. Such an extensive ceremony had never been organized in Paris and probably never will be again. It was to proclaim a new social, political and philosophical order. The date chosen was the anniversary of the fall of the Bastille, the symbol of the end of tyranny and despotism, but also of the King's reconciliation with his people on the day following this event. The subject was the Union of the French, who henceforward were to form a single nation, after the Constituent Assembly had abolished the provincial boundaries, local peculiarities, the privileges of all ranks, and customs which had existed for centuries. Federal celebrations were organized from the spring of 1790

On October 6th the royal family, accompanied by the crowd, arrived in Paris to take up residence at the Tuileries.

onwards from village to village and from province to province. In Paris, the delegates from the whole of France were to meet. But the nobility, the priests and commoners, the King and deputies, the aged, women, children, the poor and the rich were also to come together. This marked the establishment of fraternity and happiness throughout the kingdom. There were no longer to be Bretons or Angevins, dukes or serfs, powerful or weak, but only Frenchmen.

The site chosen for this enormous assembly was the Champ de Mars, the largest terrain available, at the gates of Paris where the foreign regiments camped before the taking of the Bastille. The architects' contribution was limited to the building of an enormous triumphal arch to symbolize the Revolution, and the nation's altar. Neither of these monuments, which were built with temporary materials, were very original; they were styled on ancient monuments. The painters, engravers and decorators were also busy; to mark this occasion, each company of the National Guard at Paris was to receive a new flag whose pattern had to be designed. The result was an immense riot of decorations which in general were harmonious. The processions were accompanied by songs, dances or *farandoles*. Many popular pictures were also sold and distributed.

The celebrations actually began on Sunday, July 4th. On that day, the crowd of Parisians noticed that the work of levelling the enormous Champ de Mars and the construction of the rows of seats for the spectators were very much behind schedule. Everyone set to work. Soldiers, women, federal provincial citizens, monks, colliers, wig-makers and marketeers on their own initiative carried earth day and night. Engravings even portrayed Louis XVI using a spade or pushing a wheelbarrow. In spite of the rain which fell continuously on July 14th, and in spite of many delegates being delayed, the crowd's enthusiasm was delirious, and the celebrations achieved a triumphal success. Talleyrand, the Bishop of Autun, celebrated mass in the midst of four hundred choirboys dressed in white. La Fayette took an oath of loyalty to the Nation, the Law and the King. Louis XVI followed, and then the whole crowd took the oath in their turn. Half a thousand men cried "Long live the King, long live the Queen, long live the Dauphin." It seemed, noted a republican, that the sight of

From October 7th on the Parisians gradually grew used to the presence of the sovereigns within their walls.

The National Guard's flag for the Notre Dame area carried the fleur-de-lis and the Queen's monogram.

The battalion of the Feuillans' flag showed hope for regeneration, the ship of Paris and the King's name.

this throne had bewitched all hearts and transformed patriotic spirits into royalist ones. That evening several provincial federalists wrote: "This is the end of the best day of my life."

Universal fraternity, fleeting splendour, perfect happiness, everything of which Marie Antoinette had ever dreamt and which the art of her time attempted to interpret, became reality on this revolutionary day.

But the political situation and the personal position of the sovereigns were to worsen considerably within the space of a few months. In the early part of 1791, the Assembly drafted a constitution for the kingdom which, in fact, deprived the King of all power and imposed upon him a purely representative rôle in an egalitarian democracy, which he did not want at all. Very much against his will, Louis XVI had signed the decrees abolishing

the noble titles and those of many traditional institutions, but he could not bring himself to support the Revolutionaries in their increasingly open conflict against the Catholic Church and the Papacy, for this would have meant going against his faith. During the summer of 1790, the King and Queen lived in their palace at St. Cloud which was nearer the capital. In 1791, their supervision became stricter. At Easter, a demonstration by the people prevented the royal family from going to St. Cloud, where the King had had the intention of carrying out his religious duties in secret. Beyond all question, the Revolutionary movement was becoming radical, and as it is not in a king's nature to revolt openly, a flight to the country, to the safety of the army, and if necessary, the help of forces lent by the other sovereigns of Europe, seemed

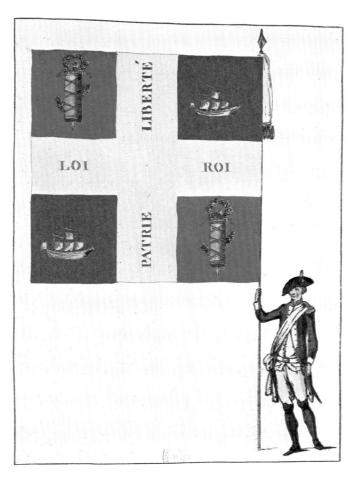

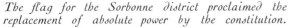

The flag for the Sorbonne district proclaimed the replacement of absolute power by the constitution.

The Petit St. Antoine flag, which carried the fasces and the ship of Paris, seemed to put its trust in the King.

to him the only possible solution. But neither Marie Antoinette nor Louis worried much about the political implications of this plan.

The idea of leaving the capital was considered by the sovereigns as a last resort in solving their problems. Exoticism and disguise were among the most popular subjects in art and literature at that time. Finding oneself under other skies, in other times, and reincarnated as other persons were common themes of inspiration in literature and painting. In Vien's pictures, antiquity was portrayed as a golden age. Russia in Leprince's watercolours; the Swiss mountains in Rousseau's writings, and Africa in those of Bernardin de Saint-Pierre, were paradises of primitive humanity. At the Salon, the painters exhibited landscapes taken from the entire world, and writers published all kinds of stories of

journeys. Without dreaming of travelling so far, Louis XVI, Marie Antoinette and their attendants nonetheless lived under the delusion that the Revolution was an event strictly limited to Paris, and that the provinces had kept their former loyalties intact. The day after July 14th, the question of rejoining the troops at Metz, the country's most invincible stronghold, had been discussed, but the army was not sufficiently reliable and this expedient was sensibly refused. The plan to leave was taken up again on October 5th, and again when the sovereigns were trapped in the Tuileries in Paris. Mirabeau, the popular democratic leader who was the King's adviser for a few months, suggested fleeing to Rouen, the capital of Normandy; the reason why this plan was not carried out earlier was that the sovereigns' optimism had always led them to

The festival of the Federation on July 14th, 1790, depicted here by Hubert Robert, was a magnificent celebration. W

re an immense crowd, the King and La Fayette swore an oath to the constitution, all hearts in France beat as one.

put off this decision. Several times, the advisers attempted to convince Marie Antoinette to leave the King, but such a separation seemed to her to be inexcusable cowardice. She would leave only with her family. Neither was there any question of alerting a part of public opinion, and preparing it to support a counter-revolution. The royal family wished to leave, but only confided in those nearest to it —in Leopold II, the Queen's brother, who had just succeeded Joseph II to the German throne; in Fersen, the Queen's lover, and a few faithful servants and a very small number of officers.

The decision for departure seems to have been taken during March, 1791, for on April lst Fersen was at work. His easy access to Marie Antoinette was an important trump card in the plot. Even at the Tuileries, noted Saint Priest, the Queen received the Count of Fersen almost every day. "I left him the means," said La Fayette, "by leaving a certain entrance to the suite unguarded, through which he could slip in without being seen and of which he took advantage." Who knows" added Saint Priest, "if this was not another trick to put her in the wrong."

Right from the beginning, the idea of keeping the flight secret was purely theoretical. The journey was planned with all the usual royal pomp. A sum of five million pounds (c. £835,000 or two million dollars) seemed necessary to finance the undertaking. The Queen ordered a second table-service and toilet articles to be made. A specially-made coach equipped with the most recent improvements was ordered. Fersen had discussed the plans and supervised its construction.

A National Guard presents arms to Louis XVI and Marie Antoinette, who urges the Dauphin to salute him. Behind them are the Tuileries, which today no longer exist.

The Marquis of Bouillé, who commanded the French army at Metz, to which Louis XVI intended to escape, was to send a few cavalry detachments to meet the travellers.

On June 20th, after several setbacks, everything was ready. To lay a false scent, Marie Antoinette had gone for a walk with her daughter in Paris that afternoon. Fersen, disguised as a coachman, waited by a fiacre a few steps from the Tuileries' courtyard. The royal family left in small groups. First of all, the children, led by Madame de Tourzel, slipped through a maze of unoccupied rooms and departed by a door which was not guarded. They settled themselves in the carriage. Madame Elisabeth, then Louis XVI followed them. Marie Antoinette unfortunately met La Fayette who had come to go the rounds, hid from him and lost her way in Paris, and thus was half an hour late. The fiacre finally arrived at the barrier at the Porte Saint-Martin, where the coach had been hidden. Three bodyguards disguised as postilions accompanied the heavy vehicle and two chambermaids followed in a light carriage. This impressive convoy got under way to Bondy. At this first halt, it was already three o'clook in the morning and dawn was breaking. Fersen now moved away from the coach, said loudly "Goodbye, Madame Korff", and as arranged left very rapidly on horseback for the Netherlands, the nearest frontier.

In the berlin which rolled towards Meaux, the atmosphere was joyful. The occupants amused themselves by distributing the rôles which had been agreed upon before their departure. The passport was in the name of a friend of Fersen, the Baroness Korff. Madame Tourzel was to play this part. The King, dressed very simply, was Durand, the steward; the Queen was Madame de Rochet, the governess; and Madame Royale and the Dauphin were the little girls Rosalie and Aglaé. The King joked and made plans. They changed horses unhindered at Meaux and at la Ferté-sous-Jouarre, then took the road to Montmirail. Louis XVI said: "My journey seems to me safe from any accident." At Chalons, the last large town on the itinerary where the coach arrived at four o'clock in the afternoon, there was no longer any question of remaining incognito. Madame Royale noted that "Many persons praised God that they should see the King and uttered good wishes for his flight." From then on, the news of the King's arrival preceded the travellers. This unusual journey also caused alarm. At Pont-sur-Velse, the Duke of Choiseul was waiting at the head of sixty hussars. A soldier learned that the King was to pass by. The excitement in the village was so great that Choiseul believed it was wiser to move his troops farther away. When the berlin arrived, it no longer had an escort. Nevertheless, everything went off without a hitch. At Sainte Menehould, the relay was made at night. The town council, which had not taken the trouble to stop the berlin, sent Drouet, the postmaster, on its heels with half an hour's delay. At Clermont, the King's coach kept its lead. The relay was carried out rapidly.

It was impossible now for Colonel Count de Duras to rally his dragoons as planned, to protect the rest of the journey. The danger, however, seemed less serious. The berlin left the highway for a crossroads where the post horses had been prepared by the army. Metz was a few tens of kilometres away. Another halt was made at Varennes. By an unlucky chain of circumstances, the horses were not at the place agreed upon. Drouet arrived from Clermont and succeeded in persuading the men of the village to barricade the road. The hussars who should have been guarding the village had completely vanished.

During this distressing night, the passengers went from house to house searching for the relay horses. They found them too late. The Varennes National Guard, a few men, made bold to forbid them to pass. The travellers exhibited their passports, and insisted that these forged papers were authentic. The town council wavered. In the attempt to reach an impossible agreement between Marie Antoinette, who wanted to pass, and Drouet who had been ordered to prevent them, the grocer Sauce, prosecutor of the Commune, proposed a solution which pleased everyone. The travellers were to spend the night in his house and the situation would be dealt with in the morning. Bouillé would thus have time to arrive, but also the Assembly's representatives who had probably been sent after the sovereigns. The hussars were there first: Choiseul's and Goguelat's soldiers who had missed the berlin at Pont-de-Vesle. By then, Louis XVI's heart had already been softened by the good citizens of Varennes. One of them who had seen him at Versailles threw himself at the King's feet. "Well, yes, I am

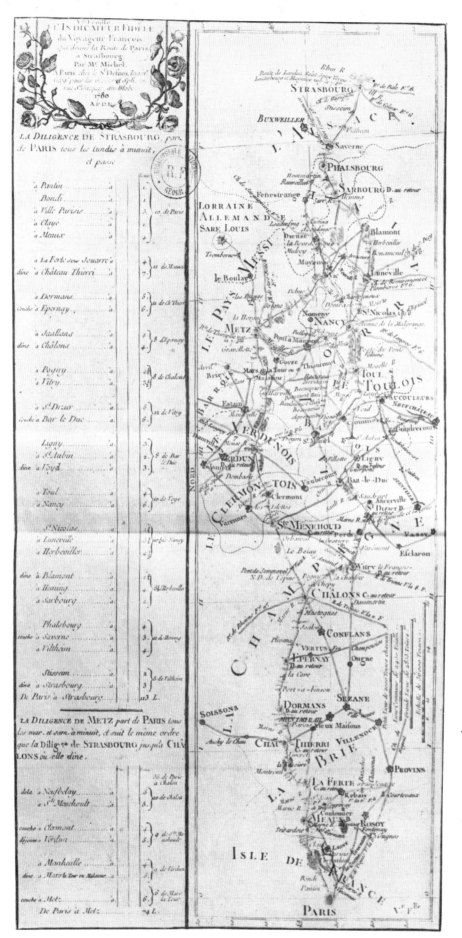

On this "Faithful Guide for the French Traveller who takes the Road from Paris to Strasburg" (1780), one can follow the escape itinerary of the royal berlin : Paris-Meaux - La Ferté-sous-Jouarre - Montmirait - Châlons-Ste-Menehould - Clermont - Varennes.

Having been arrested at Varennes, the royal family was led back to Paris in a suffocating atmosphere. Madame de Tourzel reported that one feeling united the enraged troops, that of delight at the humiliation of the monarchs.

your King," he said, and fraternally embraced all the members of the town council. Choiseul and Goguelat arrived in time to witness this touching scene. Reacting like the soldiers they were, they suggested charging the crowd to free the road. Neither the King nor the Queen would hear of it. No brutality! No bloodshed! Anyway, was it really necessary? Monsieur and Madame Sauce were getting along famously with the royal couple, as were the hussars with the crowd of villagers.

During the next night, the atmosphere slowly deteriorated; fright tinged their emotions. To free the King was Bouillé not going to massacre everyone? In the early hours of the morning, two envoys of La Fayette appeared and showed the King a decree by the Assembly suspending the King's powers and demanding that he return to Paris. Louis XVI resigned himself to the situation. "There is no longer a King of France," he cried. The Queen schemed to gain time, but

in vain. The crowd insisted that the travellers leave at half-past seven, without further ado, and to conform with a wish that seemed unanimous, the royal family settled itself in the coach again. When the heavy vehicle slowly got under way for Paris, Marie Antoinette greeted a young officer with such an air of weariness and sorrow that, as he noted a few days later, he had never before felt anything to compare with the emotions of that moment.

Several thousands of men and women ran alongside the berlin on the road to Clermont. Would Bouillé arrive? His advance guards appeared, but Bouillé did not intervene. He attempted unsuccessfully to intimidate the crowd of commoners, then beat a retreat and crossed the frontier. At Chalons, a wild mob laid siege to the coach, but the town council gave it a warm reception. Hope was reborn. The next day, while Louis XVI and Marie Antoinette were attending the mass of Corpus

213

Christi, panic and riots shook the town. Louis XVI had to promise to leave immediately. Amidst threats, howls and insults, the berlin rolled at a walking pace to Epernay; at this stop, the King and the Queen were pushed around and mishandled; Madame de Tourzel was knocked over, and Marie Antoinette's dress was torn. *"Allez, ma petite!"* a woman shouted at her, "You'll see worse than this before we've done!" A nobleman who had come to greet the sovereigns was thrown from his horse and beaten to death by the crowd. On the road again, the noisy convoy stopped out in the countryside. Three commissioners appointed by the Assembly to supervise and bring back the royal couple approached: La Tour Marbourg, a well-known figure at court and a moderate Revolutionary; and Barnave and Pétion, who were considered as having far more radical opinions. They were hailed with relief. "Let no misfortune befall the persons who have accompanied us," cried Marie Antoinette. "Let no attempt be made on their lives!" Her spirit of self-sacrifice, courage and simplicity impressed Barnave and Pétion who seated themselves, huddled together, in the overloaded berlin. Some time later, the Republican Pétion was to observe, "I noticed a simple, family atmosphere which pleased me; there was no longer any royal representation, but domestic ease and simple good-heartedness." Barnave was more timid and reserved. Marie Antoinette questioned him, amused by his confusion, and conscious right from the beginning of the attraction she exercised on the blushing young commissioner. "Do tell Mr. Barnave" she threw at Pétion, "that he should not look at the door so much when I ask him a question." Encouraged by this, Barnave launched into a political profession of faith, with which Marie Antoinette agreed. Both were surprised at their mutual moderation and their common desire to ensure the nation's happiness.

At La Ferté-sous-Jouarre, Pétion, very moved by the simple and amiable attitude of Madame Elisabeth, imagined that he had attracted the King's sister, and she agreed to take a little walk with him. Barnave talked to the Queen alone, and these private conversations were repeated at each relay.

The end of the journey, on Saturday June 25th, was very arduous. The crowd became more and more dense. The incidents increased.

Barnave and Pétion had to harangue the mob several times to avoid a tragedy. This last stage of the journey lasted from six o'clock in the morning until seven o'clock in the evening, under a blistering sun. Near Paris, they progressed in the midst of an enormous, hostile crowd in which all the men ostentatiously continued wearing their hats. The Tuileries garden was swarming with people. The mob shouted "Death!" The Assembly delegated six new commissioners to protect this tumultuous arrival. Louis XVI stepped down calmly, followed by the Queen, who was violently booed; in spite of the fright, the horror and the dark prospects which ended this abortive flight, the Queen turned to Barnave and said, "I admit that I did not expect we would spend thirteen hours together."

At the end of June, 1791, the Queen was a prisoner in the Tuileries Palace. Watched over day and night by armed guards, she was even forbidden to be alone with her husband and children. The King had been suspended from his office and even risked being dethroned. Outside, the people violently demonstrated their hatred. Marie Antoinette was accused of organizing the King's flight with her lover. The newspapers suggested that she should at least be condemned to death.

Besieged, isolated and threatened, the Queen remained splendidly herself. First of all, she had to find and reassure Fersen; she succeeded in sending a letter to him through a mysterious messenger who is still unknown. "I am alive.... How anxious I have been about you, and how I sympathize with you for all you suffer through not having any news of us! Will heaven allow this to reach you?" And on July 4th, "I may tell you that I love you, and have only time to do this.... Goodbye the most beloved and most loving of all men. I embrace you with all my heart." Fersen answered. The link between their hearts was not broken. At the same time, Marie Antoinette attempted to renew contact with Barnave. She dictated a brief letter to the General de Jarjayes, the husband of one of her chambermaids. "I desire you to try and see Barnave

Antoine Barnave had received orders from the Assembly to bring back Louis XVI after his attempted escape. He began as a convinced opponent of royal prerogatives but later grew fond of the Queen and tried to save her.

for me and tell him that, in as much as I was struck by the strength of character and the frankness which I found in him during the two days which we spent together, I now urgently wish to know from him what we have to do." Her political subtlety seemed like coquetry. Marie Antoinette asked for advice; and Barnave, at a time when La Fayette and so many others would have liked to be the Court advisers, was flattered at being put into this position. Before accepting, he asked the advice of his most faithful friends, the deputies Duport and Lambeth, and exacted complete discretion from them. De Jarjayes was to be the sole confidant. Marie Antoinette was to give him the letters, Barnave was to dictate the answers to him, and the Queen was to destroy all their correspondence after receiving it. Thus each of them would avoid being compromised.

The result of this politico-epistolary bandying was spectacular right from the start. Barnave, a young, handsome and brilliant orator, really had great influence on the Assembly; and fickle public opinion was ready to become royalist again.

From the beginning of July, a skilful declaration by Louis XVI, drawn up by Barnave, impressed the Assembly, which waived pronouncing the King's dethronement and considerably increased his powers in the Constitution drafted by the deputies.

Marie Antoinette's opinion progressed at the same time. In spite of all her protests of faithfulness to the ideal of absolutism, Fersen noted in his diary: "It is said that the Queen lets herself be guided by Barnave; this bodes no good." But she did not speak to him of Barnave. To Mercy, she indicated, "I correspond with Lameth and Barnave. In them, I have never found anything but great frankness, strength, and a real desire to restore order." At the same time, she wrote to her new friends through de Jarjayes' intermediary: "I have noted with pleasure the strength and courage with which the persons to whom I am writing have supported the monarchy. M. Barnave spoke with his usual wit and in a subtle and skilful way." And Barnave answered, "The persons to whom the Queen has been gracious enough to grant her confidence have undertaken to ensure the happiness of their country by consolidating royalty; everything they do is with the object of achieving this aim...." "The French people

keenly desire to give free reign to the feelings of their hearts. The Queen, more than anyone, has in her nature what is necessary to take possession of this favourable frame of mind. When the heart is not cold, it is always possible to recapture it."

On September 14th, Louis XVI came to take the oath to the Constitution, drawn up by Barnave and his friends, which restored his throne to him. All the royal family seemed free again. Splendid celebrations marked the new-found love between the sovereigns and the French people; theatres put on appropriate plays in which loyalty to royalist feelings was praised, with such subjects as Henry IV, the good French king, and Richard the Lionheart, whose people remained faithful in spite of his long captivity.

Marie Antoinette took advantage of this to see the plays frequently with her children and the Princess of Lamballe, who had returned from England where she had taken refuge. The newspaper *Journal Général de France* noted that "the applause at the Queen's arrival was general and prolonged, and was often repeated during the intervals".

Never at any time, however, did Barnave consider that his relationship with the Queen could be avowed. Two years later, when he appeared before the Revolutionary tribunal after being denounced, Barnave, pure, sincere and incorruptible, denied everything. "I testify on my head" he cried, "that never, absolutely never, have I set foot in the castle." Yet during the months from July to September, he increased the number of his letters, even visited Marie Antoinette secretly, and sometimes remained alone with her. Their correspondence, which Marie Antoinette later passed on to Fersen and which has since been preserved in Sweden, proves this. "Everything the Queen does bears witness to steadfast resolution," he wrote. "I am therefore full of confidence in her courage and sincerity."

The burning question for French diplomacy at that time was the attitude of the monarchs of Europe. Would the absolute sovereigns resign themselves to the establishment of a parliamentary monarchy in France? The French nobles who had sought political exile urged them to intervene with their armies; the head of one possible coalition was the Emperor Leopold II, Marie Antoinette's brother. All sides relied on him; Barnave urged the Queen to write to him and persuade him to accept the new constitution; Fersen hoped that he would come and crush the Revolution by a general massacre, and Marie Antoinette desired that he should support Louis XVI, but did not know exactly how. This resulted in Leopold II receiving warlike recommendations in Marie Antoinette's name, secret reports from the Queen's hand (written by Barnave), asking him to bring the warmongers to reason, and ultra-confidential letters in which Marie Antoinette begged him not to take into account what she was supposed to have written. Leopold II then made shift with an extremely vague public declaration on "the rights of sovereigns and the well-being of the French nation", which exasperated the political exiles and was considered in France as scandalous interference in the country's affairs.

In October, the situation deteriorated. The Legislative Assembly created by the new constitution met; its former deputies had not been re-elected and the new legislators were, on the whole, very little in favour of the monarchy. Barnave had no influence on them. He remained Court adviser but without admitting that he was now powerless. He advised the Queen to nurture her own popularity and that of the King; he committed her to relying dangerously on the Emperor Leopold II. Barnave and Marie Antoinette were more or less in agreement. Both saw the fortunes of France based on the threat of a foreign power, but they refused to accept any bloodshed. In December 1791, Barnave wrote: "The Emperor can let his intention of defending royal dignity and the constitutional prerogatives be made known." The Legislative Assembly took further steps to humiliate the King, threatened to attack the countries which had granted asylum to the French nobles in exile, and imprisoned the Catholic priests who, according to the Pope's orders and Louis XVI's wish, refused to take the oath to the clergy's new civil constitution.

There was hardly any mention of these essential problems in the conversations between Barnave and Marie Antoinette. In fact, they discussed matters of dress, or, more likely, such things as the colours of the uniform of the King's new guard. No political line emerges from this correspondence, and they did not commit themselves to anything without mental reservations. Marie Antoinette had thin-skinned or sentimental reactions and no clear-cut ideas. Barnave dreamed of the strict application of the constitution which he had drawn up, but it disintegrated when it was put into effect. Both of them showed as much good-will as insincerity. Certainly, the Revolutionary could be in the King's service and the Queen be reconciled to the Revolution; they had considered this, but did not really want it at all. Their bandying continued until neither one had any further grip on events.

In January, 1792, Barnave left Paris. The rupture between the royal couple and the new Assembly was then accomplished. The Queen was once again an object of detestation, under guard in her palace. Barnave was to return to the capital only to appear before his judges and to follow Marie Antoinette, with a few days' interval, to the scaffold.

The winter of 1791-1792 marked the end of hope. It was impossible to reach an agreement with the Revolutionaries, but since Marie Antoinette could not resign herself to being inactive, she fought by means of countless letters against everyone and everything — against the opportunist ministers, the increasingly Republican Assembly, even against the King who constantly changed his mind, and against Madame Elisabeth who had been completely won over to the cause of her brothers in exile.

Fersen, now the object of a search since it was he who had organized the flight to Varennes, decided to go to Paris. It was a chivalrous gesture, but incited by a double motive: in Paris, he would rejoin two mistresses whom he had not seen for six months: Marie Antoinette, and a former actress, Eléonore Crawford, whom he was later to think of marrying.

Fersen left Brussels, dressed as a steward, with his aide-de-camp Reuterswaerd, disguised as a diplomat. There is the extraordinary diary of that heroic and sentimental journey:

Saturday, February 11...left at 9h.30; we had a courier's passport for Portugal under false names. For my safety, I also had credentials as a minister to the Queen of Portugal.

Monday 13...left at 9h.30, stopped two hours at Louvres for lunch, arrived without mishap in Paris at 5h.30, without anyone stopping us. Left my officer at the Hôtel des Princes, in the rue Richelieu. Went to visit Her [Marie Antoinette], took my usual route, afraid of the national guards. Her suite wonderful, remained there.

Fersen then stayed about twenty-four hours with the Queen without being noticed.

Tuesday 14: saw the King at 6 o'clock in the evening; he does not wish to leave and he cannot, due to the extremely strict supervision; but in reality, he has scruples about having promised so often to stay for he is a man of honour. The Queen told me that she saw Alexandre Lameth and Duport and that they constantly told her that the only hope lay in the foreign troops.... In spite of this she does not think it is a good idea, and does not trust them.... I said that to give verisimilitude to my story, I should push on towards Spain as far as Orleans and Tours, and that I would be back on Monday or Tuesday. At 9h.30 I left her. I joined Reuterswaerd at the Pont-Royal and we took a carriage to her house [Mrs. Crawford]. At 10 o'clock, Franz [her man-servant] let me in; I was to stay with Josephine [the chambermaid] who had two rooms. He [Crawford] had gone out; we had tea together at 12h.30 and I went to bed.

Wednesday 15: fine, cold. I rose a t10h.30; Franz brought me my breakfast. When he left at 12h.30, she came to see me for a little while; they brought me a little to eat which they had taken from the table on the pretext that it was for Josephine; when they were alone, I had very little, when they had company, I had more. I had to remain quiet, for the salon was just underneath. At half-past eleven, she left me, for he came in towards midnight....

218

et vos peines sont pour moi, et par moi. Votre frère de Valenciennes a été exact à m'envoyer votre lettre elle est aimable comme vous c'est tout dire, je l'ai vue, car après trois mois de peine et de séparation quoique dans le même lieu, la personne et moi sommes parvenu à nous voir une fois sûrement, vous nous connoissez toutes deux aussi vous pouvez juger de notre bonheur elle va faire une course chez votre frère, cela étoit nécessaire, et j'avoue que j'ai préféré le moment du jour de l'an où je crois que si il doit y avoir du mouvement ici on prendra ce moment, je ne crains rien pour notre maison mais dans la ville il pourroit y avoir du train, et j'aime être tranquille sur tout ce qui m'intéresse.

vous devez avoir reçu une lettre de ma fille, cette pauvre petite est toujours à merveille pour moi en vérité si je pouvois être heureuse, je le serois

pour que deux petits êtres, le choux d'amour est charmant, et je l'aime à la folie, il m'aime beaucoup aussi, à sa manière, ne se gênant pas, je me plais à l'appeler comme cela, pour lui rappeler vous et les vôtres, je lui demande quelquefois, si il se rappelle de vous si il vous aime, il me dit oui, et alors je le caresse d'avantage il se porte bien, devient fort, et n'est plus colère, il se promène tous les jours ce qui lui fait grand bien, je ne vous parle point des affaires d'ici, je trouve qu'il faut n'en rien dire ou écrire des volumes, mon mari me charge de bien des amitiés pour vous, je crois qu'il n'y a pas longtemps qu'il vous a écrit, je viens de me donner encore une entorse à ma mauvaise jambe ce qui m'a obligé d'être une douzaine de jours dans ma chambre, mais quand on ne peut pas être où et avec qui l'on voudroit, on resteroit un an à la même place sans penser à en changer.

I was very happy, dear heart, to have news from you, and even happier to have a safe opportunity as far as Turin to write to you and tell you of my friendship. I cried with tenderness upon reading your letters.

Oh yes love me always, I will not be ungrateful for as long as I live my friendship will never cease. You speak of my courage, I assure you that I need much less for the moments of horror in which I find myself, than to have to bear our position continually, and daily, my own pains those of my friends and all who surround me, are a burden too heavy to support, and if my heart were not held by equally strong ties to my children, to you, and to two friends that I often have here I would wish to succumb, but you all hold me up, I owe this feeling to your friendship, but I bring bad luck to all of you and your afflictions are for me, and caused by me. Your valencienne brother was punctual in sending your letter to say she is agreeable as you is all that needs be said, I have seen her for after three months of pain and separation although in the same place, the person and I have managed to meet once in safety you know us both and so you can imagine our happiness, she is going to make a trip to see your brother that was necessary, and I admit that I have preferred the moment of the day of the year when I think that if there must be some movement here one will take this moment, I fear nothing for our house but in the town there could be some disturbance, and I like to be tranquil with regard to all in which I have an interest.

You should have received a letter from my daughter, this poor little one is always wonderful to me in truth if I could be happy, I

would be for the sake of these two little beings, my little "choux d'amour" is charming, and I love him madly, he loves me a great deal too, in his way, without shyness, I enjoy calling him that, to remind him of you and yours, and I sometimes ask him, if he remembers you and if he loves you, he tells me yes, and then I caress him even more he is doing well, becoming strong, and no longer has fits of temper, he goes for walks every day which does him a deal of good, I am not telling you about what goes on here, I think one should either say nothing or write volumes, my husband sends you his greetings, I believe that he wrote to you not long ago. I have just sprained my bad leg again which has obliged me to keep to my room for about twelve days, but when one cannot be where and with whom one wishes one could stay a year without thinking of changing.

goodbye dear heart, give a thousand greetings to your parents and friends for me I embrace your little boys and even the big armand, since it is so far away nothing can be said, I feel greatly comforted that M. de Guiche is with you, he is a son-in-law who by his attachment his nobility and his loyalty is worthy of you and your husband, everybody here praises him and even his enemies do homage to him by the very hate they show towards him, say hello to him from me, I cannot tell you how much pleasure your daughter's four lines gave me and how can I not be interested in her children are they not mine too, is she not my adopted daughter, I have all a mother's feelings for her, let her always love me a little and above all let her speak often to you about me, and you will both be sure of remembering a being who thinks of you without cease, and who loves and kisses her most beloved friends, with all her heart.

The intrigue was extraordinary and could be easily understood; for a week, from Tuesday, February 14th, until Monday 20th, Fersen lived in hiding at Mrs. Crawford's and in her company when her husband was away. Nevertheless, they had to take great precautions, for this British merchant was more suspicious than the King of France. On February 21st, Fersen decided to leave France and make his farewells to everyone.

At 6 o'clock, I went out; I met Reuterswaerd with whom I made all the arrangements for our departure at midnight. He took the note to Eléonore in which I appeared to announce my arrival to her husband and asked to see him. I was let in secretly, we played our parts well, he believed us; I wrote a note to Her [Marie Antoinette] that I had arrived. I told her the same story [Mrs. Crawford] as Her [Marie Antoinette] about my supposed journey. I left them at midnight. I found my little dog Odin which Reuterswaerd had been to fetch and which I was taking with me. I put on all my fur-lined coats, and we set off at 1 o'clock.

Marie Antoinette did not know of the handsome Axel's second liaison; Fersen's sister often thought anxiously about the pain which the discovery of such a secret would cause to the Queen. According to the moral principles of the times, faithfulness was not a matter of not being perfidious to one's mistress, but in not causing her any unhappiness. So much ambiguity baffles or scandalizes us. But we cannot really understand Fragonard and Laclos, or Beaumarchais and Sade without understanding that the acts and the imagery of life during this subtle and refined age had many facets....

From the spring of 1792 onwards, Marie Antoinette put all her hopes in war. She had confidence only in the intervention of the sovereigns of Europe. They would be forced to lend assistance to the French royal couple to protect their own countries against the contagiousness of democracy.

The Queen did not experience the slightest feeling of fellowship with the government, the Assembly or the Frenchmen who supported these bodies. For her, the nation was the King whose powers had been usurped. When the Legislative Assembly threatened to declare war on the Emperor Leopold II, Marie Antoinette endeavoured to pass on military information to Mercy-Argenteau or Fersen, for transmission to Vienna. For instance, she obtained a general statement of the French army, then conveyed the results of the council of ministers' debates to Mercy, who had asked her to obtain them.

The King and Queen, however, hardly needed to incite the other sovereigns to war. Leopold II, Marie Antoinette's brother, died suddenly in March and was succeeded to the imperial throne by young Francis II, who was much less level-headed than his father. The new sovereign dreamed of an easy and rewarding victory over a France in a state of complete anarchy: the French Revolutionaries hoped for popular uprisings and the rapid crumbling of all monarchies.

On April 20th, on the request of his ministers, Louis XVI suggested to the Assembly that it declare war on the Emperor, and this motion was almost unanimously adopted. For diametrically opposed reasons, this decision satisfied everyone. Naturally, no one even considered that the war would last until 1815 and would throw the whole of Europe into confusion.

There was no longer any question of the King and Queen going to the theatre, but artistic amusements were still organized with great enthusiasm amidst the circle of friends at the Tuileries. At the beginning of summer, Louis XVI's portrait was painted by the pastellist Ducreux, and Kucharski, a Polish artist, sketched a bust of the Queen. Hubert Robert visited his sovereigns and painted from life the royal family secretly attending mass said by a recalcitrant priest in a lounge at the Tuileries. As the Dauphin lacked professors to interpret the Bible and teach him French grammar and history, the Count of Paroy drew and coloured all kinds of pictures which were projected by a magic lantern system, and commented aloud on these. This was a first attempt at audio-visual teaching.

The failures of the Revolutionary armies increased the dangers run by the Queen. In May and June, events took a bad turn for France. Prussia and the whole of Germany had formed an alliance with Austria. An initial French offensive against the Austrian Netherlands turned into a local rout. The French soldiers, in utter panic, massacred their general. The road to Paris was open.

There were cries of treachery. At the Assembly tribune, the Queen was accused of collaborating with the country of her birth. Marie Antoinette, however, calmly continued

This pencil drawing entitled "Love", by Pierre-Paul Prud'hon, evokes the turbulent emotions of the Queen and Fersen during the even greater turbulence of the Revolution. Marie Antoinette to her lover on July 4th, 1791 : "I may tell you that I love you and have only time to do this.... Goodbye, the most beloved and most loving of all men." Fersen on September 4th, 1793 : "I often reproach myself even in the very air I breath when I think that she is shut up in a terrible prison, this idea tears at my heart, it poisons my life and I am forever divided between pain and rage."

her correspondence with foreign countries. On June 5th, on the pretence of a business letter, she gave military information to Axel Fersen :

I immediately saw to withdrawing your funds from the Boscaris Society. There was no time to be lost for bankruptcy was declared yesterday.... There are orders for the army of Luckner [a French general] to attack constantly; he is against it, but the minister wishes it. The troops lack everything and are in the greatest disorder.

The test of strength in Paris was imminent; the government asked the King to dismiss his constitutional guard of 6,000 men and to order the deportation of the Catholic priests who had refused to take the oath to the constitution. Louis XVI agreed to ratify the first decree, but he opposed his "veto" as he was authorized to do by the constitution, to the deportation order. He thus remained disarmed and in complete opposition to his ministers, of whom several resigned.

During the morning of June 20th, a crowd from the lower-class suburbs assembled around the Tuileries Palace and the nearby meeting-room of the Assembly, where the delegates were gathered. Madame de Tourzel, the governess of the children of France, wrote an

A year after Varennes the Tuileries was like a wrecked vessel in a storm. The royal family preferred to hear mass in one of the drawing-rooms than at the chapel and the painter Robert has left us a record of such an occasion. In the centre can be recognized the King with the Queen on his left.

222

account a few years later of these terrible hours she spent at Marie Antoinette's side:

The King, the Queen and all the royal family gathered together at the beginning of the afternoon in the King's suite, which was considered the safest place, and waited with great anxiety for the outcome of that fatal day. The King's situation was extremely critical; his only protection was the National Guard which filled the palace and refused to defend him.... Cries began to be heard everywhere, and drowned all other sounds with "Down with the veto! Long live the nation and the sans-culottes!"

The King, Queen and the royal family were in His Majesty's small bedroom, surrounded by a few faithful servants. Seeing that the doors were going to be forced, the King wished to go to meet the factionists and to try and impress them by his presence. He rushed forward and asked that the Queen and his children be kept at a distance, desiring to expose himself to the danger alone. This prince of the people gave the order to open the Oeil de Bœuf door which still separated him from the ruffians. They had already forced the opposite door to the one through which the King passed to meet them!... Cries and howls were heard on all sides. The Queen was fortunately a small distance away from the King at the moment when he decided to face the crowd, but she absolutely wanted to return to his side. She had almost to be dragged by force to His Highness the Dauphin's suite, where all the doors had been closed with hooks and bolts. The Queen hugged her son in her arms. Choking with sobs, she remained a quarter of an hour without knowing the King's fate, and continually asked to be allowed to return to him. As the first room of His Highness the Dauphin's suite had been forced and the crowd which flooded the palace

The people brandish placards in the hall of the Assembly and advance towards the president. Attributes of royalty are trampled underfoot. Locked up with some of their household in the logographer's room situated behind the president's office, the King and Queen witness the scene. A few days later they were to be led to dungeons in the Temple.

During the night of August 9th-10th the alarm-bell rang in Paris ; insurrection flared. In the small hours of the morning the Revolutionary troops, who had been joined by the National Guard, assailed the Tuileries Palace. The King took refuge in the Assembly. The Swiss guards regiment, whom Louis had ordered to put down their arms, were cut to pieces by the Marseillais. Horrifying scenes of carnage took place in the Tuileries Palace and in the Palace Gardens.

The four-storied Temple dungeon: on the ground floor and the first floor were lodged the prison guards; the second floor was occupied by the King and the Dauphin, the third by Marie Antoinette. Each of these two storeys was divided into four rooms by board partitions and false canvas ceilings. The fourth storey remained unoccupied.

were filling it, the Queen, her children and their attendants returned to the King's room, where the doors had been shut from the council room side....

One of the valets of His Highness the Dauphin, completely beside himself, ran to warn the Queen that the council room was taken, the guard disarmed, the suite's doors forced, broken and pushed in, and that he was being pursued. It was decided to allow the Queen to go into the Council room, in which Santerre, one of the leaders of the mob, had his troops parade before her to make her leave the palace. Surrounded by her children, she faced these Revolutionaries.

Her Majesty sat down at a table, with His Highness the Dauphin on her right and Madame on her left, surrounded by the Filles-Saint-Thomas battalion, which formed an unyielding wall against the muttering people, who railed her unceasingly.... Armed women threatened the Queen, but not for a second did her face lose its calmness and dignity. The cries of "Long live the nation, the sans-culottes, liberty! Down with the veto!" continued. The procession only finished at eight o'clock in the evening....

In tears, the Queen threw herself with her children at the King's feet; he kept his arms around them for some time, and this touching scene softened the hearts of all those who witnessed their happiness at finding each other safe and sound.

For the King and the Queen, June 20th represented an undeniable success. While the rioters desecrated their home, they showed courage and composure; and Louis refused to withdraw his "veto" even under threat.

Marie Antoinette's first thought was to reasure Fersen. She wrote him a short note: "I am still alive, but it is a miracle. The 20th was a frightful day. They are not after me the most any more; they are after the very life of my husband. Danger can surge up again at any moment."

In this country of France which was so sensitive to theatrical displays, and in which the Paris revolutions were portrayed as the most beautiful scene imaginable, public opinion changed again. As Marie Antoinette noted, "Courage always inspires respect"—and the applause this time was unmistakably directed toward the royal couple. From Paris and the provinces, formal addresses were sent to the Assembly to demand better protection for the life and dignity of the sovereigns. Once again, the moderates—the largest majority of the country—were ready to take up arms to defend the palace, which was threatened every day. Once again the royalists assembled at the Tuileries to resist any surprise attack. The National Guard battalions set up their garrisons on the spot. With the Assembly's agreement, Swiss guards were taken from their quarters in the suburbs and lodged in the palace's outbuildings. With respect to the decisive test which everyone knew was near at hand, the balance of power, either as concerns public opinion or from the purely military point of view, was not definitely in favour of the republicans. But the general frame of mind changed hourly, and Marie Antoinette still felt too much a queen to imagine that her salvation might come from the moderate Revolutionaries. She did not pursue a political aim, but rather followed an aesthetic line of conduct: a sovereign right until the end, she did not compromise with rebels, even though to do so might have meant her salvation.

On June 28th, La Fayette came to Paris. He spoke at the Assembly Tribunal, protested against the factional activities of republican clubs, and even presented the King with an offer to lead him to safety with his family, under the wing of his army. Louis XVI refused. "It is better to perish," Marie Antoinette is supposed to have declared "than to be saved by La Fayette and the Constitutionals." Thus was the situation reduced to absurdity; the moderates attempted to save the King who rejected their support.

The turning-point was definitely reached when Marie Antoinette wrote her last letter to Mercy on July 4th:

You already know the events of June 20th; our position is becoming more and more critical. On the one side, there is only violence and rage, and on the other, weakness and apathy.

All is lost, if the factionists are not stopped by the fear of being punished soon. They want a republic at any price; to achieve it, they have decided to assassinate the King. A proclamation should make the Assembly and Paris responsible for his life and the lives of his family.

Marie Antoinette did not wish to owe her throne to rebellious subjects; the intervention of foreign powers was therefore indispensable. But neither did she want blood to be shed. Those who would save the throne could therefore not attack; they could only threaten. It was a completely unrealistic attitude; and even though the great majority still shared her faith in the power of words, events were now about to overwhelm them. On the other hand, Marie Antoinette herself was perfectly aware of this, and the echo of her deep distress appears in the last notes to Fersen delivered by the faithful Goguelat.

June 23rd. Your friend is in the greatest danger. Her illness is making frightening progress. The doctors know no further remedy.

July 3rd. Our situation is frightening, but do not worry too much; I feel courage within me, and something tells me we will soon be safe and happy.

July 24th. A single day's delay can produce incalculable calamities.... The forces of the assassins are constantly increasing.

The prisoners in the Temple organized their lives under constant surveillance: for three months they followed the domestic routine of a bourgeois couple and seemed to adapt very well to this.

During these feverish days, Marie Antoinette did not even dare to go out into her palace garden. Like the King, she wore a bullet-proof waistcoat, a sort of armour with an exterior lining of silk material, which was supposed to protect her against possible attacks. On the insistent advice of those near to her, she left her suite at night and henceforward slept in her son's bedroom. Outside, fear also reigned. The people failed to see how the disorganized French troops could resist the imminent offensive of the Austro-Prussian army, which was well-trained and led by the Duke of Brunswick. The Assembly's reaction on July 11th was to proclaim that "A large number of troops are moving towards our frontiers; all those who detest liberty are taking up arms against our constitution. Citizens, our country is in danger!"

This proclamation was repeated in the streets, the villages and the most distant hamlets. Within a few days, France was electrified. Thousands of young men enlisted and left for the frontier. Against the background of this national epic, the tragedy experienced by a few persons in the Tuileries Palace seemed insignificant.

Neither the King nor the Queen were prepared for the final battle. The troops who remained loyal to the monarchy never at any time received orders to fire. The last letter to Fersen, dated August 1st, 1792, did not reflect the actual military and political situation, but only the despair of the royal couple who had decided not to react, and who gave themselves up to waiting to be saved:

The King's life has clearly been threatened for a long time, and the Queen's too. The arrival of about six hundred soldiers from Marseilles has greatly increased our anxiety. Precautions of all kinds have been taken to ensure the safety of Their Majesties, but the assassins prowl around the palace all the time; there is ill will among a part of the National Guard, and weakness and cowardice among the others.... If no one arrives, only Providence will be able to save the King and his family....

The final attack was provoked by the manifesto which Marie Antoinette had, with singularly poor judgement, demanded from Mercy; it was drawn up by Fersen and proclaimed by the Duke of Brunswick, and arrived at Paris on August 1st. In it, Prussia and Austria declared that they "set themselves no other aim than the well-being of France", and that they only wished "to free the King, the Queen and the royal family from their captivity". But they also threatened "that if Their Majesties the King, the Queen and the royal family suffered the slightest outrage, they would subject Paris to a military execution and total subversion".

The collaboration between the foreign powers and those besieged in the Tuileries was clear. The patriotic spirit of the people once again turned against the sovereigns.

During the first days of the month of August, a feverish atmosphere reigned day and night in Paris. Both sides organized a large number of armed patrols, and because the various uniforms often resulted in confusion, there were brawls and sometimes bloody altercations.

The Count of Paroy, one of the faithful members of the Tuileries, recounted:

On August 9th everyone seemed anxious. The streets were fuller than usual. In the evening, towards eight o'clock, the Princess of Lamballe asked me, on the Queen's behalf, to go and see if a large 24-pounder cannon was aimed at the Flore pavilion as she had been told. The call to arms was heard everywhere. A faithful medal engraver named George, who was in command of the artillery station, seemed very attached to the royal family. At nine o'clock, the alarm-bell was rung and drums were beaten everywhere; the Carrousel, the courtyard in front of the Tuileries, filled with people; I went straight to the Queen's suite, I gave an account of my mission and made as if to return to the gallery where a large number of soldiers were waiting. "Stay, if you wish," said the Queen to me. The King came for a moment and nodded to us kindly. He had had Pétion, the mayor of Paris, sent for to ask him the reason for all this noise. Pétion arrived, attempted to reassure the King, and left. The King returned to his suite; the alarm-bell doubled its ringing. Mr. Mandat, the former captain of the French guards, commanded the Paris National Guard at the palace. He constantly received notes from the Town Hall. Towards eleven o'clock, the Queen and Madame Elisabeth withdrew to their private rooms. Suddenly, shots were heard at a distance. Everyone thought that the palace was being attacked. The suites filled with soldiers of all ranks who came running to offer their services to the King.

This portrait of Louis XVI by Ducreux was made during the last weeks of the King's life. He was to be condemned to death by a majority vote of the Convention.

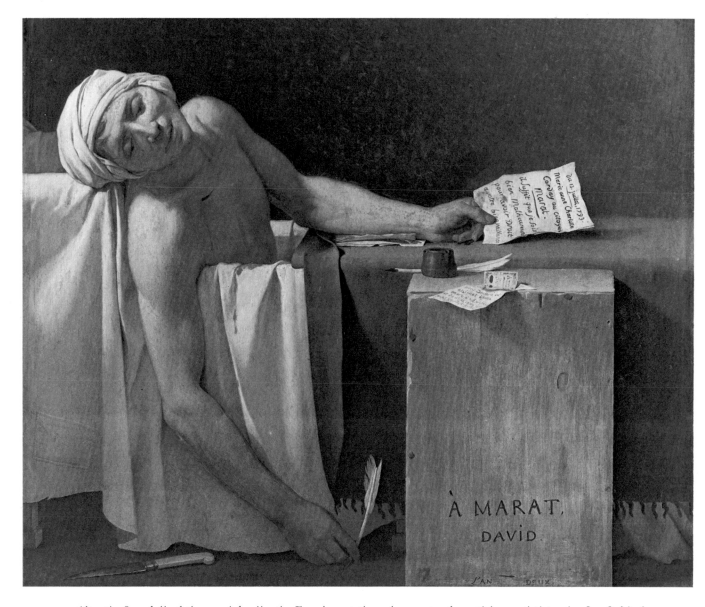

After the downfall of the royal family the French went through a spate of asceticism. Artists abandoned frivolous and elegant subjects and vied with one another to give proof of their Republican fervour. David glorified the murdered Marat, but it can also be said that Charlotte Corday, his assassin, admired the heroes of Plutarch and Corneille.

A new order then came from the town council for Mr. Mandat to go to the Town Hall; this was even more imperious than the others. The commander then decided to leave after giving his second-in-command special instructions.

By four o'clock, it was broad daylight; I was in the throne room with several lords. Mr. de Bachmann, the major of the Swiss guards, came to meet us and said: "I already see the palace becoming a vast coffin, if the King remains here. At seven o'clock, the King appeared. His Majesty was determined to inspect the guards'and the National Guards' posts, who were very pleased with this step. The King was warmly greeted with cries of "Long live the King!" As if to defy him, cheers were heard from the square of "Long live the nation!"...

Everyone was waiting in the suites when it was announced that the King and the royal family were to appear. The double doors were opened. The King advanced a step forward; we all had our swords in our hands....

230

In 1793, ten years after it had been painted, David's "Grief of Andromache" was in the news. Like the heroine of the picture, Marie Antoinette wept over the death of her husband and lamented the fate of her son. The Queen lost Louis XVI on January 21st and the Dauphin was taken from her in the following July and entrusted to a cobbler called Simon.

Half an hour afterwards, a delegation from the department was announced, led by Roederer, the Duke of Rochefoucauld, etc.... The delegation passed between our lines and returned a quarter of an hour later followed by the King and the royal family. The King stopped and said: "Gentlemen, I have just decided to give myself up to the National Assembly; let us go."

Louis XVI had decided to capitulate even before the decisive struggle for power began.

The situation was indeed impossible. Their only conceivable way of defending the sovereigns would have been to assume the offensive and to destroy the disorderly columns of besiegers who were swarming about before they attacked themselves; but neither the King nor the Queen desired this.

Early in the morning of August 10th, the King, the Queen and their children, accompanied only by Madame Elisabeth, the Princess

231

of Lamballe, the Duchess de Tourzel and the members of the department, passed through a double line of National Guards responsible for protecting them from the rioters, and covered the two hundred metres which separated the Tuileries Palace from the riding-school where the Assembly was in session. The crowd was dense and the little group had to push its way slowly through it. Madame Royale was to recount later:

On the way they assured us that the Assembly did not want to receive my father. The Feuillants terrace by which we were to pass was filled with ruffians; they heaped insults upon us, and one of them even cried: "No women, we will kill all of them!" My mother did not let herself be frightened by this threat and continued on her way. I never believed that death was so close as at that moment, and was convinced that they had decided to assassinate all of us. We were left in this distressing situation for half an hour. Finally, they allowed us to go into the riding-school and my father announced loudly that he had come to take refuge with his family in the heart of the Assembly to prevent the French nation from committing a great crime. Afterwards, we were taken to the lodge of one of the journalists. We had hardly entered this sort of cage when we heard cannon, shots and the cries of those being massacred at the Tuileries.

According to the sovereigns' way of thinking, their departure from the Palace should have prevented armed opposition. On the contrary, the first fights took place in the middle of the morning. The crowd invaded the courtyards and climbed the stairs. The defenders of the palace feared for their lives and shot to repel the invaders. The fighting became general. The Queen's women were reduced to headlong flight. Pauline, Madame de Tourzel's daughter and Ernestine Lambriquet, Madame Royale's two companions, escaped, luckily protected by a few of the people. But nearly 800 defenders of the palace—Swiss, nobles, servants or National Guards—were killed.

For three long days, the royal family, huddled together in a tiny, barred room which was generally reserved for the official stenographer who recorded parliamentary debates, silently listened to the Assembly's discussions. It was then that its fate was decided.

On August 10th the majority leader assured Louis XVI that the Assembly had sworn to die for the defence of royal authority. But on the 12th Danton spoke of kings as being the "oppressors of the people", and another

deputy of the "individuals called kings". On August 13th, the royal family was turned over by the Assembly to the Revolutionary Paris Commune, whose troops had conquered the Tuileries three days earlier. The monarchy was abolished and it was announced that a new Assembly would be elected to give France a republican constitution.

That afternoon, the King, the Queen and their children took a carriage with Pétion, who was still mayor of Paris. Marie Antoinette was penniless; one of her chambermaids slipped a roll of gold pieces into her hand. Slowly they rolled along in the midst of a hostile crowd. The vehicle stopped at the Place Vendôme, where Girardon's huge statue of Louis XVI on horseback which decorated the centre of the square had just been overturned. For Pétion, this symbolized the victory of the people over kings. But it was also the starting-point of a wave of iconoclastic fury.

In the centre of what is now the Place de la Concorde, the magnificent statue of Louis XVI on horseback by Bouchardon had been knocked down and was hastily to be replaced on its pedestal by a somewhat ingenuous wooden effigy of Liberty. Throughout Paris and then in the whole country, royal statues disappeared. The egalitarian and anti-religious fever was to cause incalculable destruction in palaces and churches everywhere. One after another, the creations of the past, the refinements of luxury, came to be considered as relics of a detestable time. Rarely in the whole of history have so many artistic treasures been scattered or destroyed in so short a time; each day, in the courtyard of the Versailles Palace, the furniture collected by three kings was auctioned, the Gothic sculptures of Notre-Dame were attacked with hammers. The ruined churches with their broken statues, whose melancholy appearance so enthused the admirers of the paintings of Hubert Robert, were now not the product of an artistic imagination but the tangible proof of the prevailing state of mind. Many water-colour painters were to find in the austere beauty of the empty pedestals and the desecrated sanctuaries a source of inspiration. Art was in the midst of a fury of self-destruction. In the same way that Rousseau imagined happiness in a society freed from all the material advantages of civilization, and David rejected the charm of

e.... will hand over to you the agreed articles for ha.... the seal imprint that I am attaching to this is another matter entirely I desire you to deliver it to the person you know came to see me from Brussels last winter, and say to him at the same time that the motto has never been so true. If you are not satisfied with h.... go and find my nephew in my name, you can also if you want see (septime) who they tell me is in London since August and ask him for what you have paid out for us if you have need of it he knows my confidence in your wife I think he must know you too but if it is necessary you could show him this and tell him what you have done for us he is too much attached to us not to be conscious of the price. for the rest I take it upon myself to make him keep account of what he will give you and if necessary I shall even use my personal means. Tell me what you think about what is going on here.

The "agreed articles" were the seal of the arms of France and the King's ring, to be delivered to the Count of Provence, now Regent; the seal imprint was of a pigeon flying with a motto "tutto a te me guida" and was for Count Axel Fersen.

colours to seek simple shapes and austere subjects, and the architects Ledoux and Boullée discovered the beauty of elementary geometrical shapes and of monuments stripped of all decoration, so the French hungered after asceticism, and thirsted for heroism and mortification. For them, this was the unexpected outcome of the impassioned search for happiness and beauty. This feeling was so strong and so widespread that it even reached the Queen and the King in their prison.

The Temple enclosure at which the royal procession arrived after a two-hour journey lay in the east of Paris. It was an isolated area where many artists and craftsmen lived, for its inhabitants enjoyed a large number of

The trial of Marie Antoinette took place on October 14th, 1793 from 8 a.m. to eleven in the evening and on the 15th from 9 a.m. to four o'clock the next morning. The Queen listened to the verdict without making the least sign, either of fear or of weakness.

corporate and fiscal privileges. In the main building, a splendid palace dating from the middle of the eighteenth century, the young Mozart had been received on his first stay in Paris by the Prince de Conti. But the Commune did not consider this palace as being sufficiently secure for a prison. A thirteenth-century dungeon, with thick walls and narrow windows, had been chosen as the residence of Louis XVI and his family, in spite of its lack of comfort. On the evening of August 13th, the work which had been undertaken to make this tower fit for habitation had hardly begun. Court dignitaries and servants had been given permission to accompany the royal couple. They all huddled together as best they could. The Commune had, however, granted large credits to arrange the rooms reserved for the dethroned king's family; although they were strictly supervised, a large household had been placed at the King's and Queen's command to ensure excellent food and to provide them with some of the comforts to which they were accustomed.

After a week during which the excitement caused by the taking of the Tuileries abated, a new tragedy occurred: all the members of the Queen's suite, and all the servants except

one, were suddenly separated from the royal couple and transferred to other prisons. For the first time in their lives, Louis XVI and Marie Antoinette found themselves alone with only their two children, Madame Elisabeth, the King's sister, and Cléry, the Dauphin's valet. Deprived of the luxury and the crowd from which the Queen had fled to her hamlet at Trianon, and the King to his locksmith's workshop, they led the homely existence of a middle-class couple, and settled down to it well. Cléry ingenuously noted the details of how they spent their days:

The King generally rose at six o'clock in the morning. He shaved himself; I did his hair and dressed him. He immediately went to his study. His Majesty prayed on his knees and then read until nine o'clock. During this time, I went to the Queen's suite; she opened her door only on my arrival in order to prevent the municipal guard from entering her room. I carried out the young prince's toilet; I arranged the Queen's hair and in the course of my duties I also went to the room of Madame Royale and Madame Elisabeth. During this time, I could inform the Queen and the princesses of what I had learned. A sign would show that I had something to say to them and one of them would then distract the attention of the municipal officer by talking to him.

At nine o'clock, the Queen, her children and Madame Elisabeth went to the King's room for breakfast.

At ten o'clock, the King came down with his family to the Queen's room and spent the day there. He busied himself with educating his son, had him recite a few passages from Corneille and Racine, gave him lessons of geography and practised drawing maps. For her part, the Queen carried on the education of her daughter. The rest of the morning was spent in sewing, knitting, and working on tapestries.

At one o'clock, when the weather was fine, the royal family went into the garden.

At two o'clock, they came back into the tower and I served lunch. After the meal, the royal family went to the Queen's room; their Majesties generally had a game of piquet or backgammon. At four o'clock, the King took a short rest. When he awoke, they continued their conversations; His Majesty made me sit near him. He watched me give writing lessons to his son, and played ball or shuttlecock with him.

At nine o'clock in the evening, the King had supper, then went for a moment to the Queen's room and gave her and his sister his hand to wish them goodnight. He withdrew to his study and read until midnight. The Queen and the princesses closed themselves in their suite.

Communicating with the exterior and evading the vigilance of their guard was one of the royal family's amusements. Turgy, a former servant of the King, entered the municipality's employment as a kitchen boy. Since at that time the decanters were closed with paper plugs, it was possible to pass on notes with the drinks. Other letters, rolled around a ball of lead and protected by stronger paper, were hidden in the food.

There were also days of terror. After the mass uprising and the departures of many young men for the army, the announcement of the Austro-Prussian successes gave rise to tragic scenes in all the Paris prisons. Tribunals formed by rioters decided, in the prison courtyards, to massacre hundreds of men and women. During one afternoon, a shrieking crowd besieged the entrance of the Temple. The guard was powerless to repel this tidal wave of unleashed anger. A commissioner of the Commune, a painter named Daujon, then went forward alone and unarmed to meet the rioters, and succeeded in convincing them not to force the doors.

Upstairs, the King became worried. He questioned a national guard. "Well," was the reply, "since you wish to know, they want to show you the head of Madame de Lamballe." A cry was heard. The Queen fell down in a swoon. "This was the only time," Madame Royale noted later, "that her strength of heart left her."

The bloodthirsty population had indeed dragged the body of the Princess of Lamballe, who had been massacred in the Abbaye prison, to the Temple. Now her head, stuck on the end of a pitchfork about which her blond hair was entwined, wavered for endless minutes before the window of the room where the royal family was grouped. The rioters, drunken with atrocities, howled that they wished to see the Queen embrace the head of her best friend. It was again Daujon who managed to divert the frightful procession to the Palais-Royal.

The victory of the French armies at Valmy momentarily calmed the fears and passions. On December 7th, however, a decree ordered that "all sharp tools, scissors, razors, and knives belonging to prisoners who are presumed to be criminals" were to be taken from them. This was followed by a decree by the Convention, the new assembly elected after the fall of royalty, which forbade Louis XVI any further communication with his family. Indeed, the former King was to appear before the deputies, acting as his judges, on the charge of treason. A part of his correspondence with Austria had been discovered at the Tuileries in a secret casket which Louis XVI had made himself with the locksmith Gamain, who had worked with him for twenty years. It was Gamain who had betrayed him. His crime of collaborating with the enemy was proved.

On December 25th, Christmas Day, the King had hardly any doubt that his end was near. He drew up his will with care:

I entrust my children to my wife; I have never doubted of her maternal love for them; I particularly enjoin her to make good Christians and honest men of them, and to make them consider the splendours of this world, if they are condemned to experiencing them, only as dangerous and perishable goods. I beg my wife to pardon me all the unhappiness which she suffers through me...as she may be sure that I do not hold anything against her if she believes that she has anything to reproach herself with. If my son has the misfortune to become King, I enjoin him to be aware that he owes his life and soul to the happiness of his fellow-citizens!

On Sunday, January 20th, after long debates and endless votes, the King's sentence of death was voted. At the end of the afternoon, a pathetic scene, worthy of Greuze or Prud'hon, took place. Cléry gave the following account:

It was half-past eight in the evening. Marie Antoinette appeared first, holding her son's hand, and followed by Madame Royale and Madame Elisabeth. They all threw themselves into the King's arms. For a few minutes, the silence was only broken by the sound of sobs. This painful scene lasted seven quarters of an hour, during which it was impossible to hear anything; through a glass door, we only saw that after every sentence of the King's, the princesses' sobs increased, and that the King then gave up trying to speak. It was easy to gather from their gestures that he himself had told them of his condemnation.

At a quarter to ten, the King rose, and they all followed him. They took a few steps towards the entrance, uttering the most sorrowful wails.

"I assure you" said the King, "that I will see you tomorrow morning."

"Do you promise?" they all repeated together.

"Yes, I promise."

The next day, at seven o'clock the King came out of his study and called me. "Tell the Queen, my dear children and my sister, that I had promised to see them this morning, but that I wished to spare them the pain of such a cruel separation."

The Queen waited one floor below. Since five o'clock in the morning on this day of January 21st, 1793, the call to arms had been heard, for the troops were to mount guard all along the King's passage. Then later during the morning, drums and trumpets announced that Louis XVI had left his prison and was going to the scaffold. Artillery salutes and oft-repeated cries of "Long live the Nation! Long live the Republic!" announced the death of her husband to Marie Antoinette.

Since the beginning of her captivity in the Temple, Marie Antoinette dreamed of escape. This is certainly the case of all prisoners, but in the royal family she was the sole instigator of numerous plots. Her weapons were always the same: weary, old before her time, and humiliated, she nonetheless continued to exercise an undeniable fascination. Her lack of prejudice was pleasing, and her desire to please attracted. But the delegates of the Paris Commune who were responsible for watching the royal couple day and might were chosen from the avowed anti-monarchists.

The final chapter began with the encounter of Marie Antoinette and an extraordinary individual, François Adrien Toulan. A hero of July 14th and August 10th, a fierce Republican, and a Commune commissioner at the Temple, he in no sense favoured the monarchy's cause, but rallied to that of Marie Antoinette. Toulan was from Toulouse, a fine orator, an intelligent and courageous man. The Queen had always had a taste for gambling and risks. Both of them amused themselves in hiding their very real liking under the cloak of mutual repulsion. Toulan was to keep up his pretence for ten months.

After the King's death, Toulan succeeded in his first exploit. Before going to the scaffold, Louis XVI had charged Cléry with giving Marie Antoinette his ring engraved with his wife's initials and the date of their wedding, a packet containing locks of his children's hair, and a seal, the last symbol of his royal authority. But the Commune council had opposed the King's desire and these objects had been placed under guard in the Temple itself. Marie Antoinette, who had been informed of this by Cléry, desired to recover them. She told Toulan of her wish. Without hesitation, the Commissioner, one day when he was on duty, broke the seals, stole the treasures and secretly gave them to the Queen who hid them in her room; he then accused imaginary thieves of the crime, who were naturally never found.

On February 2nd, 1793, the Chevalier de Jarjayes, who had remained in Paris in the hope of one day being able to be of use to the Queen, received a visit from a stranger. It was Toulan, who gave him a note: "You may trust the man who will speak to you on my behalf. I know his feelings; he has not changed during five months...."

De Jarjayes recognized the Queen's handwriting, but was sceptical about the chances of escaping. To convince him, the Commissioner suggested smuggling him into the Temple. Toulan had the ingenious idea of having de Jarjayes replace the lamp-lighter who came to light up the buildings for an evening. Disguised in this way, de Jarjayes reached Marie Antoinette, his sovereign.

The problem of letting four persons escape from a fortress which was watched day and night by several hundred men does not seem to have intimidated any of the plotters. They only needed to win another commissioner to their plan. The Commune's representatives were always in pairs when guarding the prisoners, but Marie Antoinette pointed out

The artist Louis David watched the procession conveying Marie Antoi-
nette to the scaffold from the window of a Representative called Jullien. He
drew this pen-portrait of the Queen during the last hours of her life.

The Greatest of all the Joys of the Père Duchesne

Having seen with his own eyes the head of the female Veto separated from its fucking tart's neck.
Detailed account of the interrogation and judgment
of the Austrian she-wolf, and his great anger against the two devil's advocates who dared plead this monkey's cause.

In the days of the do-nothings, which are not far away, fuck, when the wild animal called the king came out of the Versailles menagerie, either to burn a candle before the shrine of the patron saint of Paris, in whom he believed no more than in Jean-de-Verd, and to give the impression of thanking her with regard to the birth of a freak, of whom he was only the sham father; or that after a bloody war undertaken for the smallest pleasures of his whores and for the whims of his pimps, he was at last coming to declare peace, when the poor people had nothing left but their eyes to cry with; then, fuck, all the red-nailed rabble took great care to cry *long live the king*, *long live the queen*, *long live monseigneur the dauphin* along his route. "You see Sire," said these motherfuckers to him, "how happy your people are; how they love you." The royal ogre took their word for it and that evening he went back into his cuckold's nest, all joyful, not because of the blessings he thought he had received, but delighted to see the Sans Culottes so well disposed, and as soon as he got to his council chamber he ordered the levy of another tax, and felicitated himself for plucking the hen without making it cry.

The Pompadours, the Dubarrys, the Antoinettes, when these do-nothings had formed a chorus and bawled to show their joy to the two-horned monster, in whose name they reigned, they congratulated themselves for making the frogs (this is what they called the Sans Culottes) sing, but, fuck, when the misery was at its peak, when the crushed people groaned and murmured low; in a word, when the frogs kept silent in spite of the fat sous and sausages tossed to them, as to famished dogs to stop them barking; then, fuck, the kings and their cliques were in a sticky situation. The people is never so great, so terrible as when it is calm in its anger.

I would have liked, fuck, all the crowned brigands to have seen, through a cat-trap, the interrogation and judgment of the Austrian tigress. What a lesson for them, fuck! How they would have trembled to see two or three hundred thousand Sans Culottes, surrounding the palace and waiting, in silence, the moment when the fatal decree was to be pronounced! How small they would have been, these so-called sovereigns, before the majesty of the people! What would they have thought on seeing themselves subjected thus to the law, they who can only make themselves obeyed through terror. No, fuck, no, one never sees such a sight. Tender mothers, whose children have died for the republic; you, cherished spouses of the good fellows who are fighting right now at the frontiers, just for a moment you stifled your sighs and dried your tears when you saw appear before her judges the infamous trollop who caused all your pain; and you, old men, who languished beneath despotism, witnessing this terrible scene took twenty years off you. "We have also lived," you say to yourselves, "since we have seen the last day of our tyrants."

The days follow on, they say, and one is never like another. What a difference between these moments of vengeance and those times of idleness, when all the French had not eyes enough to admire their dauphine, not voice enough to sing her praises; she could not take a step without being followed by an immense crowd who made the air ring with cries of joy; when she appeared at a show, the music, the dancing, all was forgotten in order to applaud her and attend to nothing but her. The poor Sans Culotte who sweated blood and water from one sun to the next, to pay for all their gorging, thought no more of the taille, the corvée, the gabelle, of the hunt, of procurators, lawyers and all the vermin that gnaw his living body, when he saw this monster, whom he looked upon as a divinity, crossing the fields watered by his tears. Who would have ever said, fuck, that the object of so much love would come to so bad an end! But hunting is in the blood of all dogs. It is as natural for kings and their blackguardly progeny to devour men as it is for wolves to devour lambs.

For the price of all the good deeds that they have squandered on this termagant, the French have been reduced by her to within two fingers of ruin. Since she began to reign she dreamed of nothing but murder and carnage. More than a million men have been her victims and the crimes she has committed are still only rose water in comparison with those she has meditated. There was no punishment great enough to expiate them and the judges were right when, in pronouncing her death sentence, they reminded her of the kindness of the law, since a new punishment had not been invented to avenge France and humanity. In spite of yourself, hussy, you have had to feel the benefit of equality since your punishment was as gentle as that of the other guilty parties.

Is it possible, fuck, that a hardened enough blackguard could be found to dare defend her? And yet two palace louts had that audacity. One of them even had the effrontery to say that the nation had too many obligations towards her to punish her, and to hold out that without her, without her crimes with which we reproach her, we would not be free. I cannot conceive, fuck, how it can be suffered that these curs of Bazoche, lured by the stripping of villains, by a box of gold, a watch, some diamonds, should betray their consciences and try to throw dust in the judges' eyes. Have I not seen these two devil's advocates not only jig like hens in a hot griddle to prove the innocence of the monkey whose cause they pleaded, but even dare to lament the death of the traitor Capet, and say to the judges that it was enough to have punished the fat cuckold, that at least mercy should be shown to his slut. Show mercy to a villain covered with the blood of the French, let such a monster live! is it then so that she may immolate more victims? But I felt a joy I shall never be able to repay when I learned that these two motherfuckers had been arrested by an order of the convention's general security committee. I hope that they will keep them in quod at least until peace.

All you who have been oppressed by our former tyrants; you who weep for a father, a son, a husband dead for the republic, be consoled, you are avenged. I have seen the head of the female Veto fall into the sack. I should like, fuck, to be able to express the satisfaction of the Sans Culottes, when the archtigress crossed Paris in the thirty-six-door carriage. Her fine white horses, so well plumed, so well harnessed, were not pulling her, but two old nags were yoked to Master Samson's vis-à-vis, and they seemed so satisfied to contribute to the deliverance of the republic that they seemed to want to gallop in order to arrive earlier at the fatal spot. The trollop, furthermore, was audacious and insolent until the end. Nevertheless her legs gave way at the moment for the tipping, for playing at hot cockles, doubtless in the fear of finding, after her death, a more terrible punishment than that she was about to undergo. Her cursed head was eventually separated from her tart's neck and the air resounded with cries of long live the republic, fuck.

238

Je suis le véritable Père Duchesne, foutre !

LA PLUS GRANDE
DE TOUTES LES JOIES
DU
PERE DUCHESNE.

APRES avoir vu, de ses propres yeux, la tête de véto fémelle séparée de son foutu col de grue. Grand détail sur l'interrogatoire et le jugement de la louve autrichienne, et sa grande colère contre les deux avocats du diable qui ont osé plaider la cause de cette guénon.

Du tems des badauts, qui n'est pas

299.

De l'Imprimerie de la Cour des Miracles, rue Neuve de l'Egalité, ci-devant Bourbon - Villeneuve.

The first and last pages of a Revolutionary paper by Jacques Hébert, a full translation of which appears opposite. Yesterday's tyrants are dead and the new queen, Madame Guillotine, is soon to count Hébert among her victims.

a certain Lepitre among her jailers, a young, ambitious man without deep political beliefs and de Jarjayes took it upon himself to bribe him. Henceforward, Lepitre was to form a team with Toulan at the Temple.

It was planned to disguise Marie Antoinette and Madame Elisabeth as municipal guards; it seemed easy enough to bring in the uniforms secretly and gradually. Madame Royale was to leave with de Jarjayes who would again replace the lamp-lighter, who was sometimes accompanied by a child. They hoped to hide little Louis XVII in a basket of washing. Light carriages would transport the escaped prisoners to the Normandy coast, where they would embark for England.

But unforeseen difficulties arose. The precautions at the Temple were increased: Lepitre, in spite of the sum he had received, hesitated and took fright. He suggested to Marie Antoinette that she leave alone, for of the four prisoners, she was the most threatened. She refused. Once again, Marie Antoinette enjoyed planning an escape without really wanting to carry it out successfully.

"We have had a beautiful dream, that is all," she wrote to de Jarjayes. "But I have gained very much in finding a new proof of your complete devotion to me on this occasion." She asked him the supreme service that he leave France and bring to the Count of Provence, who was now the regent of the kingdom, her last souvenirs of Louis XVI, and to give a ring to Fersen. "Tell him," Marie Antoinette enjoined de Jarjayes "that the motto has never been more true." This ring was a present from Fersen to the Queen; inside it, these five words were engraved in Italian:

Tutto a te mi guida
(Everything leads me to you)

De Jarjayes faithfully carried out these two missions. Fersen and the Count of Provence were to receive the objects intended for them. Toulan, betrayed and pursued, was to die on the scaffold shortly after the Queen.

On July 13th, 1793, a slightly-built woman from Normandy, Charlotte Corday, aged twenty-five, stabbed to death a Revolutionary journalist, Jean-Paul Marat. This heroine was condemned to death and guillotined; shortly after, the dethroned Queen was sent to the Conciergerie, a prison in the Palais de Justice, seat of the Revolutionary Tribunal before which she was to appear. Marie Antoinette arrived there on August lst, very ill physically and morally broken by the separation from her children. Her material situation improved, however, thanks to the sympathy she inspired among the prison staff. She was given a decent wardrobe. Meals specially designed to tempt her were prepared. The flowers in her cell were renewed every day. But she was not allowed to be alone either by day or night; soldiers and a chamber-maid kept a constant watch over her.

In spite of these extraordinary precautions, one last plot was being hatched to prepare her escape, and once again Marie Antoinette agreed to play her part. Michonis, a commissioner of the commune who had already attempted to arrange her escape from the Temple, was at the heart of the intrigue. His duty of inspecting the prisons allowed him to enter all the cells. On August 28th, he took a companion with him, a royalist, the Knight de Rougeville, who had taken part in the defence of the Tuileries on June 20th, 1792. Rougeville, in a gesture straight out of operetta, dropped a carnation at the Queen's feet. He had hidden a note in the flower. In reply, Marie Antoinette traced letters by pricking holes with a pin in a paper; she entrusted this message to her bodyguard Gilbert, who was doubtless part of the plot, and charged him to give it to Rougeville or Michonis. But after five days, nothing had happened, and Gilbert, to avoid any responsibility, drew up an accusation.

On being questioned, Marie Antoinette gave evidence of a great strength of character. First of all, she denied everything. Confronted with the facts, her only care was not to reveal the name of Rougeville, and to minimize the part played by her accomplices. Her defence was so skilful that no serious sentence was pronounced.

In a dungeon which was henceforward darker and less comfortable, Marie Antoinette spent the last weeks of her imprisonment in reading heroic adventures. Those who came near her were surprised at her calm. She probably did not know whether she was to find the happiness she was seeking on earth or in heaven. A survivor of the Terror noted:

Her light-heartedness of which we saw so many signs was in strange contrast to the awe-inspiring seriousness of the situation. She was often inspired by it: among the jewels worn at that time by women, one saw delicate pictures of the guillotine which they wore in their ears or around their necks; their dresses were given names corresponding to the circumstances; they wore their hair *à la victime*; they took revenge on their executioners beforehand by composing songs about them. The women studied how to climb the scaffold without showing their legs.

Marie Antoinette did not greet the prospect of a trial with horror, but with a kind of relief. A prevailing mood at that time was an overwhelming desire to judge oneself and to be judged. Just as Rousseau wrote his *Confessions* and the artists painted their self-portraits, everyone published his memoirs, and drew up autobiographical testimony. Marie Antoinette, who had been called heedless, keenly felt the need to justify herself, for the happiness which she had desired for herself and for others did not seem to her to be corrupt, but only what was due her.

This is why she answered so well and so precisely the questions of a tribunal which, even before hearing her defence, had decided to send her to the scaffold. At this time when she had ceased to be of any importance, Marie Antoinette expressed herself like Joan of Arc in addressing her accusers. She did not refer to God—she was far too impassioned by life on earth—but she found words of a sublime candour.

Her first questioning took place on October 12th. Marie Antoinette appeared before Fouquier-Tinville, the public prosecutor. He tried in vain to make her admit her hatred of the Republic and of her adopted country. Urged to choose a lawyer, she accepted in advance those who were to be officially appointed for her.

Tronçon Ducoudray and Chauveau-Lagarde, to whom this difficult task fell, were energetic, skilful and devoted. But the trial was organized with a haste which made the work of the defence counsel ineffective. The two lawyers were advised on October 14th; they immediately contacted the Queen; the dossier was enormous and the hearing was fixed for the next day.

The debates began on October 15th, 1793, at eight o'clock in the morning. Marie Antoinette was elegantly but simply dressed. There was no sign of fear on her face. She was

The King was dead, the Queen was dead : the statue of liberty had replaced that of Louis XV. But the Place de la Révolution, rendered bloody by the guillotine, was soon to become a symbol of new hope, the Place de la Concorde.

dignified, firm and calm. The act of accusation was extremely vague. The most serious assertions were made without proof. The procession of witnesses turned to her advantage : they were a collection of fantastic gossips. Marie Antoinette conducted herself with skill and evoked sympathy. She avoided recognizing her accusers in order not to compromise them. Several of those who came to the bar, and even some of her prosecutors, tried to prove her innocence.

The official minutes of the trial show some of the questions asked. The President demanded of her :

"Where did you get the money with which you had the Little Trianon built and furnished, in which you gave celebrations of which you were always the goddess ?"

"They were funds intended for this."

"These funds must have been considerable, for the Little Trianon must have cost an enormous amount."

"It is possible that the Little Trianon cost an enormous amount, perhaps more than I would have wished; we were gradually drawn into undertaking this expense; anyway, I wish more

than anyone that people should know what happened...."

"Was it not at the Little Trianon that you met the la Motte woman [the heroine of ill-repute in the Necklace affair] ?"

"I have never seen her."

"You persist in denying that you knew her ?"

"My intention is not to deny; I have told you the truth and will continue to do so."

A delegation from the Comité de Sûreté Général, the Criminal Investigation Department, to which David had belonged, questioned the little dauphin for a long time. He had probably been indoctrinated by his jailers and spoke of his mother's secret conversations with a few commissioners of the commune, and also made wildly absurd and hateful accusations. His mother was supposed to have tried to have incestuous intercourse with him. An account of this examination was given. Marie Antoinette remained silent.

"Citizen president," asked one of the jury, "I request you to be so good as to bring to the accused's attention that she has not answered what has been said with regard to

241

what happened between her and her son." The president then questioned the Queen. "If I have not answered," she said, "it is because my very nature refuses to answer such an accusation made against a mother. I appeal to all such who may be present."

A wave of emotion swept through the room. Throughout the debates, there had been neither murmurs or hostile cries, but at critical moments, the same irresistible bonds were fashioned between Marie Antoinette and those around her as when she had first arrived in France, and at other decisive moments during her brief life.

"Did I not put too much dignity into my answer? she asked Chauveau-Lagarde. "Madam, be yourself," answered the lawyer, "and you will always be perfect."

Nearly twenty uninterrupted hours of questioning had affected her energy and optimism not at all. When the president asked the accused whether she still had anything to say in her defence, she declared: "Yesterday, I did not know the witnesses; I was not aware of the charges they would bring against me; well, no one has uttered a single concrete fact against me!"

It was after midnight when the jury withdrew to consider. Marie Antoinette waited for several hours for their verdict.

She was unanimously declared guilty: Marie Antoinette was condemned to death.

Chauveau-Lagarde noted:

The Queen listened to the sentence calmly; and it was only then that we could notice that a kind of revolution had just taken place in her heart which seemed remarkable to me; she neither gave the slightest sign of fear nor of indignation nor of weakness. She was as though dumbfounded with surprise. She came down the steps without saying a word or making a gesture, and crossed the room as if she saw and heard nothing, and when she arrived in front of the barrier where the people were, she lifted her head majestically. Was it not clear that, until that moment, the Queen had nourished hope?

It was already about five o'clock in the morning of October 16th, 1793 when Marie Antoinette went back to her cell for a little while. Her execution was to be that day.

Many fictitious accounts have portrayed the Queen's last hours. There is the report of the *Moniteur*, the Republic's official newspaper, which is moving in its very baldness. It was written on the day of this event and published on the next day:

At five o'clock, the call to arms was sounded in all sections. At seven o'clock, the whole armed force was ready; at ten o'clock, a large number of patrols made the rounds in the streets. At eleven o'clock, Marie Antoinette, the widow Capet, wearing a white, quilted gown, was taken to the scaffold in the same way as other criminals [i.e. in an open cart] accompanied by a constitutional priest dressed as a layman, and escorted by a large number of gendarmerie detachments on foot and on horseback. Marie Antoinette, all along the way, appeared to regard with indifference the armed forces forming a double line along the streets through which she passed. Her face showed neither despondency nor pride, and she appeared insensible to the cries of "Long live the Republic", "Down with tyranny" which she heard all the way. She spoke very little to her confessor; her attention was caught by the tricolour flames in the streets of Roule and Saint-Honoré. She also noticed the signs placed on the frontispieces of the houses; on arriving at the square of the Revolution, she looked towards the National Garden [the Tuileries garden]; signs of keen emotion were then noticed on her face; she then climbed the scaffold with considerable courage. At a quarter past twelve, her head fell and the executioner showed it to the people amidst long drawn-out cries of "Long live the Republic".

A new prisoner was soon installed in the cell which the Queen had just left at the Conciergerie. He was Mgr. Salomon, the Pope's representative in Paris. He saw a little dog come into the room. "It is the Queen's pug," he was to note in his memoirs, "Richard, the Conciergerie guard, has given him a home. He comes to smell his mistress's bed. I see him do this every morning for three whole months."

Her flowers, her dog and her elegance bear witness to Marie Antoinette's faithfulness to the last to an ideal of happiness and beauty of which art is only the highest expression. Since time immemorial, art and happiness have never ceased to fascinate men. But artistic passion has often opened up the dream of a world where perfect happiness would at last reign supreme, and the striving for this Utopia has engendered revolutions which have destroyed works of art and sacrificed the artists. Perhaps, as Marie Antoinette's life bears witness, supreme refinement is but a prelude to barbarity, a passion for happiness can lead to despair, and an excessive love of life may end in massacres.

"For happiness," as the French poet Laclos wrote, "sometimes also brings death."

INDEX OF ILLUSTRATIONS

247

GENERAL INDEX

Edited and produced by Edita S.A., Lausanne, Switzerland,
under the direction of
Ami Guichard, Joseph Jobé and Charles Riesen

Text translated by ITES, Geneva
and captions by Valerie Green

Text and illustrations printed by
Imprimeries Réunies S.A., Lausanne

Photography by Atésa S.A., Geneva

Binding by Maurice Busenhart, Lausanne

Printed in Switzerland